T. E. Cochran

KEEPING A SOUND MIND

THE MACMILLAN COMPANY
NEW YORK · BOSTON · CHICAGO · DALLAS
ATLANTA · SAN FRANCISCO

MACMILLAN & CO., Limited
LONDON · BOMBAY · CALCUTTA
MELBOURNE

THE MACMILLAN COMPANY
OF CANADA, Limited
TORONTO

KEEPING A SOUND MIND

BY

JOHN J. B. MORGAN

PROFESSOR OF PSYCHOLOGY
NORTHWESTERN UNIVERSITY

NEW YORK
THE MACMILLAN COMPANY
1934

SET UP AND ELECTROTYPED BY T. MOREY & SON

PRINTED IN THE UNITED STATES OF AMERICA

PREFACE

The point of view which underlies the content of this book is that mental health is dependent in large part upon the formation of certain mental habits and the elimination of certain others. It is believed that it is just about as easy to form the beneficial habits as it is to fall victim to the detrimental habits if the person involved can be given a clear conception of their relative significance. Furthermore, it is believed that the practice of those habits which bring mental health is just as enjoyable, or more so, than the practice of the pernicious mental habits which lead to mental disease. It is ignorance that does the damage.

Through infancy and childhood the formation of these habits is dependent upon the guidance of parents and teachers but in later years the individual is thrown upon his own resources and discretion, and his mental development must be directed primarily by himself. How is he to know which of the things he has learned are not for his best interests or how is he to initiate others which might be beneficial to him?

This book therefore is addressed to the college student primarily and puts in understandable form the basic principles involved in the preservation of one's own mental health. It is offered as a basal textbook for courses in mental hygiene. Because of the absence of technical language it is hoped that it may also be used in freshman hygiene courses covering mental as well as physical aspects of health.

The theories presented here are no arm-chair theories. They do not represent the pet hobbies of the writer nor the biased viewpoint of some partisan in the field. They are the essential principles which have come out of a great amount of work by specialists in mental disorders, stripped of their abstract terminology, and presented in a simple, straightforward manner.

Most mental diseases come from faulty adjustments to the problems of life. Patients with such diseases demonstrate by their life histories just where they began to make these faulty adjustments and why. Certainly, the way to prevent other persons from following in their footsteps and arriving at the same pitiable end is to direct them so that they do not make the same mistakes. To suggest to students as early as possible in their college careers that they substitute certain healthful forms of adjustment in place of the ones which produced the dire results in victims of mental diseases seems to be a sound policy. To carry out this policy is the purpose of this book.

JOHN J. B. MORGAN

EVANSTON, ILL.,
December, 1933

CONTENTS

KEEPING A SOUND MIND

CHAPTER I

HOW TO EVALUATE YOUR MENTAL HEALTH

Marian had graduated from college at the head of her class. Her record in high school had been unusual. She was cheerful, industrious in her academic work, an excellent tennis player, a star in dramatic performances, she was chosen president of her class, and was much sought in all social affairs. In college she was even more conspicuously successful. For three years she edited the college paper, was head of the student council, was again selected president of the class, and finished her academic career with great promise of success in the hard, cold world.

However, opportunity did not seem to beckon her when she left college. She drifted aimlessly for a time and eventually took an inferior position with a woman who seemed to delight in humiliating her. She left this position, took another even more inferior, began to break in health, returned to her home, grew despondent, and attempted suicide. Her family, thoroughly frightened by this change in her, put her in a sanitarium where she remained for six months. Shortly after her discharge she made a second attempt at suicide and then developed a serious condition which necessitated her second commitment, this time to an institution for mental disorders.

This girl's break was wholly unnecessary and was due to ignorance of and consequent failure to apply some

1

simple principles of mental health which would have
made such an outcome practically impossible. Her mental
break was just as unnecessary and foolish as the total
decay of excellent teeth because of failure to care for
them, the development of digestive disorders due to
improper diet, the destruction of physical health due to
failure to take adequate exercise, or the contraction of an
infectious disease because of failure to obey the simple
laws of sanitation.

It is not necessary to become a physician in order to
learn the essential rules of healthful living. We need the
physician to help us when we have failed to comply with
the rules of health. He is necessary to help us regain our
health, but the more significant result of the study of
physical diseases is the formulation of prophylactic
measures which will enable us to evade ill-health. It
takes the chemist, the pharmacologist, the physiologist,
the histologist, and the clinical work of the practicing
physician to dig out of the facts of physical disease the
rules for physical health. As these become more thoroughly
understood, they can be more and more clearly formulated and can be expressed in simpler and simpler terms
so that the layman can understand and apply them.

The principles of mental health can be clearly stated.
The same principle holds in connection with mental
health. It takes the work of the laboratory psychologist
to formulate the principles of mental life and the clinical
work of the psychiatrist, who deals with cases of mental
disease, to show how the failure to apply the principles of
mental health results in mental disease. But the real
value of the work of these two professional groups lies in
the eventual formulation of the laws of mental health in
such terms that they can be applied by any person who

possesses a modicum of intelligence whether he is trained in psychology or not.

How much knowledge of mental life should one possess in order to maintain his mental health? The more one knows the better, but it cannot be expected that every person should acquire enough information to make him an expert before he can remain mentally balanced. On the other hand, the statement of rules of health with no explanation of why they are effective results in a dry pronouncement of mere platitudes. One needs to know enough of the principles of mental adjustment to understand why to apply the rules and how one rule is related to the others. The general outlines are logical, and simple enough for any person to grasp without burdening himself with the details which the professional should possess.

Knowledge eliminates fear of mental diseases. Adequate knowledge involves an understanding of the dangers to be avoided as well as of the positive aspects of adjustment. The important thing is to get a wholesome balance. It would be folly to stress the dangers unduly. Such a procedure breeds unwholesome fear. At one time a white cross was erected on the highways throughout the state of Ohio wherever a person had been killed in an auto accident. These ghastly crosses were supposed to instill the drivers with such fear that they would drive carefully. But fear did not make for careful driving. The fear thus aroused made for less assurance in driving and resulted in increased accidents. The crosses were removed.

The object of showing dangers is not to instill fear but to increase knowledge. If we know where others have made mistakes, we can guide ourselves more wisely because of such knowledge. Fear results from a knowledge of danger without clear understanding as to the nature of the danger.   Knowledge of the significance of the danger eliminates the fear. If a person finds that he is afraid of a mental break he should not avoid the subject of mental hygiene. He should study it until he knows enough to maintain his mental health without fear.

Importance of mental hygiene. The average man or woman invests a third or a fourth of his life span—a vast store of energy and considerable money—in the improvement of his mind. He spends years sitting in class rooms receiving instruction from teachers. He gleans from books the knowledge accumulated by his forefathers through the ages. He consumes endless hours practicing skilled acts of one sort or another. His mind becomes his greatest treasure, far outweighing in importance all the other benefits of life. Why should he not give a little time to learning how to take care of this treasure?

The world is full of examples of men who have developed great minds only to lose them because of sheer ignorance of some simple fundamental principles of mental health that would have made such a fate almost impossible, The average man knows less about taking care of his mental integrity than he does about safeguarding his money. The time to learn the laws of mental balance is in the prime of life before any damage has resulted from ignorance. Every person should, in his teens, stop long enough to take account of stock, to develop a consistent program of mental health and efficiency which will safeguard him in later life and enable him to live a life of happiness, of personal and social accomplishment, and increased ethical merit.

Can mental health be measured? The evaluation of mental health must be on a basis of relativity because there is no definite scale of measurement which can be applied. We have all degrees, from the complete lack of health which may be witnessed in extreme mental disease to the opposite extreme of ideal mental balance. If we had a calibrated scale extending from one extreme to the other, self-evaluation might be relatively easy; but no such scale exists. We can only compare ourselves with those who are unbalanced or with the ideal of perfection. Which is the better plan?

In our self-analysis we might fix our attention on the possible kinds of ill-health and, as a result, we should emerge from our study either with a feeling of exaltation that we are in fairly good condition or with a hidden fear that we might succumb to some of the disorders we have discovered. On the other hand, we might compare ourselves with the ideal and thus provide ourselves with a powerful incentive to improve or with a feeling of discouragement because we seem to be so far from the ideal.

It is obvious that two of these attitudes should be avoided. We should not permit ourselves to fear dire possibilities nor should we be discouraged because the ideal seems so far from our reach. We should be able to survey our position with equanimity and use our knowledge in an intelligent program of improvement. We can do this if we recognize that our mental condition is never static. Our position on the scale of mental balance is sure to change with the passage of time whether we attempt to change it or not. Knowledge will enable us to move in the direction of mental health, whereas ignorance might carry us in the direction of deterioration. Knowledge should not bring fear. It should banish fear; and should breed the hope and energy needed to effect an improvement.

True insight usually does naturally give rise to a program of improvement. If self-analysis ends in a feeling of self-pity or in arrogant pride the possibility of such improvement will be checked. The first step toward mental health is to get rid of any such emotional reactions. True insight must be cool, calm, rational, and balanced.

How to make a personal survey. If you will answer the following questions sincerely and carefully, you will obtain a relative evaluation of your mental health.

1. *Are you happy?* If you are unhappy you may be sure that there is something wrong in your mental life. The unhappy are always wrong. Happiness is a symptom, a sign that things are going well with you. Unhappiness is a sign that things are not well. The degree of happiness which you experience is as accurate an indicator of mental balance as the temperature of your body is of your physical health.

If happiness is such an important sign should you not then strive always and only to be happy? Not directly. You should attempt to attain such perfect adjustment that happiness will become a habit but if you permit basic maladjustments to be present and attempt to attain happiness in spite of such maladjustment you are merely working at cross purposes. If, when unhappy, you merely try artificial means for convincing yourself that you are happy, you are paving the way for ever increasing bitterness and for mental illness.

Do not ignore unhappiness when it comes. It is an extremely significant index of maladjustment. But do not try to attain happiness as an end in itself or use artificial devices to convince yourself against evidence that you are happy. Unhappiness should be a goad to prod you on and on in your search for the basic cause of your discomfort and, when you have found the cause, to continue to prod you until you gain courage to right the conditions which caused the trouble.

May not this be demanding an impossible achievement for you? Are not some conditions beyond your control? How can a person control such inevitable and unavoidable calamities as disease, illness, the death of one's loved ones, loss of property through fire and storm, and the like? To be sure, a person cannot avoid being unhappy under such circumstances, but the person with virile mentality immediately sets about adjusting himself to the events of life, no matter how calamitous they are. It is to be expected that a person will be unhappy if death takes his best friend, but it would not be normal for him to spend the next fifty years wholly absorbed in self-pity because of this loss.

The essential task of life is to adjust to anything and everything that comes, and happiness or unhappiness is merely an index of the degree of success or failure one is having in making such adjustments.

2. *Have you breadth of vision?* One of the prime tasks of youth is to get acquainted with life as it is. Youth should have a wholesome appetite for new experiences, a curiosity as to the significance of each new experience as it comes, a fairness in the evaluation of each new viewpoint which is presented, and a willingness to relate each experience to what has gone before. Breadth of vision does not come from flitting from one experience to another in a superficial manner, nor does it come from avoiding certain aspects of life; on the contrary, it comes from a true evaluation of each situation and a relating of it to all others which have preceded it.

Suppose life has hurt you. Is that any reason for hiding from it and living in a world of fancy? Suppose it has failed to measure up to your expectations and your ideals have been shattered. It is better to admit that it is not up to your expectations than to deceive yourself into believing that it is different from what it is.

Narrow vision is unwholesome. If it is the result of limited experience the normal way to correct it is to widen your contacts with life. If it is the result of biased vision and prejudice you must change your emotional bias to tolerance and honesty.

You must, because of local and temporary circumstances, align yourself with certain organizations, beliefs, and factions, but it is a sign of mental imbalance when you can see no virtue in the connections and positions of others. You may be an American, but other political boundaries may have just as much value for an ongoing world. You may have a religious preference, but there is value in other religions than yours. You may have joined a particular fraternal organization, but that is no excuse for snobbery. Even a self-righteous person may have a more shriveled soul than one who has succumbed to some of life's temptations. Narrowness, no matter how cleverly cloaked under the guise of virtue, is a sign of weakness, cowardice, or lack of experience. If you find yourself to be narrow, try to view it as the result of a lack of experience and do not let weakness or cowardice prevent you from remedying the deficiency.

3. *Can you do things easily and smoothly?* Adjustment to life involves more than seeing things broadly; it rests upon reacting to experiences wholesomely. A large part of your life as a child was taken up with learning motor performances. This should continue through

life. You have not completed your motor adjustments when you have learned to eat, to walk, to talk, to write, and to play a few games. Your bodily activities become a more and more intimate part of you as you grow older until they express your personality better than anything you may think or feel inwardly.

Speech, for example, displays your mental balance and integrity in unmistakable fashion. If you stammer in the presence of others you thereby display your lack of poise and self-control. If your voice rises in pitch with the slightest excitement you thereby loudly proclaim your emotional tension. Fluency of speech, an adequate choice of words, and a clearness of expression are the best indicators of clear and unified thinking. Here is a form of motor expression which lends itself to improvement as long as life lasts.

At the other extreme nothing so clearly shows when you are breaking mentally as your speech. Blocking, hesitation, repetition of ideas, dwelling on some hobby, incoherence in expression, or vulgarities betoken varying degrees of disintegration.

Excitement provides the best test of motor coördination. Even a poor driver may guide a car successfully on a straight open paving. The crucial test of our driving skill comes when we encounter some foolhardy driver or get mixed up in traffic. Spilling soup at a formal dinner, knocking over furniture, or treading on others' feet are all betrayers of inward panic, excuse them as we may. The body of the well-trained man never gets in his way. It gets him out of tight places automatically.

4. *Do you enjoy solving problems?* Is a difficulty a challenge which brings out the best in you? Or, are you the kind of person who cringes unless fate presents good

fortune to you on a silver platter? Fears, as we shall
show later, are behind most mental disorders. They may
make one retire from a problem situation or may impel
him to attempt to solve it in feverish haste. In either
case he is likely to make a poor solution and, of course,
each failure to solve a problem satisfactorily makes the
next one more difficult of solution.

The one thing about life which is absolutely sure is that
it is ever changing. This changing nature of events makes
continuous readjustment essential. You scarcely have
time to get your breath after one conflict before the next
one is upon you. Life is a game with a continual challenge
which you must meet if you are to keep alive. Stagnation
and death come when you cease to rise to the challenge.
Increased confidence and vigor result from accepting it.

Success in a game is measured more by the attitude of
the contestants than by any reckoning of victories or
defeats. If you play valiantly you have succeeded. If
you play unwillingly, with fear of the outcome, or hatred
for your contestants, you have lost the real value of the
game. Your attitude toward the problems of life is a real
measure of your mental health.

5. *Have you a manifest objective in life?* If your past
life has been unsuccessful you may be afraid to look
ahead because you fear a repetition of past failure. If
you have been successful you may be so intrigued with
your success that you prefer to gloat over it rather than
to look to what the future may hold for you. Either
attitude is unwholesome and may lead to serious disintegration. It is unwholesome to dwell too much on the
past. You may learn from the past lessons which will
guide you in the future, but these lessons have value only
as you put them to use.

One great barrier against the forward outlook is our disappointment that things do not always turn out as we expect them to do. We plan ahead with high hopes only to find disillusionment and disappointment. This should mean only that we have miscalculated. The value of the forward look does not depend upon achieving what we set out to attain but in the fact that it incited us to do *something*. The man who is doing something is thereby enriched mentally. The man who does nothing stagnates and dies. It is the forward look which keeps him going.

If you spend more than a small amount of time going over your past you need to revise your mental program. We shall find that looking back leads to a very pernicious form of mental disruption.

6. *What factors in life motivate you?*   In childhood the motives which actuated you were simple and obvious. As you grew older and life became more complex your motives became correspondingly complicated and very often, perhaps, were of a nature that you could not understand.

The difficulty of comprehending our motives lies in the fact that we are taught to evaluate them. Some, such as patriotism, loyalty, industry, and the like are regarded as noble and we try to interpret all our actions as the result of these drives. Others, such as selfishness, pride, passion, and hate, are considered ignoble, and we do not wish to admit that they play any part in our lives.

If, in spite of ourselves, some of the ignoble impulses play a part in our behavior, we tend to delude ourselves into thinking they are inoperative or we distort our thinking so as to overemphasize the noble impulses. Such distorted thinking plays some part in most of our behavior, but if it takes too great a grip upon us it is a sign of unwholesomeness and should be avoided.

It may not be so serious if we do some things from unconscious motives but, if we permit our reasoning processes to become violently distorted in an attempt to excuse such behavior, the resulting irrationality becomes a habit and spreads to all phases of our lives. We shall, in later chapters, show the significance of such distorted thinking and present more specific means for correcting it. We merely mention it here to show its significance as an index of mental unsoundness. The man of sound mentality does relatively few things for reasons which he does not understand. Insight into motivation is one of the best indices of mental soundness.

These motives become crystallized into attitudes or principles, into systems which some call a philosophy of life, and these attitudes become the guiding principles which direct us in all our behavior. There is nothing in life which it is more important for you to understand and to control than the development and influence of your fundamental attitudes.

7. *Do you get along with people?* Do you like people? Do they like you? Are they at ease when you are in their company and do they enjoy your actions and conversation? Are you at ease when with other people? Do you feel that people are kindly disposed toward you and would help you in a crisis, or do you think people would, as a rule, hurt you if they had the opportunity? Do you like advice or do you shun it? The answers to these and many other similar questions will indicate to you the degree to which you have adjusted yourself socially.

In the last analysis, the psychopathic patient who becomes so seriously deranged that he must be confined in an institution is merely one who has not learned to get along with others. Queer ideas or unusual forms of conduct do not, in themselves, constitute grounds for segregation; it is only when behavior becomes extremely annoying to others that segregation becomes necessary. Sanity can be measured only in terms of social tolerance.

Consequently, if you cannot get along with others, do not blame them, for that is what all abnormal people do. If they are out of harmony with the whole world they consider the world out of tune and think that their music is perfect.

The growth from egocentricity to socialization is, again, one of development. It was normal for you as a child to be relatively egocentric, but normal life should have enabled you to integrate with society. For this reason, do not think that any minor social maladjustment is an index of a pending psychosis; it may merely indicate the necessity for more social education. Each social blunder should teach you to behave in a more wholesome fashion next time just as each fall of the child should enable him to learn to walk more steadily.

Finally, when you are socially matured you will enjoy the society of other people. If adjusting to other people is still a task which provokes considerable worry on your part you have yet a long way to go before you can consider yourself socially mature.

The causes of maladjustment. If you are unhappy, narrow in your outlook on life, awkward in your execution of acts, afraid of meeting problems, lacking in any objective in life, if you are unmotivated, or if you cannot get along with people, what can you do about it?

There are two sensible things to do. The first is to gain

a clearer understanding as to the cause of your poor adjustment and the second is to organize a rational plan to correct the trouble at its source. The manifold mental disorders that are found can be traced to a failure on either of these two counts.

If one attempts to do something to correct his maladjustment without a clear conception of why he is maladjusted he is not very likely to succeed. To be sure, the very fact that he does something may cause him to stumble on a corrective measure. It is better to do something than to sit idly by and let the maladjustment grow worse. But it is not good policy to trust one's destiny to chance happenings in this fashion.

An analogy may make this point clearer. A young man was once given the task of locating and repairing trouble in the circuits in the switchboard of a telephone exchange. He knew little about the circuits but was told that trouble might result from a broken connection or broken insulation which would permit a short circuit. After making his tests, if he found trouble, he would go up and down the switchboard hunting for broken wires or short circuits. There were thousands of wires and thousands of possibilities of short circuits. He did not know exactly where to look for any specific trouble but he always made a general search. Strangely enough, he often was able to correct the trouble but, if it came from any unusual source, he could never trace it down and correct it.

That is the way some people order their lives. Given an indication that something is wrong they proceed to do something. They go on a trip, they lose themselves in social activities or work, they laugh it off, take to drink, take up religion, play golf, become reformers, or do some similar thing. Sometimes they effect an improvement just as the boy often found a loose wire in the switchboard. If, however, such random behavior brings no relief, they end in a worse condition than before.

To do something, anything, is better than to do nothing, but one needs to use intelligence in applying these various forms of behavior. Consequently, a large part of mental health involves learning the significance of various snags which we encounter in our adjustments. The fact that we understand their significance will indicate the proper remedy. Remedies applied indiscriminately may be worse than no remedies at all.

Can causes of mental maladjustment be removed? If we are to apply our remedies to the causes of mental disorder we must look squarely at these causes and attempt to evaluate them. This evaluation will involve a relative estimate of the part they play and the degree to which they can be changed. We should recognize clearly that no mental condition is produced by any one factor but by a large number of interacting elements. If we discover several causal elements in any one situation and know that one of them cannot be changed we still have the possibility of changing the others and thus bringing about an improvement. It is a mistake to hunt for the element which is beyond our influence and then to use this fact as an excuse for lack of endeavor toward improvement.

Heredity. What bearing has one's heredity on his mental health? The customary procedure when one propounds this question is to go off into an academic discussion of the relative importance of heredity and environment. Such a discussion leads nowhither and must inevitably end with the conclusion that both are important and that one cannot definitely state the relative value of either.

What we often fail to realize is that the particular emphasis given by the contestants in such an argument is dependent upon personal emotional bias. While the academic answer has little bearing on mental health this bias has extreme importance.

If a person is making what he considers a good adjustment to life and has a commendable heritage he is very likely to become complacent in his viewpoint and give great emphasis to the value of inheritance. This attitude may be very helpful in that it builds up self-confidence and stimulates its possessor to further achievements. Its danger lies in the tendency of the complacent person to develop a static self-satisfaction which kills initiative. When he contemplates his endowments and assumes that they presage inevitable success why should he exert any effort to accomplish what others seem to be having such a struggle to attain? Regardless of original endowment such an attitude is the inevitable cause of failure to make the most of himself. A man can never rest on his laurels, whether they were handed to him through heredity, or won through his own efforts, without finding himself drifting downstream. Even if a person thinks he has a fortunate heredity he cannot afford to gloat over it.

An excessive emphasis upon heredity with an accompanying feeling that one is *not* fortunately endowed has an even more pernicious result. It furnishes its victim with a ready excuse for every failure. Instead of being stimulated by failure to attempt to be more successful in the future, this type of person hides behind the excuse that he was cheated in his heritage and feels that there is nothing he can do about it. His chagrin is accentuated by the attitude of relatives and friends who know his family. They treat him as though they were convinced that he would never amount to anything; they help him to celebrate every failure, until this united atmosphere gives birth to a fatal pessimism which it is almost impossible to eliminate.

This pessimism is fostered because it has still another value for its possessor. We are all taught that we are responsible for our behavior, for our moral conduct, and for our vocational success or failure. Should we happen to do some immoral act, or if we are even tempted to do so, we feel a sense of guilt which requires some sort of recognition and adjustment. An easy way to rid ourselves of this feeling of guilt is to blame some circumstance for which we have no responsibility. What a ready scape-goat heredity can become if we can believe that it is extremely significant in human life and inflexible in its control of our conduct?

This escape from guilt not only operates upon the victim of the unfortunate heredity but upon his teachers. We recognize that those whom we influence—whether as parents, teachers, or moral advisers—depend largely upon our teachings. If our teachings fail we may either acknowledge that our methods have been faulty or hide behind the excuse that our pupils are unteachable. Having failed to make the proper impression upon a student, it is very satisfying to present the excuse that he has a poor heredity and, consequently, our failure was due to no fault in our teaching technique.

Environment.   What may be the effect of overemphasis upon the influences of the environment? It is very difficult to conceive of any mental injury resulting from such overemphasis. The effect of the belief that the environment is important in achievement is an incentive to greater and greater efforts toward accomplishment. He who emphasizes his opportunities becomes incited to make the most of what he has without undue consideration as to what his endowments might be.

It has been discovered by students of mental health that the tendency to look forward is wholesome while the tendency to look backward, to live in the past, is unwholesome. Overemphasis upon the importance of heredity is, from the mental hygiene standpoint, only another method of regression, a living in the past, while emphasis on the importance of the environment typifies a fighting, forward looking attitude and, for that reason, a wholesome one.

Each one of us has to face many situations in life which require initiative and independence. The extent to which we face such situations squarely is a good index of mental stamina. Any device which enables us to shrink from a direct facing of real life is a weakening element. How can we achieve such independence? We are born not independent, we must achieve it.

The achievement of independence. Probably the most significant thing about human life is the fact that the human infant is born helpless. He can do nothing for himself and if it were not for the protection of his parents and others he would become the victim of his environment and would surely perish. The pathway from this utter helplessness to the independence and skill of manhood and womanhood is a long, arduous path beset with many dangers. We learn at first to do things through the instruction of others and with their help. Some of us never get beyond this stage of requiring help; we are eternally dependent upon others. A few

attain the goal of becoming masters of themselves and of
their environment. These few have learned the most
vital lesson of human life.

Adulthood is synonymous with self-reliance, a condition which does not come necessarily as a concomitant
of increasing years. It should be a gradual process beginning with birth (or perhaps before birth) and continuing throughout life. Some writers have felt that the
time to achieve this freedom was at adolescence. The
child who has been too much repressed and restrained
may make a valiant effort for freedom at this stage of his
life, but to one who has made normal progress before
adolescence the struggle at this period is not likely to be
so violent.

The pathway from helpless infancy to adult independence is beset with many dangers, some of which we shall
consider later in detail. These dangers are partly from
our objective environment, but largely from our social
environment. The greatest obstacle to the achievement
of independence is the interference of other persons.
What makes this interference so subtle and so vicious
is that it is usually accompanied by kind motives and
good intentions on the part of the persons who cause the
greatest interference. We need the help of those around
us but we do not need too much help. How is the infant
to decide how much to accept or who is to guide the
adult in how much he should give?

We have already stated that happiness is an index of
normal development and unhappiness is a sign that something is wrong. Can this be used as a guide to tell the
growing child whether he is progressing properly? Unfortunately this index is not always accurate in indicating
danger until the damage has been done. We tend to

continue the conduct which brings us comfort and to discontinue that which causes us discomfort. The child may enjoy too much the over-solicitous care of adults.

It is very satisfying to have things done for us, at times, and we may relax with satisfaction when we are waited upon. When such service interferes with the freedom of our conduct we will resist such help. As a result, the physically robust child is more likely to struggle for freedom than is the physically weak or ailing child. When a child fights his mother and yells, "Do it by self! Do it by self!" he is making a wholesome struggle against too much service on her part.

If, on the other hand, the child learns to become too dependent, he must await future discomforts, which often come too late, to make his struggle for freedom. The teasing of comrades, the taunts that he is tied to his mother's apron strings, that he is a sissy, a weakling, and the like, provide discomforts which stimulate him to achieve freedom or which discourage him so that he fears to make an effort. A poor adjustment will eventually cause discomfort and unhappiness but temporary contentment may cover a situation which should not, in his best interests, be satisfying, over a longer period of time. It is very easy to mistake complacency for the happiness which is the resultant of a fortunate adjustment. One should welcome a jolt which spoils his complacency.

Defense reactions. We can assume that progress will not be smooth and regular. What should happen when a crisis arises? The sane thing to do is to survey the whole situation so critically and rationally that we arrive at a plan of action calculated to eliminate the trouble and assure future progress of a smoother sort. What we are likely to do is to act in each crisis in the same manner as we did in some previous difficulty.   If this new situation responds as the former one did we tend to think we have a means for meeting all difficulties.   Such a habitual means for solving problems may be good or it may be bad, but it will make us trouble if we tend to use it on all occasions regardless of its suitability.

These habitual ways of solving problems have been called variously defense mechanisms or dynamisms. A large part of our discussions in this book will be of these dynamisms. We merely wish at this place to indicate their nature and to show how they may work effectively or unfortunately.

We have said that the immediate occasion for the use of a dynamism (or defense mechanism) is some sort of discomfort.   Now, reason and sanity suggest that we delay any action until we have decided what is best to do. Such a delay will probably accentuate the unhappiness and if we are misled by emphasis upon our immediate feelings we will not tolerate any such delay but will do something impulsively, only to awaken later to the realization that we have brought upon ourselves still greater unhappiness.

In some situations such a delay and rational analysis is impossible. If I am chased by an angry bull I cannot afford to sit in the middle of the field, contemplate all the factors in the situation, and then decide what to do. The bull might unfortunately decide it for me should I delay in such a plight. I will do the first thing that occurs to me and, if I happen to be fortunate in my hasty choice of alternatives, I may have the opportunity at some later time to consider whether I did the best thing I could have done. Obviously, in some situations, I must do

my thinking after I have acted if I hope to do any thinking at all. Granted that some emergencies require action
without previous contemplation, the great proportion of
situations do brook delay. When confronted with a bull
it may pay to remember the aphorism, "He who hesitates is lost." In deciding a career it may pay to "Look
before you leap."

These maxims illustrate our point. Each of them may
be supposed to represent a defense mechanism. Suppose
a person has found that it pays to act without hesitation
on several instances. He thereupon unhesitatingly adopts
action as a rule of life. He benefits in some instances and
loses in others. On the contrary, the man who has learned
(probably through some accidental early experiences)
the value of waiting may find that he suffers by using
hesitation in situations where action is demanded. One
must learn to have a large repertoire of dynamisms at
his command if he would attain mental stability.

How does this principle relate itself to mental health?
It illustrates very clearly the first and most important
principle of mental health: namely, that one should look
clearly at every situation which confronts him. This
analysis may be during, before, or after we have acted—
best of all, at all three times—but look we must if we are
going to attain and retain mental balance.

Looking itself may cause pain, but we will soon learn
that it pays to take a little pain now in order to avoid
much more pain in the future. Facing life squarely is
the first principle of mental health.

Insight a stimulus to activity. But such facing of life
must always be a preliminary to doing something. A
life spent in self-contemplation is not a wholesome life.
You may sit in the valley looking at the mountain top but

looking will never get you to the top. You should start
to climb whether your attention is directed toward the
pitfalls that will face you or whether you fix your attention on the glories of achieving the climb to the top.
You will not get anywhere so long as you sit. We are
told that the positive sort of contemplation is better than
the negative sort which dwells only on dangers, but its
value lies only in the fact that it is easier to make the
jump from hopeful anticipation to action than from
negative fear to action. The goal is action regardless of
the means taken to produce action. The wholesome life
is the active life.

Where the discomfort which incites to activity has its
inception in objective circumstances or in the behavior
of other persons, the achievement of normal behavior
designed to remove the discomfort is relatively easy.
One can view frankly such situations, can rationally
decide the reason for the pain, and can organize some
rational behavior to meet the conditions. When, on the
contrary, the source of the pain is from within, when it
is due to the fact that certain of our impulses or certain
acts run counter to the ideals and standards of conduct
which we have established, the rational program is not
so easily followed.

Conflict with the external environment does not tend
to produce as severe a disruption as a conflict with ourselves brings about. It is here that we are apt to develop
dynamisms which are inimical to our welfare. We adopt
behavior patterns not primarily to adjust to our difficulties, but to deceive ourselves as to the true nature of
affairs.

Dangers of self-deceit. The person who gets into
social difficulty may plan to deceive others in order to

escape a dilemma. He may declare war upon his environment but at the same time maintain his mental integrity. War within oneself is fraught with much more dire consequences because it is difficult to fight a straightforward battle with oneself. In short, the most important causes of mental disintegration come from the attempt to deceive oneself or from a failure to make a straightforward adjustment when some internal conflict is discovered.

To be sure, one does not set out to deceive himself in a gross or exaggerated fashion. Such a method would be apparent even to oneself and thus be ineffective. The process starts in a very subtle and insidious fashion and gradually grows until the deceit is not recognized by its victim even though it is extreme and easily recognized by outside observers. Mental health does not depend upon hunting for evidences of gross maladjustment but upon recognizing the significance of minor beginnings of maladjustment and in correcting them in these early stages.

Some persons express a fear that they may suddenly lose their minds. They seem to think that a perfectly balanced person may suddenly become deranged. Such cases are very rare. If there is a gross injury to the brain due to some physical violence, to some disease such as meningitis, brain tumor, or to some sort of poisoning, derangements may appear suddenly. But these cases constitute a minor portion of mental disorders. The great majority come from mistakes in using the nervous system rather than from accidental injury or brain disease.

For example, suppose a student fails in an examination. The rational attitude to take toward such failure is frankly to admit the failure and to search for its causes. He may have been ill, lazy, worried about some personal difficulty, lacking in background, or too busy with other things to have studied sufficiently. Regardless of which of these might have been present the real truth would probably not be very gratifying to the one who failed. Honesty would force the admission of some personal lack and such an acknowledgment would be painful. It is easy to succumb to the temptation to hunt for some reason which is not painful. To blame the failure on some one else, for example, might be quite gratifying. If one can make himself believe the teacher had a grudge against him, or was unfair for some reason, one's pride and self-esteem would be safeguarded. The attempt to avoid pain would make it easier to accept the latter reason rather than any of the former ones.

To be sure, a person does not lose his mental balance by one such escape from chagrin, but in the next and succeeding situations where failure is encountered he is very likely to adopt the excuse which satisfied him before; he hunts for some one else to blame. Soon the tendency to blame others becomes habitual. Instead of endeavoring to improve himself, he spends his time hunting for evidence that he is being persecuted by those who, he fancies, dislike him. He becomes less and less efficient and finds it more and more necessary to blame others and gets an ever increasing delight from the feeling that he is the center of persecution.

Finally, he develops the delusion that he is the victim of an organized effort to keep him from succeeding. He asks himself why they are so interested in this pursuit, why do they want to keep him from succeeding. The answer is that he is a great man. His enemies recognize his

greatness and are afraid of him. They dare not let him
succeed for such success would encompass their ruin.
In brief, his delusions of persecution began with a failure to face his own weakness and as a substitute he has
convinced himself that he is truly great. Having reached
this stage he finds it so satisfactory to acknowledge his
greatness (although there is not the slightest foundation in fact for his belief in his ability) that he can never
admit any weakness or failure.

Such a person becomes potentially dangerous because
he may go so far as to attempt to punish his imaginary
enemies. If he should eventually break out and commit
an act of violence against these supposed persecutors he
is placed in custody and those who witness his plight
suppose that he has suddenly become unbalanced, making
their judgment because of his final acts of violence. The
truth is that this behavior began when he was younger,
in his first attempt to blame others for his initial failures.
The remedial steps should have been taken years before
he developed to the extent that he attempted to injure
others.

The defense mechanism so briefly outlined is but one
of a great number which we shall study in detail. It is
given at this point to illustrate the danger involved in
failure to view one's life and mental processes with
frankness. Dynamisms are very valuable when adopted
to adjust to a situation which has been rationally
analyzed; they become pernicious when they are unconscious devices adopted to maintain an unjustified self-
esteem.

Summary. What you need to know to assure mental
health for yourself is whether you are proceeding in the
proper direction in the conduct of your life. You may

get an answer to this question by determining whether
you are happy, whether you have a broad perspective
of life, whether you have developed your body into a
machine which is capable of doing your bidding, whether
you enjoy the challenge of life's various problems, the
nature of the goal toward which you are working, the
degree of urge you have to attain that goal, and the
degree to which you are able to get along with other
people.

In the second place, you need to know that any event in
your life is dependent upon a great number of factors,
some of which are beyond your control—they are past
history—and some of which are subject to change. The
criterion you must use in evaluating the various factors
must never be: "How can I find an excuse for my behavior?" You must continually ask: "What influences
can I discover which I can control and change?"

In the third place, you must recognize that there are a
great number of possible things to do in any situation.
You will tend to do the easiest thing, the thing you have
been accustomed to do, or the thing which will bring the
quickest results. You will need to learn the relative value
of all sorts of conduct and use all the intelligence you
possess to do the wisest thing.

Keep before yourself the questions: "What am I
doing? Why am I doing it? What is the wisest thing to
be doing?"

QUESTIONS

1. Give some instances to prove that clear understanding facilitates
simplicity of statement.
2. Defend the statement: If a law is true it may be applied by one
who does not know why it is true.
3. Why are people so afraid of mental disease?

4. Suppose a skeptic contends that mental health is not important. How could you convince him that it is?

5. What emotions should be avoided in studying the problems of mental health?

6. Memorize the seven indices of mental health given in this chapter.

7. Gather some incidents from life to demonstrate the truth of the statement: The unhappy are always wrong.

8. What should one do when he finds himself to be unhappy?

9. How does one gain breadth of vision?

10. What are the two most prominent causes of narrow vision?

11. Why is a broad outlook an ideal which may be approximated but never completely achieved?

12. Give some instances of motor coördination being disturbed by emotional excitement.

13. Why cannot we ever hope to have complete stability in our mental lives?

14. Life involves continuous readjustment. Is there any reason to think we would be happier if we were once and forever adjusted?

15. What danger is likely to result from success?

16. What danger may come from failure?

17. Why is a forward look more wholesome than a backward look?

18. When we find ourselves actuated by some ignoble impulse, what do we tend to do about it?

19. What is meant by a philosophy of life?

20. Explain the statement: Sanity can be measured only in terms of social tolerance.

21. What is involved in social maturity?

22. What two things are involved in correcting a maladjustment?

23. Why is a blind attempt to correct a difficulty better than idle submission?

24. Why is it imperative to get at the cause of mental difficulties before they are corrected?

25. What danger results from blaming all mental disorders upon heredity?

26. Why does overemphasis upon heredity breed pessimism?

27. Why is there less danger from overemphasis upon environmental influences than from overemphasis upon heredity?

28. What part does the achievement of independence play in mental health?

29. Why must independence, of necessity, be learned gradually?

30. Why is social interference with independence so dangerous?

31. State the various dangers that one encounters in his struggle for independence.

32. What is meant by a defense mechanism or dynamism?

33. Show how rational analysis prevents the unwise development of defense mechanisms.

34. What is meant by insight?

35. Distinguish conflict with the external environment from conflict within the self.

36. Show the importance of correcting a mental difficulty in the early stages of its development.

37. State in your own words the three divisions into which the problems of mental health are divided in the summary of the chapter.

CHAPTER II

MENTAL CONFLICTS

What do you do when you get into a tight place? Does an emergency stimulate you to mobilize all your energies so that they work harmoniously toward a satisfactory solution of your difficulties? Or do you find yourself going to pieces, one part of yourself fighting against another, with the vast portion of your energies wasted in an internal struggle, instead of being directed against the immediate emergency?

Conflicts the measure of the man. The wholesome individual welcomes an emergency; it is a challenge which calls out the best in him. Anybody can drift with the tide; but it takes a strong man to fight against the current. How does a person achieve such strength? It is not by chance that one is able to meet an emergency while another fails miserably. Mental virility is the result of the sort of training which is gained from minor conflicts in life. If a person has learned the rules of the game from his childhood battles, if he knows how to handle his mental abilities in minor emergencies he can face the most difficult situations with confidence.

The unwholesome individual grows fearful with the approach of an impending crisis. He loses control of his powers, finds that he is out of harmony with himself, habitually makes the wrong decisions, and realizes what he should have done only when it is too late. The wholesome life is not one that is free from conflicts. It is filled with them. But these conflicts are not fearsome things,

they are events in a great game, the glorious game of
living.

Anyone who looks forward to a time when his life will
be free from conflicts is fostering a silly ambition. The
virile man desires only to achieve greater skill in handling
himself in the great game of life and only hopes that he
may be able to continue in the game until death signalizes
that the game is ended.

A man must fight in order to win, but mere fighting is
not enough. He must fight intelligently. To develop some
intelligent principles for facing life's emergencies is the
purpose of this chapter. A grown man should know more
about handling his mental forces than does the child, but
this knowledge is the outgrowth of childhood experiences.
Consequently, we shall begin with a description of the
struggles of the child; we shall try to show why he meets
opposition as he does, we shall study the effect of his
various responses on the formation of his later behavior
and finally contrast with this infantile behavior the attitudes which the adult individual should achieve in
order to conduct himself most effectively. It takes zeal
to win, but it takes intelligent zeal, and intelligence is
the most vital part of our fighting equipment.

The form of the infant's struggles. The tensions which
result in activity on the part of the child may be caused
by various irritations: hunger, pain from the prick of a
pin, discomfort from excessive heat or cold, restraint of
his bodily members, intense sounds, difficulties in breathing, and the like. Despite the diversity in the irritating
situations, his reactions are very similar: a combination
of kicking, waving his arms, and crying. He reacts in
a very vague and diffuse manner and has no specific
ways of dealing with particular forms of irritation. The

success of his endeavors depends not so much on his own activities as upon the intervention of adults who respond to his signals of discomfort. He cannot relieve his own hunger, he cannot remove the pin which is pricking him, he cannot change the temperature, and he has not physical strength enough to remove physical restraint. He can simply grow tense and emit cries, thus broadcasting his distress.

Despite his impotence in dealing effectively with specific irritations the child does not passively submit to them. He is wholesomely intolerant of discomfort and is a fighter. What he lacks in knowledge as to the most effective way of fighting he makes up with zeal. Fortunate is the child who can retain a generous portion of this zeal while accumulating knowledge!

The child learns through random behavior. What he learns about fighting depends upon what happens to him when he does various random things. If, when a pin pricks him, he kicks his legs vigorously and if, the more he kicks, the more intensely the pin hurts, he will soon learn to kick less and to do something else more vigorously. If, in the same situation, he finds that when he yells loudly his mother comes and removes the pin, he will learn to yell when he suffers the irritation of a pin prick.

This illustration gives the pattern for a great part of our learning. We learn to give up that type of activity which accentuates our discomfort, which increases the irritation from a definite situation, and we learn to repeat the type of behavior which decreases our discomfort. In short, the ways in which we respond to opposition from our environment are the results of habits which had their beginning in infancy. To be sure, these infantile habits are modified by every succeeding experience, but we can understand these later modifications better if we trace the process back to the simple beginnings.

What the child learns is thus dependent upon the environment in which he happens to find himself. If his discomforts are always removed through the interventions of a solicitous mother, he will learn to do the things which will make his mother respond. If he must always extricate himself he will learn to do things for himself rather than depend upon others. If, no matter what he does, his discomfort remains undiminished or is intensified, as could happen if he were ill for long periods, he might learn to endure suffering and to fight less.

Typical reactions to opposition. The range of habits that it is possible for a child to learn is as wide and as complicated as life itself. No two persons will develop over exactly the same pattern and we should not attempt to place any grown person we know into any well-defined classification. Nevertheless, classification helps our thinking and so, with the warning against trying to fit persons into our system, we may outline the general reaction trends of people.

1. *Blindly persistent or stubborn fighting.* When the environment fails to yield to our plan of attack, the sensible thing to do is to change our tactics. Exactly how long to persist and when to make a change no one can say. Only the final results can answer this question.

There are persons who, once started on a line of attack, cannot find it in themselves to change, and will persist doggedly, in the face of overwhelming evidence that they are wrong, until they are forced to admit defeat. They are blind instead of intelligent in their persistence.

Such persons may defend their conduct by eulogizing

persistence as a virtue. Persistence may be a virtue when used wisely. It is a sign of weakness to give up too soon, but it may be foolhardy to persist in the same trend too long. Instead of dwelling on the virtues of persistence it would be instructive for persons who are blindly persistent to understand how this tendency develops in infancy. Such a survey will show that persistence is merely a habit, developed like any other habit. Habits should be evaluated on the basis of the results they accomplish and not on the pride of possession.

Persistence is developed because the infant is repeatedly thwarted, usually by an adult who is trying to teach him submission and discipline, and not persistence. To the adult with this aim in view the child's behavior is not a sign of persistence but an indication of perversity and stubbornness. As an illustration, suppose a mother is told that her child should be fed regularly, that it is a fatal mistake to feed him until the appointed time arrives. The child may become hungry and cry for food for a five-minute interval preceding the scheduled time. The mother makes the child wait until the hour arrives and thinks that she has taught him to be regular and to wait for his appointed feeding. From the child's viewpoint, he cried for five minutes and was fed. The feeding was, for him, a reward for five minutes of crying. Suppose in succeeding periods he wakes up and cries for gradually increasing intervals; five minutes, ten minutes, fifteen minutes, twenty minutes, and so on. In this way it would be easily possible to teach the child to cry an hour for his food. The mother is still adhering to her schedule. She may think she is making him learn to wait, but she is teaching him to fight for his food.

The mother who does this in connection with the child's

feeding is likely to use the same tactics in other directions. The child is taught that if he persists long enough in a steady protest against thwarting he will eventually get his way. As he grows older he tries the same tactics with other persons and in other situations. Unless such learning is tempered by other means of breaking down opposition he may become narrowly and doggedly persistent. Persistence may be intelligently applied to meet certain obstacles in life but it should not be the only weapon. Unintelligent persistence is stubbornness.

2. "*Quitting.*" In order to understand the person who tends to give up too easily we must overcome the customary habit of recrimination and attempt to understand how he developed this habit. The one who submits passively to every opposition he encounters is no more to be blamed than the one who persists too blindly. Both tendencies are the inevitable outcome of certain childhood experiences, although each results from a different type of situation.

Passivity results from too much kindly assistance or from too much domination. If a child is pampered too much he finds it much more satisfying to depend upon others to fight his battles than to attempt to fight for himself, while if he is dominated too much he learns that it is useless for him to fight against persons who are too uncompromising and tyrannical to give him any opportunity for self-expression.

The passivity of the pampered child is likely to be quite different from that of the dominated child. The pampered child does not lose his battles, he learns how to induce other people to fight for him. Sometimes he continues childish methods of getting help from others; crying, whining, appealing to their sympathy and pity, becoming an obvious parasite. On the other hand, he may develop very subtle techniques for influencing others to do all his work for him.

The dominated child is likely to resent the interference of his well-meaning friends; he does not want their assistance and yet cannot meet his problems himself. He becomes a complete failure so far as any active resistance to the difficulties of life are concerned, withdraws more and more from objective and social life and, in the end, presents a very pathetic spectacle, a complete failure.

If a child is unfortunate enough to be surrounded by persons who are overbearing and aggressive it is much better for him to become a fighter, even though he may develop excessive persistence, than it is to become an abject coward.

3. *The delayed attack.* Most of the child's reactions are immediate and spontaneous. As we grow older we learn from experience that the passage of time often changes the combination of circumstances so that our course of behavior becomes more clearly defined. If, in addition to waiting for the future to throw more light upon our problem, we fill the interval with thinking about the various things we might do under the circumstances, our reaction is more likely to be adequate. Thus we learn the value of withholding some of our actions.

But the value of waiting comes not in the waiting itself but in the possibility of a change of circumstances or in the intellectual work that we do while we wait. Some persons do not see this aspect of waiting and seem to be convinced that waiting in itself has some virtue. They acquire the habit of putting off decisions, delaying their activities, vacillating between the various possibilities, sure of nothing except the feeling that they should wait.

When such a person does act it is usually with unbounded vigor, a vigor backed by a fear of hesitating lest he again be caught in the web of indecision.

The great value afforded by the delayed reaction is that it enables us to get a perspective. It provides an opportunity to weigh the different possibilities and to arrive at some hypothetical solution. This solution should then be tentatively tried with a keen outlook as to its suitability as we progress. Should the beginnings of our response show that it needs to be modified, such a change should be made immediately. It cannot be made if we merely wait for the sake of waiting and then close our eyes and leap.

When we are infants we demand the immediate satisfaction of our wants. Time teaches us that gratification depends upon chains of events which consume time, we learn to wait for things. The child either fights to get what he wants immediately or gives up in despair; the grown person looks ahead to the time when he can gratify his desires and plans a course of activity to fill the interval so that he will eventually arrive at his goal. He learns to wait not because there is any virtue in waiting but because he has discovered that valuable things can be acquired only by a complex route which it requires time to travel. His waiting is really not waiting but substituting the intermediate steps which he has learned he must take in order to get what he wants.

4. *Modifying the reason for fighting.* Probably nothing indicates the maturity of an individual so much as the circumstances which stimulate him to fight. The infant is stimulated only by physical discomfort. Fill his stomach, provide him with a comfortable bed, and remove all physical irritations and he will relax into sleep. The grown

man or woman who has no ambition but to obtain physical comfort is not much superior to the infant.

Normally the child soon becomes sensitized to other environmental conditions and demands social approval and the feeling of achievement before he is content to relax. He begins this learning in a very simple way. The mother is instrumental in relieving his physical discomforts and, instead of striving only for physical comforts, he seeks to gain her approval as a means of achieving physical comfort. As he extends his experiences he includes other persons and is directly concerned with gaining their approval.

Furthermore, he develops different ways of gaining the approval of his fellows. He may begin by childish tricks, but later he learns the intricate likes and dislikes of those around him and strives to measure up to their standards of achievement and conduct. He may learn that others dislike people who are dishonest, so he strives to be honest to please them. Others like those who are industrious, so he works hard to please them. In short, his moral conduct is, in the first instance, the result of his efforts to gain social approval.

Finally, he makes a further step in advance. Having accepted the demands of others in respect to conduct, he sets up standards of behavior for himself based on the demands of those he respects and whose approval he strives to attain. Working from his knowledge of the acts which his friends approve and disapprove, he formulates his own moral code. He measures himself according to this code and becomes exceedingly uncomfortable if he fails to conform to its mandates.

The fight of the mature adult is thus transformed from the childish attempt to resist all conditions which produce physical discomfort to the battle against any infraction against his self-imposed standards of behavior. He has transferred the battle ground from the outside to within his own being. The battle of the adult is with himself rather than with objective conditions or even with other persons.

The irritations arising from the demands of one's standards of conduct are much more violent than any which bring about mere physical discomfort. The remorse, the feelings of guilt, and the recriminations which one levels against himself produce the keenest type of anguish and cannot be easily ignored or circumvented. The conflicts based on this internal struggle submerge the more primitive battles and an individual will undergo all sorts of physical anguish in order to procure the internal harmony that comes with the sense that one has measured up to his own moral standards of conduct.

If we are to understand these internal conflicts we must never lose sight of the fact that the ideals and standards which give rise to them are learned. They are learned in our attempt to act in a way that will be pleasing to those we love and respect. Their disapproval brings us pain and their approval brings us comfort. If it has been our lot to be nurtured by those who have high and rigid standards we will be forced to adopt rigid standards if we are to gain their approval and our conflict will take on more severe forms. If we happen to have been trained by those with easy standards we will not have such a severe struggle to gain their approval. But the fact that we have learned ideals does not make their demands less rigid. The greatest part of this learning occurs when we are very young and is consequently deeply implanted into the intimate fiber of our personalities.

Subjective conflicts. Another complicating factor in the battle of adjustment is due to the fact that the standards we learn to adopt as our own are often inconsistent and incompatible. One ideal may be at variance with another which is on the same ethical level.

For example, a man may be caught between the alternatives of being false to a friend or being untruthful, between being loyal to his mother or to his wife, or between his loyalty to his country or to his Christian principles of peace. What shall he do under such conditions? Whichever alternative he chooses, he must violate some established and accepted principle of conduct. He must either attempt to evaluate his codes anew, make an arbitrary decision, or establish some sort of compromise.

It is these internal conflicts which cause personality disruption if they are not faced squarely with the full implications of either course plainly apparent. Failure to meet the issues squarely may cause irreparable harm. The frank facing of the issue may be the means of strengthening the character as nothing else can do. The way in which these internal conflicts are met determines more than anything else whether a man shall achieve mental health or succumb to mental disease.

Conflicts should be wholesome. While it is internal conflicts which cause rupture of the personality, this is due to the faulty manner in which these conflicts are handled rather than to the fact that there is a conflict. From the preceding discussion it should be clear that it is only through conflict that progress is effected. All that a conflict implies is that we have encountered a situation for which we have no ready response. It contains some new elements which require a different response from any we have made heretofore. If we attempt to meet this new situation by treating it as though it were the same as some similar previous experience, we find that we are mistaken because it does not yield to our response. This failure brings about an increase in tension, an emotion, and we are stimulated to act more vigorously and in different ways until we do find some way of meeting the new experience. Having found this satisfying response the emotional tension subsides.

The emotional tension and the initial failure are signals to us to warn us that we are wrong. Being in the wrong is not fatal unless we persist in staying in the wrong. Being in the wrong should be a forerunner to getting in the right. If I am walking blithely across a field, gazing at the beautiful sky, whistling in the sheer ecstasy of living, quite pleased with myself, and suddenly bump into a barbed wire fence, I am likely to suffer some discomfort. This pain is a signal to me that I must do something different from what I have been doing. For the time being, I must forget how good life is and set about meeting this new emergency; I must change my course, find some way of getting over the fence, or tear it down. It would be immature on my part to sit by the fence and cry because I was hurt, or to bemoan the fact that I have been suddenly disillusioned, that life is not as grand as it seemed a moment ago. The fact that I bumped into the fence is not nearly as important as what I do about it after I have experienced the accident.

Furthermore, having solved this immediate problem I should have learned how to conduct myself better next time. While I may enjoy the beautiful heavens in the future I learn to keep my eyes open for mundane obstacles as I walk. Has my life been impoverished by such an experience? Should I long for a return of my

innocence of barbed wire fences when I could walk along
in blissful ignorance? No. My knowledge of the dangers
and my learning to meet them has enriched me and I
should be able to get more pleasure from walking because
of such experiences.

This analogy applies to the more intricate events in
life. Each obstacle I encounter, each conflict I resolve,
gives me that much more knowledge of life, and it should
accomplish this end with no diminution of enjoyment
but rather an accentuation of it. A conflict is not an
excuse to whine and give up, but a challenge to do something different, and an opportunity to gain the pleasure
which comes from having been able to meet an emergency successfully.

The development of attitudes. Reverting to our illustration, we said that the experience of the fence should
teach us how to revise our principles of behavior. We
might formulate it in some such words as, "Watch your
step." We adopt this as a rule of conduct and learn
that when we adhere to it we are less likely to meet with
unfortunate injuries than when we ignore it. It is experience which has made it mandatory, and should we
be tempted to abandon it we find the emotional tensions
that accompanied the accident, and which taught us the
precept, make it very hard for us to do so. We have
developed an attitude toward walking which we are
afraid to change because of the memory of the time when
we did break it or when we were ignorant of it.

This is the way in which all attitudes must be learned
no matter how complicated they are. They have to be
learned by experience. Does this mean that we have to
suffer to learn any attitude? Do we have to be immoral
in order to learn a moral attitude? Can we not tell a child

what attitude he should take and thus enable him to avoid conflicting situations and the concomitant pain?

Experiments have demonstrated that teaching a child verbal precepts, if they have little or no relation to experience, is virtually ineffective in formulating attitudes and consequently in controlling behavior. An attitude is a habit and a habit cannot be taught by telling a child about it; he must practice it. But the pain can be minimized by permitting the child to learn from minor experiences. He can be taught to generalize from these so that they carry over to more intricate phases of life.

A verbalized attitude is of value only to the degree that it expresses habitual activities. For example, it is often found that a child will glibly tell you that "Honesty is the best policy," while his behavior tells you that his belief is that it pays to steal. The best way to test an attitude is to place a person in a situation in which his conduct will demonstrate what attitude he actually has adopted.

Attitudes, in the sense of formulated codes of action, provide the basis of an adequate understanding of conduct, whether it is the conduct of ourselves or of others. The overt behavior of a person can only be understood in this way. Suppose, for example, a person has taken some money which did not belong to him. To jump to the conclusion that this is stealing, and that the person is dishonest, is unwarranted. You must discover why he took the money, and the reason must be in terms of the attitude or code of behavior which motivated the act. He may have had no sense of property rights and have the attitude that anything belongs to him if he can appropriate it. He may have stolen it to help some person in distress and his attitude may have been that the end justifies the means. He may have had a grudge

against the owner and an attitude of hate and retaliation for a real or fancied wrong. Thus we could go on
indefinitely enumerating hypothetical attitudes which
could actuate stealing. The overt behavior is compre-
hensible only when we understand the attitude or attitudes which were behind the act.

Attitudes are the dynamics behind behavior but it
must be remembered that there is no particular force
in an attitude except the force of habit. Every attitude is
the formulation of a habit of conduct which the individual
has learned through his own experience.

The changing of attitudes. The question which confronts us is not whether we can change our attitudes.
They will change in spite of anything we might do to
keep them stable. Every experience which we undergo
must change them in some respect. The problem which
we must face is whether we can exercise any guiding
influence upon the formation and modification of attitudes
so that the end results will be more favorable to us than
if they were permitted to grow wildly.

Before any change can be effected the exact nature of
the attitude must be determined. If it is dependent upon
unconscious factors these must be discovered and duly
considered in any reëducation program.

In some cases the attitude is a vague feeling—a feeling
of approval or relaxation when we have done one thing
and a feeling of dissatisfaction or tension when we have
done the opposite. In some cases the attitude is clearly
formulated into an abstract principle of behavior. This
expressed conception of the attitude may be in the nature
of an ideal—a statement of what we should like to do or
to be. In others the attitude may be an expression of
what we habitually do.

Whichever of these forms the attitude may take, there is one common element which will serve to guide us in changing it. That common element is the fact that it has been learned. Good or bad, conscious or unconscious, vague or clearly defined, idealistic or realistic, the attitude must have developed as the result of experience of one sort or another. If we ascertain how it came to be learned we have taken the first step toward modifying it.

Watson has shown the value of knowing the origin of a habit in his illustration of the psychopathic dog. He says: "Without taking any one into my counsel, suppose I once trained a dog so that he would walk away from nicely ground, fresh hamburg steak and would eat only decayed fish. . . . Instead of licking my hands and becoming lively and playful when I go to him in the morning, he hides and cowers, whines and shows his teeth. Instead of going after rats and other small animals in the way of hunting, he runs away from them and shows the most pronounced fears. . . . Instead of smelling every tree trunk, he growls and fights and paws the earth but will not come within two feet of the tree. He sleeps only two hours per day and sleeps these two hours leaning against a wall rather than lying down with head and rump touching. . . .

"Then I take him to the dog psychopathologist. His physiological reflexes are normal. No organic lesions are to be found anywhere. The dog, so the psychopathologist claims, is mentally sick, actually insane. . . . Everything that a dog should do—as compared with what dogs of his type usually do—he does not do. And everything that seems foreign for a dog to do he does. The psychopathologist says I must commit the dog to an institu-

tion for the care of insane dogs; that if he is not restrained
he will jump from a ten-story building, or walk into a
fire without hesitation.

"I tell the dog psychopathologist that he doesn't
know anything about my dog; that, from the standpoint
of the environment in which the dog has been brought
up (the way I have trained him) he is the most normal
dog in the world. . . . Then I take the psychopathologist
into my confidence. He becomes extremely angry. 'Since
you've brought this on, go cure him.' I attempt then to
correct my dog's behavior difficulties, at least up to the
point where he can begin to associate with the nice dogs
in the neighborhood. If he is very old or if things have
gone too far, I just keep him confined; but if he is fairly
young and he learns easily, I undertake to retrain him.
. . . Soon I get him to eating fresh meat by getting him
hungry, closing up his nose and feeding him in the dark.
This gives me a good start. I have something basal to
use in my further work. I keep him hungry and feed
him only when I open his cage in the morning; the whip
is thrown away; soon he jumps for joy when he hears my
step. In a few months' time I not only have cleared out
the old but also have built in the new. The next time
there is a dog show I proudly exhibit him, and his general
behavior is such an asset to his sleek, perfect body that
he walks off with the blue ribbon."[1]

The queer attitude of this hypothetical dog toward
his master, toward meat, and toward trees is clearly
understood when we know how he learned to have those
attitudes—through a peculiar type of training. The
modification of those attitudes is clearly defined as well.

[1] Watson, John B., *Behaviorism*, W. W. Norton and Company, 1930, pp. 298–
300.

He must be taught to change his attitude by giving him new and different concrete experiences in similar situations to the ones which developed the original attitudes.

If an attitude is to be changed, the result is obtained by objective experience and not by any introspective study of the attitude itself. Attitudes grow as a result of experiences and they are changed only by changing the type of experience of the individual to the sort which will effect a different attitude.

If a person is dishonest you teach him honesty by placing him in situations where he has the opportunity to be honest. If he hates people, and you desire to make him love them, you give him objective experiences where he gains satisfaction from loving them in place of hating them. If he has race prejudices which you would like to eliminate you must give him experiences with individuals of the despised race which will result in his satisfaction.

Diversity of attitudes. Attitudes are literally mental postures, guides for conduct to which each new experience is referred before a response is made. Since life is exceedingly complicated there is no one attitude which will apply to all situations, rather each new problem must be solved by reference to a combination of principles or codes.

Some of these attitudes are more deeply rooted than others and are given greater weight, some are absolutely inviolable and others still subject to modification, some lead directly to action and others will brook some delay before a response is made, some are almost independent of others and some are contingent upon related attitudes.

If we had accurate knowledge of the dominant attitudes of a person we could predict much of his behavior in various situations. If we understood our own attitudes our lives would cease to be the riddle they sometimes are to ourselves and to others. If we could keep open-minded toward our attitudes, being willing to have them modified in the light of our varying experiences, we would find ourselves making more progress than if we attempt to make them rigid and unchangeable.

The person who has a simple set of rules to guide his life is sure to lead a narrow life; the one who has a rigid set of rules is sure to lead a bigoted life; and the one who is ignorant of the rules which guide his behavior is sure to lead a disjointed and abnormal life.

Evaluation of attitudes. Even a superficial survey of our attitudes will reveal the fact that some are evaluated much more highly than others. Those that we value lightly play a relatively small part in guiding our actions and are easily modified by each new experience which has any bearing on them. Others are held sacred, resist all change, and play such a dominant part in our lives as to determine very serious issues. There are attitudes, or moral principles, for which we would gladly give up our very lives.

There is a tendency to assert that these highly valued attitudes possess some intrinsic merit outside of our experience, that they need no defense or support of reason. Their very formulation seems enough to warrant their acceptance. How do we form such judgments? Are they purely arbitrary? Is there any sound way in which attitudes can be evaluated?

If we had a measuring scale of attitudes our behavior would be much more rational. When we come to an issue in which two attitudes are in conflict, it would facilitate matters if we had some standard by means of which we could weigh each one and come to some rational conclusion before we act. We have no precise norms but the following criteria should help us to some extent. If we apply all of them to each attitude which we formulate, the mental conflicts which confront us should not be so severe and our eventual solution should be more conducive to development and to internal harmony.

1. *Where did the attitude come from?* If it grew from actual experiences, and is a correct abstract formulation of the lessons learned from a large number of these experiences, it should be rated high.

How many experiences did it take to arrive at its formulation? A hasty generalization based on a very few incidents should be viewed with suspicion. If one man with red hair deceived me, I should not take an antagonistic attitude toward all red-haired men. If I was cheated by a Japanese merchant, this one experience should not determine my attitude toward the Japanese race. The only way to correct such biased attitudes is to increase the number of experiences with red-haired men and with Japanese people.

If we look at our attitudes critically we shall discover that many of them are based on too few experiences, and that they are held tenaciously not because they are logical deductions from those experiences but because they represent the results of a dominant emotion which came with those limited experiences. The excessive emotion resulting from one experience of being cheated by a red-haired man will overpower a dozen experiences with little emotion when red-haired men treated us fairly.

Search your memory to discover how many of your own experiences underlie any attitude you wish to evaluate. After you recall all such experiences that you can, attempt to evaluate the emotional intensity of each ex-

perience. If the attitude proves to have resulted from a
wide experience and is not unduly determined by a few
situations with a high emotional setting, then you may
value that attitude highly. Discount the value of any
attitude resulting from a few intensely emotional experiences.

2. *Is it held by others?* Which should be valued more
highly, the attitude which is markedly different from the
attitudes held by others or the attitude which conforms
to social opinion? Some persons get an emotional thrill
from being radical while others get a similar thrill from
being conservative. In support of this thrill the radical
person argues that it is only through changing attitudes
that progress is made, the conservative defends his emotional bias by urging the opinion that through conserva-
tism man avoids many foolish blunders.

The truth is that an attitude is neither justified or
condemned because it has few or many adherents. It is
a mistake to adopt an attitude merely to be different from
others and it is a mistake to be too complacent because
everyone agrees with you.

It is probably wise to criticise very carefully any attitude which differs from all your fellows. This difference
does not prove that you are wrong in your departure from
the conventional attitude, but it does mean that you are
more likely to be wrong than if you had some support from
others. Be very slow to believe that you are the only one
in the universe who is in the right.

On the other hand, beware of complacency which is
unsupported by indisputable evidence. You can be complacent in your belief that $2+2=4$ because you have
logic in addition to common acceptance to support your
belief. But you have little reason for doubting a belief

just because a great many people hold it; universality of belief is not grounds for doubting it. In the realm of attitudes, on the other hand, where rational proof is scarce, too much agreement is often evidence of stagnation.

3. *Has it been greatly modified by historical setting or racial boundaries?* We may discover that an attitude which we hold in great esteem is not so regarded by other races or nationalities. We may learn that our forefathers regarded lightly those attitudes which we honor, and died for attitudes which we now think trivial. It would seem that an attitude which has been steadfastly held by all races through all time is more deserving of acceptance by us than one which has had a brief and limited following. Here, again, we have no absolute criterion, but one which it would pay to consider.

4. *What results will follow rigid adherence to the attitude?* Some attitudes are essentially pernicious in their effect upon the one who holds them, as well as on others with whom he comes into contact. They may be adopted in an attempt to adjust to some difficulty but they turn to destroy the one who entertains them. Living in memory of the past is an example of such an attitude. It may begin innocently enough, when a person who has failed in some enterprise dwells in memory upon some earlier period of his life, to compensate for the present failure. The memory of the past success drowns the present disappointment. Such an attitude, if persisted in, kills all initiative and paves the way for other failures.

Another illustration of a pernicious attitude is that of hate. Hate may seem to benefit its host temporarily by enabling him to hurt the one who caused him suffering. An attitude of revenge may seem justifiable for a time

but, in the end, it does more harm to the one who entertains it than it does to his enemies.

It is <u>a sound principle to avoid any attitude which
eventually brings failure to the one who adopts it or discomfort to those he meets.</u>

This criterion should not merely be applied in its negative aspect. It is not enough to avoid those attitudes
which might have a pernicious influence but it would be
wise to attempt to cultivate those which give promise of
being of positive advantage to its host and to others.
Honesty, for example, is a valuable attitude not merely
because it does no harm to anyone but in that it is of
positive benefit to all concerned. In other words, an attitude may have varying degrees of value, as measured
by the effects it produces, from the most pernicious to
the most beneficent. It would pay to attempt to determine where, on this scale of values, any particular attitude falls.

5. *Is it workable?* If a person's attitudes are correctly
formulated they are an actual expression of the way he
really does act. There is a tendency on the part of all of
us to have formulated attitudes somewhat better than our
conduct would warrant. This raising of the standard of
our conduct is an expression of our hope and our expectation that our behavior in the future will be of a better
order than it has been in the past. It becomes an incentive
toward improvement and as such has value. We are not
satisfied with the way we have acted so we formulate a
higher standard to guide us in order that time will register
an improvement.

These reformulated attitudes, ideals they are usually
called, are of value only so far as they fulfill their purpose
of improving our behavior. If they are merely a means of

deceiving ourselves as to our actual conduct they become harmful. Self-deceit is always harmful. An ideal is, consequently, an attitude which expresses the sort of person we would like to be.

An important problem that arises in this connection is how great a gap should exist between the actual behavior of a person and the idealized expression of what he would like to be, if that gap is to provide the maximum incentive for improvement. Some persons have thought that the greater the gap the greater the urge to reach the ideal. If carried to an extreme this procedure leads to the erection of all sorts of impossible standards. But impossibility of reaching the goal seems, for these advocates of high ideals, to provide no lessening of the pulling power of the ideal. They believe that it is a very worthy endeavor to reach for the moon. You may know that you can never get the moon, but the important thing is to reach.

Is this theory sound? It is unsound for the reason that a person will never continue, for long, to reach for something which he has no conceivable hope of attaining. The discouragement which results from a futile attempt to do the impossible kills all incentive, and a person who has learned to entertain too high ideals, when he learns that he cannot get what he had hoped for, is very likely to give up all striving.

A much better plan is to formulate ideals which one has some hope of achieving. If the end goal is in the far distant future then one should formulate intermediate goals which may be attained in a reasonable length of time. There need be little fear that, if a lesser ideal is attained, one will become content with this lesser goal and cease effort. The effect of achievement is usually

quite the opposite, the erecting of higher goals with an
added urge to reach them. Where one rests on his laurels
it is not so much because of success in reaching a minor
goal as because of failure in attaining one which is too
high. The falling back upon the satisfaction of a lesser
goal is the result of failure and not of success.

The pragmatic test of an attitude, the question of
whether it will work or not, is a very important one. A
good rule to follow is: Be sure that you evaluate your
present position honestly, formulate clearly how you
would like to change this position, and make sure that
your immediate objective is within reasonable distance,
no matter how high you may place your ultimate goal.

6. *Does it harmonize with other essential attitudes?* We
have already indicated that a relative degree of internal
consistency and harmony between various mental attitudes is essential for mental health and balance. Perfect consistency is an ideal which is probably never completely achieved in any virile individual, but it provides a
guide for the toning down of some attitudes and the
strengthening of others.

It is a mistake to close our eyes to glaring inconsistencies in our various attitudes. Some persons go through
their lives living a compartmentalized existence. They
have one set of attitudes to guide them in their religious
life and another set to guide them in business, failing often
to see the total lack of harmony between the two. Some
persons are honest in their dealings with individuals but
seem to have an entirely different attitude toward honesty
in dealing with corporations. Some men will have an
attitude of love and respect toward their mother, wife,
and sisters, but seem to have quite a different conception
of womanhood when they meet a strange woman. It

takes a change of situation to bring home to these people
the fact that they lack internal harmony. A man may
discover he has cheated a member of his church; another
may find that in his dishonesty with a corporation he
inadvertently robbed his best friend; another may find
that the woman with whom he flirted is a highly respected
member of his own social circle.

Life should be a process of continually ironing out these
inconsistencies. They are sure to occur and merely indicate our limitation in experience and a lack of insight
when they do occur. Severe conflicts of this sort may be
avoided if new attitudes are measured on this basis of consistency when they first appear.

This does not mean that an attitude should be discarded merely because it is radically inconsistent with
other attitudes we possess. It may be that the new attitude is the correct one and the old ones should be modified or discarded. But if we attempt to retain the old
ones in an unmodified form and at the same time attempt
to accept whole-heartedly an entirely diverse new attitude we are sure to have trouble. It is folly to deceive
ourselves into thinking that we can entertain mutually
antagonistic attitudes at the same time and avoid an
active conflict between them.

7. *Is the attitude an expression of your behavior or an
excuse for something you would like to do?* The formulation of an attitude should be designed to give us more insight into our lives. It should express the principle or
principles which control our conduct. At this point we
encounter a temptation to refer acts which were motivated by ignoble impulses to attitudes which we consider
more worthy. If we can account for an act of flagrant
dishonesty by referring it to our principle of loyalty to a

friend we may justify the dishonesty to ourselves. At times this may be a real issue but we can easily deceive ourselves into believing that we have been impelled by the principle of loyalty where it never existed, merely to justify our ignoble act. We can wreak vengeance on a friend in the guise of duty to our country or some moral cause. Beware of emphasis upon an attitude or principle of conduct when the acceptance of that principle works to your own selfish ends. It is very easy to distort values in this fashion.

Unconscious attitudes. The correct evaluation of attitudes and the modification of the different attitudes so that they will harmonize and provide the basis for an integrated personality presupposes that we are aware of the different attitudes that motivate us. It has been demonstrated, on the other hand, that many of the attitudes which influence our conduct are unconscious. We do many things for reasons of which we are totally unaware. These unconscious attitudes provide the basis for much queer conduct and much inner disharmony. For this reason, the healthy minded individual is on the alert for such motivating influences and takes them into account wherever he obtains evidence that they are operative. He tries to become conscious of these unconscious influences. It is unwholesome to keep these in the realm of the unconscious and still permit them to influence our behavior.

Life is full of these influences and we shall merely cite a few to illustrate our point. The reader can discover many similar incidents which demonstrate this principle in his own life and in the lives of those around him. Incidentally, it may be noted that it is much easier to see these influences in the lives of others than in ourselves.

If we like a person it is hard for us to see any faults in him, if we dislike him it is difficult to see any good in anything he may do. If an opponent beats us at cards we are likely to believe that he held good hands and we held poor hands; if we win it was because of our good playing. If another accumulates money it was because of his questionable business ethics; if we get ahead financially it was because of our industry and business acumen.

Our attitude toward relative strangers is colored by their resemblance in some particular to those we have known. One business man distrusted every man with a gold tooth because he had once been deceived by a man who had a particularly prominent gold tooth. Prejudices for or against blondes or brunettes are probably based on childhood experiences with individuals who may have been light or dark in coloring. We may tend to overvalue things beyond our reach and undervalue things which we already possess or which seem to be easily attained. We fail to see that this is an expression of our desire for achievement and not the true evaluation of the objective.

In more subtle form this distortion of attitudes because of unconscious elements may operate as follows: We may be hostile to some movement because some friend opposed it or because some enemy of ours sponsored it. We may be friendly to some individual because some one we love favors him or because he is an enemy to some one we hate. The real motive for our antagonism or attachment is usually so subtly disguised that we are totally unaware of it and base our estimation on supposedly sound evidences. It is well known that a loving mother can see little of worth in any young lady whom her son loves. The interesting part of such a situation is that everyone can see the meaning of such behavior excepting the person manifesting it.

Bringing unconscious attitudes to awareness. We have given rules for the evaluation of attitudes to serve as a guide in building an integrated personality; now we state that some of the most significant of our attitudes are unconscious. We certainly cannot evaluate an attitude which is outside our field of awareness. Does this dilemma provide an impenetrable barrier against a unified growth? There seems to be but one way around the difficulty; bring the unconscious attitudes to consciousness. How?

If we become familiar with some of the clues which indicate that an attitude is dependent upon subconscious factors we shall be better able to detect them and thus to cope with them. Some of these indicators are:

1. *Resistance to change.* We have already shown that it is characteristic of attitudes to be modified by every experience which relates to them. Abnormal rigidity in the face of situations which should bring about changes indicates that the attitude is probably determined by subconscious elements.

2. *Degree of emotional fervor in defending the attitude.* Beware of the attitude you feel called upon to defend with emotional fervor. If your defense is overdone in this fashion it probably indicates that you are not only answering the objections of some critic but at the same time you are answering the objections of some subconscious urge to agree with your external opponent. You are afraid of his opposition because part of you wants to agree with him and therefore you must make his defeat as crushing as possible, thereby defeating your subconscious agreement with him.

Of course, this oversimplifies the subconscious factors,

and you cannot hope to come to a clear understanding of their operation in such an easy way. The significance of the emotional fervor lies in its power to indicate that there is a subconscious element and not in its ability to give a clear identification of it or to bring out its actual relation to conscious factors.

3. *Sensitivity to disagreement.* While a person may not go so far as to defend aggressively his attitude he may manifest the presence of subconscious elements by his sensitivity to disagreement by others. He looks for little signs of approval. When he fails to discover them he takes subtle means for discovering how the other person feels and is very much chagrined if he finds that he does not agree with him.

If an attitude is built solely of conscious factors, having developed through objective experiences, one is not likely to be sensitive about it no matter how much it may differ from that of others.

4. *Urge to convert others.* It is the subconscious attitude which drives a person to get converts to his idea. We can attempt to change the viewpoint of another person when we have discovered by cool analysis that his viewpoint is likely to be harmful to himself or to others, but this is quite different from the attempt to change him merely because he disagrees with us. When you cannot tolerate disagreement it means that you are none too sure of your ground yourself. If you are sure that your hat is becoming you need little confirmation from others as to its beauty. It is when you question its becomingness that you are driven to seek the approval of others.

When the uncertainty is based on unconscious factors it multiplies this urge many times and prevents one from developing a normal amount of tolerance. We cannot endure the viewpoint of a person when it agrees with some subconscious view which we have discarded and relegated to the field of unawareness in ourselves. In being intolerant of the other person we are really disclosing our intolerance of our own subconscious attitudes.

Keeping mental conflicts wholesome. It should be apparent that a person may have intense conflicts within himself and still be sanely balanced. It is not the fight which makes the trouble but the fact that the fight may not be fought in a straightforward fashion. In ordinary life one meets all sorts of different situations and acts differently in the face of each. One day I shiver with the cold, the next I melt in the heat. One moment I am starved for food and the next I suffer from having eaten too much. The sun hurts my eyes and I strain them in the dark. I bump my head and stub my toes. Do I become insane because I am so buffeted? By no means, I adapt myself to each changing circumstance.

So can I adjust myself to the changing attitudes which comprise a large part of my mental life if I but remember that these attitudes are the result of ever changing experiences. It is when I distort these attitudes, when I honor some and think that they must be adhered to though the heavens fall, when I discount others, when I deceive myself as to the real nature of them, and permit myself to be dominated by unconscious attitudes, that I get into difficulty.

All attitudes come from my own experience, I learned every attitude I possess. I can only evaluate them correctly when I check them against other experiences and permit them to change freely with the addition of still other experiences. Then, when they come into conflict

I settle them in exactly the same manner as I would adjust any objective conflict. I make an unemotional, intellectual study of the relative merits of each contestant, pit them against each other and say: "Let the best attitude win."

QUESTIONS

1. Describe the way a wholesome personality should face a difficulty.
2. Why does not mental health imply freedom from conflict?
3. In what way must zeal be reënforced if one is to win life's battles? *by intelligence*
4. Describe the typical struggle of an infant.
5. What is the most prominent characteristic of the struggles of an infant?
6. Describe the process of the infant in getting relief from his discomfort.
7. Show how the child can learn different ways of getting rid of the same unpleasant situation.
8. State four different ways in which persons may meet opposition.
9. Why is it that people differ in the way they meet difficulties?
10. How is persistence learned?
11. Distinguish persistence and perversity.
12. Why or why not should persistence be considered a virtue?
13. How is passive submission learned?
14. What two different types of treatment may produce the habit of submission?
15. What is the value of waiting in the presence of a difficulty?
16. What danger may arise from learning to wait?
17. Why is it that a person who vacillates usually acts with great vigor when he does act?
18. What is the justification an adult has for waiting in the presence of a dilemma?
19. Show the process by which a simple childish irritation is transformed into a moral code or precept.
20. Why is the irritation from an internal conflict more violent than that from an objective irritation?

21. How does it come about that our own standards of conduct are often inconsistent?

22. What should be the attitude toward an internal conflict?

23. How can internal conflicts be made wholesome?

24. Why must attitudes be learned by experience?

25. Show the importance of understanding the attitudes which underlie conduct.

26. What is the process for changing an attitude?

27. What explains the fact that some attitudes appear to be queer?

28. Give a definition of attitude.

29. Memorize the seven rules for evaluating an attitude.

30. Show how an intense emotion may lead to a faulty evaluation of an attitude.

31. To what extent should we permit ourselves to be swayed by the opinions of others?

32. Is there any particular virtue in conformity or non-conformity? Why or why not?

33. Give some illustrations of attitudes which lasted through centuries being discarded by the present generation.

34. Why do some persons persist in living upon memories of what is past?

35. Why do we develop ideals?

36. Define ideal in terms of attitude.

37. Is it wise to make ideals as lofty as possible?

38. Why are intermediate ideals valuable?

39. Should one demand consistency in attitudes? Why or why not?

40. Show how an attitude may not be a real expression of behavior but an excuse.

41. Describe the way in which unconscious attitudes influence conduct.

42. What are the clues which indicate the presence of an unconscious attitude?

CHAPTER III

THE MASTERY OF FEAR

"Late Thanksgiving afternoon in Seattle, a little Filipino named Julian Marcelino made his way to the Midway Hotel, small downtown hostelry. He walked into the room of an elderly acquaintance, Pito Gualto, stabbed him over the heart. He turned and stabbed Pito Gualto's nephew. Then Julian Marcelino, a slightly dazed expression on his small brown face, descended into the street and quietly, efficiently, went amuck. Proceeding at an even dog trot, a knife fashioned out of a bolo (native blade) in each hand, he skewered an aged grocer as he stood in his store doorway, then an amazed bystander on the sidewalk, then three Filipinos in a row. People ran screaming in all directions. When officer Gordon Jensen, returning from a football game, saw him, Julian Marcelino was busy on a Japanese. By this time reserves had been rushed to the scene from all over Seattle. Officer Jensen and two colleagues finally overcame the little madman. Summoned from every hospital in the city, ambulances clanged up to the carnage. Julian Marcelino's incredible record for the afternoon: six killed, 15 seriously wounded."[1]

As you read this account a creepy feeling runs up and down your spine, perhaps you shudder, look around apprehensively lest the little madman should be in your vicinity. You wonder that such things can happen in a civilized community; you ask yourself whether some-

[1] *Time*, December 5, 1932, *20*, No. 23, p. 13.

thing could not be done to prevent outrages of this sort; you wish you could do something, but recognize that you cannot; then, in your impotence, you develop a feeling of irritation and resentment that I should have begun this chapter with such a gory illustration.

Such an occasion is an adequate cause for fear. You experience this emotion in a small degree as you read the account; you would have experienced it in large doses had you been an eyewitness. What chance would you have had, unarmed, against a wild man brandishing a deadly knife in each hand? You shudder to think about it. Fear is inevitable in such a situation. We fear when we are powerless to cope with an obvious danger. Fear has a valuable function to perform on such occasions, it gets us out of the way. There is nothing to do, so we get out of danger in the best manner possible; by running, hiding, feigning death, or swooning. Fear is the name given to the various forms of running away from a conflict when we are powerless to cope with it.

Fears are sometimes valuable. Fear is essentially an escape reaction and there are times when it is highly necessary for us to escape; ruin stares us in the face if we do not. The various bodily reactions that occur in a condition of fear are all designed to aid in this process of escape. If the thing which we do when we are afraid is appropriate the danger will, as a result, be less imminent; we can catch our breath again, we can take a calmer look at the events which precipitated the fear, analyze the factors, and perhaps decide how we can deal effectively with the situation. The natural result of this calmer view is to substitute a fighting reaction for the fear one; we retrace our pathway and engage the danger anew. In short, fear is a temporary reaction and should pave the way for a renewed struggle. Fear should be but an interlude in our fight with the difficulties which surround us.

Fear in itself is never a satisfactory form of adjustment. It is an index of temporary failure. It is a warning that we had better do something different, that we should learn more about our difficulties. It makes us retreat so that we may have a better opportunity to win because of the temporary retreat.

Fears should be temporary. Fear should occupy but a small portion of our lives. If it becomes a habit it indicates that we are becoming habitual failures. The way to change such a habit is to become successful and the fear will disappear. Some persons continue to fail, giving little attention to improving their means for overcoming the objective danger, and instead, set about to overcome the fear itself. Continued failure and increased fear is the only possible result of such a procedure. Suppose you were a witness to the ravages of a madman bent on killing everyone he saw. Would you tell yourself that you must overcome your fear? Certainly you would do better to ask yourself how to overcome the madman. The only way to master a fear is to discover what it is that caused the fear and to meet that situation adequately.

Allies of fear. Any factor which tends to prolong fear beyond its stage of usefulness is dangerous and should be avoided.

1. *The strongest ally of fear is ignorance.* Our forefathers were afraid of thunder storms because they did not know what caused them or how they operated. They thought that the gods were fighting with each other and that thunder was caused by Thor's hammer. We have built devices to protect ourselves from lightning, our

casualties from that source are few, and we are no longer afraid. Thousands of other fears of natural events, such as eclipses, meteors, comets, cyclones, diseases, volcanos, and the like, have been eliminated or have been lessened in their intensity, through understanding. Fears of silly superstitions, such as ghosts, devils, fates, vampires, and the like, have vanished.

2. *Superstition accentuates ignorance.* But this progress away from fear through learning is a halting affair due to a queer quirk in our mental processes. We fear a thing originally because we do not understand it, but this fear becomes changed to a fear of investigation of the thing which causes the fear. We become superstitious, that is, we explain the event in a manner which precludes any further study. The study of the feared event is assumed to be a wicked act which can only bring destruction upon the investigator. What a vicious circle this creates! We fear because of our ignorance and then make our ignorance a virtue and develop a fear of knowledge, the only thing which will dissipate the fear.

3. *Superstitious friends provide a fear threat.* The history of thought demonstrates that progress has been made, and this vicious circle broken, only when some hardy soul finds it more satisfying to run the risk of being injured by his pursuit of knowledge than it is to spend his life doing what the majority of persons are doing, living an existence of fear and superstition. When such a courageous individual begins to discover the laws which determine a fearsome event he finds himself confronted with a worse danger than those inherent in his field of investigation; he discovers that his fearful comrades turn upon him like a pack of wolves and tear him to shreds because he is not willing to remain in ignorance with them.

So it comes about that, while ignorance means fear, wisdom means even greater danger—the danger of vengeance from all of one's ignorant comrades—and consequently is a greater occasion for fear than was ignorance. In comparison to this latter danger one might really enjoy the fear that comes with ignorance because it is so much less than the fear which accompanies wisdom.

How can one escape this double threat: the Scylla of ignorance on the one hand and, on the other hand, the Charybdis of vengeance from superstitious and ignorant contemporaries? The great majority of people escape by joining the ranks of the ignorant and superstitious and by engaging in the persecution of the few who have the temerity to combat ignorance and superstition. One avoids trouble by such a procedure, he avoids any personal conflict by joining the majority and permitting the mob to fight his battles for him. This avoidance of any personal conflict may enable him to maintain his mental health but it is a feebleminded way of doing it.

Every advanced idea has brought suffering to its early advocates. We accept the notion of the plurality of worlds, but Giordano Bruno, the Italian astronomer of the sixteenth century, after six years of imprisonment and two years in the dungeons of the Inquisition at Rome, was burned at the stake for teaching it. Galileo, who discovered that the earth moves around the sun, saved his life only by recanting and asserting that the sun moved around the earth. History is filled with instances of humiliation, near-martyrdom, and martyrdom because men have sought the truth rather than submit to humiliating fear. "Truth, crushed to earth, shall rise again," but it leaves behind it a trail of suffering and death. Is it any wonder that people actually enjoy the fear that accompanies ignorance rather than face the added dangers which accompany learning? Mobs will pray, in abject terror, for deliverance from the plague of some disease they do not understand and murder the man who, in his laboratory, is discovering a cure for the disease.

Through our knowledge of the laws of nature we have been enabled to eliminate to a great extent fears of natural events. If, perchance, some new phenomenon in the physical world is beyond our comprehension, we at least take a rational attitude toward it, and our fear is merely a temporary expression of our inability to cope with it. Few persons in this present period of civilization lose their mental balance because of a chronic and uncontrollable fear of natural events.

Present need is knowledge of human nature. On the other hand, modern man is profoundly ignorant of the laws governing human behavior, and because of this ignorance is much more likely to develop fears and superstitions about human relationships than he is about physical events. This ignorance covers both our own behavior and the conduct of others.

When we have performed an act we know little about why we did it. Our attempts to explain our behavior are usually silly and unwarranted. The folly of such explanations we cannot discern very clearly when we account for our own conduct but we can easily see how superficial such explanations are when proffered by others. We form plans for the future and with all the determination in our power decide to carry through the project only to find ourselves unable to persist in our determination.

In the face of this extreme ignorance of our own behavior and our inability to control our conduct, some of us may become blithely indifferent. Many of us are openly afraid of ourselves and those of us who conceal such fears usually find them lurking in the background ready to pounce upon us at the first opportunity. Some of our own thoughts may so terrify us and surprise us that we cannot understand how they can belong to us.

If we are ignorant of our own behavior, we are more profoundly ignorant of the reasons for the conduct of others. All of us develop some rule of thumb formulas to guide us in our relations to others, but they are only makeshifts and we soon learn that we cannot rely upon them. When they do not hold, we can blame the failure on the perversity of our friends, we can avoid human contacts, or we can give the same sort of superstitious explanations that our forefathers gave in attempting to explain thunder and lightning.

The way to overcome fear of people is to learn more about human conduct. Knowledge of natural laws dispelled for man the fear of natural law; knowledge of the laws of human conduct will enable him to eliminate his fear of himself and of others. Ignorance and uncertainty breed fear; knowledge and assurance dispel fear.

How fear may become a habit. Having been pursued by a vicious dog a number of times you may develop the habit of being afraid of that particular dog. Such a habit is a purely reasonable one and indicates that you have not learned how to handle that dog. The fear may not stay confined to that specific dog even though you have no similar experiences with other dogs. You may carry over the fear of one dog so that it becomes a fear of all dogs. Indeed, the fear may spread further and may include all four-legged, hairy animals. It is very easy for a fear to spread from one single object to a large number of related objects.

Furthermore, the fear may readily spread to relatively unrelated objects, or to incidents which merely happened to be connected with the fear situation. If you chance to have an object hit your head when you are in the dark and in an empty house, you are likely to become afraid, not only of the object which hit your head, but of the dark, or of all empty houses, or of being alone. In fact, anything which reminds you in any way of the previous fear experience may arouse in you all the effects of a repetition of the experience.

To make matters still worse the fear element from a number of vastly different experiences may combine in their effect on their victim. The following fearful events all happened to one boy in the course of a week. He was frightened by a tornado and thunder storm in which the barn was carried away; he was chased by an angry bull; he fell from a horse and narrowly escaped being crushed; he failed in his lesson and was ridiculed by the teacher before all the other pupils; he was teased unmercifully by the other boys because they had caught him giving an apple to a little girl; and, as the result of this teasing, he got into a fight with a boy much bigger than himself and was badly beaten. Is it any wonder that, when we saw this boy somewhat later, he had a hangdog, beaten expression? He had developed the habit of fear and failure because all these experiences had combined in their effect upon him. He did not know what was going to happen to him next, but he was sure it would bring disaster to him no matter what it was.

Finally, it may be possible to develop the habit of being fearful even though you have had no specific fearful experience from which to develop fear. You may absorb a fear attitude if you are forced to associate intimately and for long periods with a person who has a morbid or depressed outlook on life. The absorption of attitudes from those around us is not inevitable. Indeed, it is possible to compensate and tend in the opposite direction; we may see how silly it is for our mother or friend to be depressed and be over-optimistic as a result of this insight. Nevertheless, it is easily possible to find ourselves being fearful if we have to live with those who are in a state of constant dread and anxiety. When young people show an unusual tendency to be fearful at the slightest provocation it is very reasonable to expect that they have mothers or fathers of the worrying, anxious type.

What a range of possible causes may be behind the habit of fear! All the way from a series of dog bites to the contact with a brooding father or mother! What to do about it? There is just one thing to do, no matter where the habit came from, and that is to substitute a fighting habit for the fear habit. It will do no good to attempt to bolster up courage by "sheer determination" to be brave. Fear is built upon experiences in which failure is a large factor; courage is built upon experiences where success is a large factor. The way to overcome fear is to substitute the habit of success for the habit of failure.

Vague versus specific fears. The application of the principle which we have just stated for overcoming a fear will vary in accordance with the nature of the fear. Building up the habit of success in connection with dogs is quite different from building the habit of success as a substitute for the vague fear which developed from contact with a worrying father or mother. The difficulty lies in the fact that the more vague the fear happens to be, the less likely is the person to know what caused it. If a mother has developed a worrying attitude for reasons which are not clear to herself and if her daughter has developed a morbid attitude because of contact with her, it is apparent that the daughter will have little realization of why she is afraid. She may tell you that she is afraid she will become sick, that she will not be able to support herself, that she will fail in her studies, and the like; but the truth of the matter is that she has no notion of why she is depressed and fearful.

On the other hand, if a boy has a fear of a dog which is based on several unfortunate experiences which he remembers vividly, he has something very concrete and tangible with which to work. He watches dogs from a safe distance, he studies their behavior—their psychology, if you please—discovers that some dogs are very affectionate and harmless, distinguishes the vicious ones from the good-natured ones, and builds up rational behavior patterns for himself instead of his unreasoned fear patterns. When he has learned how to conduct himself rationally with dogs his fear of them disappears. Such specific fears do not disrupt mental life. If they are not overcome in the method just outlined they may remain indefinitely, but they do little harm—they merely make for inconvenience at times. If they become too disturbing they can be overcome with sufficient practice of the right sort.

A vague, intangible fear cannot be handled in this way because one cannot get acquainted with, and learn new reactions toward, something which exists not at all or in an extremely shadowy or tenuous form. If your fear is nothing more clear than a foreboding of some dire happening, you cannot get acquainted with it unless you trace it back to its real meaning. Vague fears do have real meaning and the first task is to get behind their mask and see them in their true light. Then they can be handled in the same simple fashion as a fear of some harmful object in our environment.

How fears disguise themselves. When a fear cannot be diminished by straightforward dealing with it—by getting acquainted with the object of fear and learning new ways of acting toward it—when you recognize that it is foolish to have the fear while acting in a fearful manner, it is evident that the real cause of the fear is disguised and that you are dealing with a superficial manifestation of the real fear or with some symbol which merely suggests the fear without disclosing its identity. It is because fears can be disguised that they become harmful to the mental life of the one who possesses them. The first task is to penetrate that disguise and see the fear in its true light. When this is accomplished the task of mastering the fear is relatively easy.

Not all disguises are the same. In fact it is quite probable that in each case they are so different that it is impossible to describe the true fear by a description or analysis of the disguise. All we can do is to describe some of the forms of true fear which tend to disguise themselves in order to give ourselves some sort of clue as to how to study each disguise as it comes. The forms of hidden fear which we shall discuss are only illustrative and the individual differences are multitudinous.

1. *Fears from infancy.* Fears may be established in infancy before the child has knowledge of any words with which to designate the object which causes the fear. It is not necessary to have a name for an object in order to be afraid of it. The results of such fear experiences may exist in later life as vague, indefinite fears which seem to the owner to be silly, meaningless affairs. Their obscurity is accentuated because there is no memory of the

experiences which gave rise to them. Sometimes a fear attaches to some irrelevant object connected with the infantile situation and all that is manifest is the possession by the adult of a paradoxical fear of some specific object.

One young man had an abnormal fear (phobia) of rubber. This fear existed from the earliest remembered years of his childhood. While later experiences may have accentuated this fear, the original fear experience must have been an infantile one because he recalled experiences which indicated that he was already afraid of rubber at the age of three. A possible hypothesis is that the original fear began by his experience with the rubber nipple of his bottle. This boy's mother had very great difficulty in weaning him. He became sick when given artificial food, had a long period of malnutrition and rebelled against the bottle with great emotional fervor. We have no way of proving this thesis as to the cause of this fear, of course, but it seems reasonable to guess that his fear of rubber might be part of his antipathy to being weaned and his emotional reaction against the nausea.

John B. Watson did some experiments which indicate that the establishment of definite fears in infancy is possible. He found that a sudden, loud sound caused fear in a child. He also found that children are not afraid of furry animals, such as dogs, cats, rabbits, and the like. In experimenting with one child he produced a sudden, loud sound every time the child attempted to touch a tame rabbit. By repeating this experience several times he made the child so afraid of the rabbit that he would cry and withdraw every time he saw it, even when no sound was made. This is called by psychologists a conditioned reaction. The child was at first afraid of the sound but he was not afraid of the rabbit. By repeatedly presenting the fearsome sound in conjunction with the rabbit the child learned to fear the rabbit when the sound was absent. Many things are learned in this manner and thus many fears become established.

Suppose that no steps had been taken to change the child's fear of the rabbit. It is easy to see that he could have developed into a grown person with an intense fear of rabbits and no memory of the experiences which produced this fear. The owner of such a fear would merely be able to tell you he was afraid and would probably accompany his confession with a qualifying statement that the fear was silly. He would tell you that he knew the rabbit to be harmless, that he knew he should be able to overcome the fear, but that he could not.

Watson went further, however, and showed by an experiment how to eliminate such a fear. He permitted the rabbit to appear as a minor part of a very pleasant situation—the situation being a very tasty dessert which the child was eating. By making sure that the pleasant part—the dessert— was always stronger than the fearsome part—the rabbit—by keeping the rabbit at a respectable distance, he gradually overcame the fear. Eventually the child was taught to like the rabbit.

This experiment provides the principle which should enable even a grown person to overcome a fear, provided the fear was established in the simple manner described, and provided the only disguise is a lack of memory of the specific incidents which caused the fear.

Make the object of fear a minor part of a pleasant and desirable situation and it will gradually partake of the emotional tone of the desirable situation as a substitute for the emotional tone of fear. The change will, it must be clearly recognized, be a very gradual one.

2. *Fear of insecurity.* Normally every person should progress gradually from the helplessness of infancy to the independence of adult life. This journey should be accomplished with such smoothness that the individual has no feeling that he is achieving anything extraordinary when he is developing independence and, certainly, he should have no accompanying forebodings of the evil consequences of losing the protecting help of his mother, father, or other adults who have provided an infantile haven for him. Some young people, nevertheless, view with apprehension their insignificance in relation to the growing complexities and responsibilities of life. Leaving home produces virtual agony in some persons. Even intelligent students are sometimes so tormented with the contemplation of the responsibilities that fall upon a college graduate that they adopt all sorts of devices (failure in studies, "nervous breakdowns," infractions of discipline, and the like) in order to prevent their graduation and so avoid the inevitable thrust into the "hard, cold world." In varying degrees others are afraid of marriage, parenthood, or executive responsibility.

Such fears are very common, but seldom do you hear persons acknowledging them. They will give all sorts of excuses to explain ther failure in college, their choice of celibacy, their failure to have children, or their refusal of a position of responsibility. The nobler the "reasons" these persons give the less likely they are to be the real ones. In most instances the real cause of their conduct is fear—a fear of insecurity. They are unable to tear loose from their traditional moorings and trust to their own powers to undertake the voyage of life. They must cling to home, to some loved one, to some institution, to some law, custom, or tradition to give them stability and some measure of confidence. These persons are pitiable spectacles because they are afraid and do not realize that they are afraid, much less what it is they fear. The various social institutions should provide means for hardy individuals to accomplish more by means of co-operation than they could single handed; their function is degraded when they become solely a refuge for fearful individuals who have learned no measure of independent activity.

What conditions of infancy foster these fears of insecurity? They may be the result of too much love and affection from mother, father, or nurse. Such extremes of affection beget in the child an expectation that everyone whom he meets will bestow the same unselfish devotion upon him that he was accustomed to receive from his mother. When he discovers that such extreme solicitude is not forthcoming he feels totally lost and must either run back to his mother or, if this is impossible, is filled with a vague dread—a feeling of being lost. He must have some one to whom he may cling.

A second infantile situation which may lead to this fear of insecurity is the sudden removal of affection. This may result when a first child who has been accustomed to an excess of attention is dethroned by the appearance of a second child. The jealousy which this situation creates may set up an attitude which follows the dethroned child through life. He judges everybody by the degree of devotion they give to him and is continually looking for signs of slights or fancied injustices when there are none. He must have love to be secure, he is sure that no one loves him devotedly, he accuses his best friends of insincerity, his wife of infidelity, pretends not to care whether anyone loves him or not; but behind all this is the hidden fear that he will eventually be stranded, a lone creature in a world of enemies.

A third reason that might underlie the feeling of insecurity is the tendency on the part of some parents to hold up before their children standards which are too high. In their attempt to make their children reach these standards they take the rôle of judges or critics, goading them always to do better by showing them the defects in what they do accomplish. So treated, a child is sure that he can do nothing correctly. Being always reminded of his faults he can never build up a feeling of confidence. The parents think their constant emphasis on perfection is motivating their child to do better, but in the end such treatment is more likely to build up an attitude of utter helplessness, failure, and the futility of trying to improve.

To overcome the feeling of insecurity one must make a study of the form it takes in him and try to get behind the disguise to the probable situation which caused it. If you can get a little perspective and look at yourself coolly you will realize that a grown person should not demand the same extreme devotion from any person that a helpless infant gets from his mother; the grown person should get more fun from taking care of some other person than in being cared for himself. If your fear of insecurity is largely tinged by jealousy and you can see the infantile nature of this jealousy you will understand that one does not get love from others by picking flaws with them or by demanding more love. Jealousy always drives people away from us and destroys the hopes of filling the very void that started the jealous process—the lack of love. Finally, if the insecurity is based on the insistence by your parents upon too high a standard of perfection,

you can set about getting a more sane view of human accomplishment. Success is not to be measured by the
attainment of some arbitrary goal which we set up in
infancy, or which we have had set up for us by some doting
admirer, but by the courageous adjustment to every difficulty which life presents to us.

3. *Fear of guilt.* Remorse, the sense of sin, the feeling
of guilt, the pangs of conscience—these are all names for
one of the most intense and persistent forms of fear that
man can experience. The fears that one undergoes in
the face of an objective danger are usually less intense
and surely less persistent than the fears that are based
on a sense of sin. The anguish that victims of conscience
suffer is of extreme poignancy. Moralists tell us that such
pain is deserved and that the victims are paying their
just debts in such suffering. Indeed, there is a tendency
on the part of "good" people to gloat over the agony
of "sinners," probably because they have a subtle feeling that the "sinners" have experienced some pleasure
in their "sins," of which they have been deprived, and
their gloating is a form of jealousy.

The "sense of sin" is not a just retribution for stolen
pleasures. This is evidenced in the fact that the degree of
suffering is not usually in proportion to the degree of sinfulness of the victim. Many a hardened "sinner" suffers
no pangs of conscience at all, while a holy person, one
who has lived an exemplary life, may suffer untold agony
because of some tiny lie or some very minor indiscretion.
If the agony of conscience is a payment for wrongdoing
the observer is led to the conclusion that it must be administered by a most inequitable judge. Close analysis
of individuals would lead one to the opposite conclusion,
that conscience is largely a fear which brings suffering to

"good" persons and which causes relatively little suffering to "bad" persons.

The feeling of guilt and the fear of sin may be exaggerated as a preventive, a barrier against the possibility of committing some undesirable act. This is especially likely to be adopted by a person who has already made a mistake, although the mere possibility of such an error may be enough to cause the accentuation of the feeling of sin. When a temptation arises it leads to an increase of the feeling of remorse so that the remorse so fills the horizon that there is no room left for the recognition of the temptation of the present moment. Such persons are likely to confess to many persons, to bewail their past sins and wickedness, and to manifest such agony of repentance that the hearers are filled with sympathy and are too likely to have their attention centered on the exaggerated past of the confidant. They will think that the poor sufferer is paying the just rewards for a past transgression, whereas he is exaggerating what has happened because he is afraid of himself at the present moment.

Such a person needs not so much consolation for his past as he needs encouragement to face the present and the future with assurance.

In other words, the persons who are most firmly enslaved by their fear of guilt are usually the ones who have the least need of such a restraining influence; they are the ones who are already circumspect in their behavior. The ones who need most to be restrained by their conscience are likely to have it developed least. The sense of sin cannot be explained as a form of retribution for sins committed nor as a device to keep one from committing evil acts. The conscious part of the feeling of guilt may be accentuated when one feels that he is about to be discovered in some error and to be punished for it, but there is a large part of the guilty feeling which cannot be explained in this simple fashion—it is not wholly chagrin at being caught.

The greatest part of the sense of sin is a wholly unreasonable fear which, in each individual case, is a relic of childhood. The child's first fear of sin comes when he has brought down upon himself the disapproval of his mother or some loved one. He probably has no rational explanation of why they are angry—he merely knows that they are and is afraid that the outcome of this anger will be his exile from the bond of affection upon which he has learned to depend.

Even at this early stage the degree of his fear of guilt is not in proportion to the enormity of the act he has committed, but to the degree of his emotional attachment to the beloved person and the severity of the threat that this bond will be broken. The child's first fear of guilt is the fear that he will lose his mother—that she will leave him in disgust. He begins to study the things that displease her and these things are to him immoral, no matter what the rest of society thinks about them. The emotions which are begun in this fashion adhere to him and color his adult reactions to related acts. He does not know why he has such a guilty feeling when something trivial happens; he may argue with himself, but the emotion persists. Witness the man, who gloats over the fact that he just smashed another's fender, blushing and feeling abjectly humiliated when he spills a little coffee on the tablecloth. Tell most men that their hands are dirty and they will laugh. Tell them that they have dirt behind their ears and they will become crimson.

In short, when we judge our conduct by the degree of

guilt or self-approval which we feel upon committing an act, we are judging ourselves by infantile standards. The feeling is an unconscious remnant from infancy. Our feeling of guilt is no adequate measure or guide to tell us to what extent others dislike our behavior. The fear of guilt began with a fear of displeasing others and persists as a silly fear of displeasing ourselves when we have no conscious or rational notion as to why one act pleases us and another displeases us.

How can the victim of a tender conscience train himself to rational behavior in place of his silly fears? By remembering that fear of sin is in the last analysis the fear of displeasing others and of losing their esteem as a result. If he makes a rational study of the likes and dislikes of others he will have a rational basis for his behavior. He refrains from certain acts because he learns that these acts injure other persons either physically or emotionally. He cultivates those forms of activity which he learns will bring happiness to others. He can thus substitute a social basis for morality for the irrational feeling of right and wrong which he learned in infancy and to which he still clings when he lets his conscience be his guide.

Bertrand Russell gives some good advice in this connection: "Whenever you begin to feel remorse for an act which your reason tells you is not wicked, examine the causes of your feelings of remorse, and convince yourself in detail of their absurdity. Let your conscious beliefs be so vivid and emphatic that they make an impression upon your unconscious strong enough to cope with the impressions made by your nurse or your mother when you were an infant. Do not be content with an alternation between moments of rationality and moments of irrationality. Look into the irrationality closely with a determination not to respect it and not to let it dominate you. Whenever it thrusts foolish thoughts or feelings into your consciousness, pull them up by the roots, examine them, and reject them. Do not allow yourself to remain a vacillating creature, swayed half by reason and half by infantile folly. Do not be afraid of irreverence towards the memory of those who controlled your childhood. They seemed to you then strong and wise because you were weak and foolish; now that you are neither, it is your business to examine their apparent strength and wisdom, to consider whether they deserve that reverence that from force of habit you still bestow upon them. Ask yourself seriously whether the world is the better for the moral teaching traditionally given to the young. Consider how much of unadulterated superstition goes into the make-up of the conventionally virtuous man, and reflect that while all kinds of imaginary moral dangers were guarded against by incredibly foolish prohibitions, the real moral dangers to which an adult is exposed were practically unmentioned." [1]

4. *Fears as disguised wishes*. One of the most subtle forms of disguised fear is the fear of our own desires. The moral code which we have been taught to adopt precludes certain forms of conduct. We know we dare not do these things and so tell ourselves that we do not want to do them. These acts are "undesirable" and we assure ourselves that we do not desire to do them but, in spite of this assurance, there may be a lurking suspicion that we do desire them. We fear that if we did desire to do them we probably would do them, so we must shun the very thought that they might bring us any pleasure. We dare not desire them for fear we might perform them.

[1] Russell, B., *The Conquest of Happiness*, Horace Liveright, 1930, pp. 102–103.

But if we admit that we are afraid to desire to do some untoward act, it is tantamount to admitting that we do want to do it, so we have to disguise the fear in order to reassure ourselves as to the impregnability of our moral position and stamina. Fears of our own desires consequently seldom show themselves in their true light, but appear as fears of other things.

This disguise often takes the form of fearing just the opposite of the thing we are really afraid of; the thing we say we are afraid will happen is precisely the thing that we wish would happen. For example, when a woman says she is afraid that her sick husband will die, she may be expressing a real fear of losing one whom she dearly loves; or she may be expressing a fear of a hidden desire that he would die. In the latter event her fear would likely be overdone, she would show extreme and unwarranted solicitude and, in the event of his death, would show an extremely exaggerated sorrow, which is really remorse for her unconscious disloyal thoughts.

Again, the girl who protests a great fear of being pursued by some man, may be really afraid of such pursuit or may be disguising a wish to be pursued. The elderly maiden lady who looks under her bed each night for the villain may be covering a desire to find some assailant. The man who is extremely afraid that he may forget a financial obligation may be hiding a wish that he could forget to pay his creditors; he is afraid of a possible dishonest act because he wishes, unconsciously perhaps, for the advantages which might come to him were he dishonest. Life is full of illustrations of such fears.

The most striking criterion of the disguised fear is its exaggeration. But even an exaggeration is easily mistaken for a genuine emotion. If the wife overdoes her ministrations to her husband it will be more likely to be interpreted by herself and by outsiders, including her husband, as an intense love rather than as a disguised dislike. The girl who overdoes her fear of being pursued by the villain will consider this fear as evidence of unusual virtue rather than as a hidden desire which would be abhorrent to her.

It is this very exaggeration which makes these disguised fears potential threats to our mental health. If we could successfully disguise undesirable wishes and could gain more peace of mind by so doing, there would be no reason why we should not continue any such disguises which we may have and even to cultivate others. Why not continue in our sublime ignorance and bliss? For the simple reason that the more persistent the hidden desire becomes the more we need to accentuate the fear which serves to hide it until the fear becomes an energy-consuming force which may tend to disrupt our whole peace of mind.

Now let us go still deeper. Suppose we could dig out all these hidden desires and look at them squarely. Would we find that these desires in and of themselves were bad? Quite the contrary, we should find most of them very worthy and even those which, at first sight, might appear to be unworthy would probably be so merely because they have become distorted by some queer thinking on our part. When hidden behind a disguise of superstition and uncertainty the most wholesome desire can look like a specter and frighten the most hardy individual. When we penetrate such a mask we shall find that it is not the desire itself but the emotional attitude which we have built up around it which should be changed. It may be that we have conceived a poor way for attempting to attain our desires, in which case the mode of endeavor should be corrected rather than the desire relegated to the limbo of forgetfulness.

Certainly there is no reason why a young girl should be afraid to face her desire to be attractive to young men to such an extent that she must show it only in the perverted fear of being pursued by any strange man she happens to see on a dark night. She would do much better to tell herself that she desired to be attractive, and then calmly to look around to select the men upon whom she could make an impression and at the same time maintain her personal dignity.

What fears do to their victims. Fears do drastic things to their victims.

1. *Physiological changes.* Fears cause, in the first place, mighty physiological changes. The heart beats faster, breathing is increased, digestive processes are retarded, blood pressure is increased, there is an increase in muscular tension, the pupils become larger, the speech organs are affected so that the victim may emit cries or be paralyzed into silence, and certain internal glands increase their activity and accentuate general activity. These effects occur in spite of any attempt on the part of the victim to stop them. One may argue that he is not afraid but, if he is afraid, he will experience these violent reactions within himself. For example, a small boy, being frightened by a dog, ran to his father and attempted to hide his fear of the dog. His father asked him if he were afraid, to which he replied: "No, I am not afraid, but my stomach is."

Furthermore, these changes do not immediately subside when the occasion of the fear is removed. Many persons have had the experience of being frightened in a traffic tangle. They may extricate themselves almost automatically and in a few seconds find the crisis over with their car safely landed at the side of the road. Having passed the crisis with little evidence of fear, they now sit, with no immediate occasion for fear, filled with tension and overcome with trembling. It takes longer by far to calm down from the emotion of fear than it did to get out of the traffic jam. In fact it may take hours, or even days, to get completely over a violent fear reaction. This is normal.

2. *Motor incoördination.* Because of its very nature fear makes impossible the smooth operation of our muscular apparatus. After such a shock as the foregoing it would be hard to conceive of the driver being able to be as smooth and deliberate in his handling of his car. His hand would shake, his foot would tremble on the accelerator, he would look anxiously and nervously this way and that, he would sit more erect in his seat, grip the steering wheel more firmly, and make a zigzag trail. If he tried to carry on a conversation it might easily happen that his voice would be unsteady—he might even stammer. If the shock were extreme he might be totally incapable of driving. One should not be apprehensive because of such violent reactions. They indicate that the subject has made a healthy reaction to the accident. It would be unwholesome if he could maintain his poise and have absolutely no reaction to such a violent experience. All he needs, to overcome this trembling and lack of motor control, is time. If he admits he is afraid, joins with his friends when they laugh at his trembling, and watches with a little scientific curiosity his various performances, he will recover more quickly than if he attempts to fool himself and others into thinking that he was not frightened.

3. *Self-consciousness and blushing.* Most of us try to conceal from friends any fear which we may feel. One reason for this is our realization that persons admire strength in others and look with disparaging eyes upon the fearful individual. This supplies an impelling motive to hide any manifestations which might reveal fear. We may succeed in suppressing trembling, stammering, crying, or other indices of panic, but the fear will then play the traitor to us and reveal our true feelings in the form of manifestations of self-consciousness—blushing and the like.

The usual procedure of a person who recognizes his self-consciousness is to attempt to conceal it. Usually he is not very successful in this and to his original fear is added the fear of what others are thinking of him. His blushing is increased and he is forced to retire from the scene in the most extreme humiliation and chagrin.

Such discomfiture is the result of dealing with self-consciousness in the wrong manner. The contemplation of a fear-inducing object without doing something about it only accentuates the fear. One may argue with himself that he is not afraid in such circumstances but argument is of little avail and the fear will increase. Now, in self-consciousness the object of which one is afraid is oneself. It does no good to reiterate that one is not self-conscious— such affirmations only serve to keep the situation at white heat. Something must be done, some active and satisfactory reaction must be made. What might that be? Think of something else besides yourself and self-consciousness will depart.

When you are trying to make an exceptionally good impression upon some one who is held in high regard this situation is seen at its peak. You are afraid that you are not making a good impression and keep thinking about

yourself. Divert your attention from yourself to a study
of the interests and personality of the other person and
you will find that this will take your attention from yourself and the self-consciousness will disappear.

4. *Worry and exhaustion.* Fear which is not circumvented by the method of doing something definite to the
fear-inducing stimulus results in a great expenditure of
energy which grows with the strength and persistence of
the fear. The fatigue which results from this useless expenditure of energy is often explained as the result of
overwork but it is seldom that this fatigue condition can
justly be attributed to work. The work may be excessive
because the subject is using it as a distraction device—
something to enable him to forget his fear. But the work
without the emotion would seldom cause excessive fatigue.
It is the internal tension produced by the fear which has
the real debilitating effect.

If the fear is one of the subtle disguised fears we have
described, the fatigue is accompanied by excessive worry
about all sorts of trivial things. Chronic worriers are
seldom helped by removing the cause of the worry about
which they complain for the good reason that this factor
is seldom the real cause of the fear. It is a disguise in
itself. The chronic worrier needs to get at the underlying
cause of his feeling of failure and when he has dealt it the
death blow the tendency to worry will disappear with it.

5. *Queer compulsive acts.* Disguised fears are quite likely
to lead to ill-timed, spasmodic, overdone, and queer behavior. The fear drives its victim to do something. Not
knowing why he is afraid, he will most surely do the wrong
thing, but he will still be driven to continue to act, even
though it is apparent to himself and to others that his
behavior is silly. Such conduct is known as compulsive

activity. The victims of such an urge will tell you that they are acting in a peculiar manner, they will tell you that they do not know why they act as they do, but that they have a strange impulse to continue the conduct.

Instead of attempting to control the compulsion, the victim of such an impulse should search for the real cause of the fear if he ever expects to make his conduct rational. For example, a person may be filled with a fear of moral guilt. This fear may take the symbolic form of a fear of having his hands defiled. To correct this guilt he will feel an urge to cleanse his hands and may continually wash them. He can argue that his hands are clean, he can find no trace of dirt on them, but he will wash and wash them incessantly.

Such a compulsive act may be the sequel of a wrong act or it may be the expression of a fear of committing an act by a person whose conduct is faultless. In the first case it is backed by a fear of getting caught, a fear of suffering the consequences of the act; in the second the fear of the consequence is exaggerated as a safeguard against it.

How to overcome fears. Throughout our discussion we have given incidental suggestions as to how to deal with fears. We shall now bring these together and give them coherent, practical form.

1. *Do not be afraid of fear.* Fear is not an enemy, it is an ally. It is a device to make you stop fighting when you are getting the worst of it. It has the same value in the mental world as pain has in the physical world. A man with no pain sensations might easily burn his hand off. A man with no fear might easily go to his ruin.

2. *Use fear as a preparation to fight.* The period of inactivity which the fear imposes should be used as a preparation to fight. The sequence should be: fight—victory

or fear—reason—fight—victory or more fear—reason—
fight—victory or more fear—and so on. The use of reason
should make each fight different from the preceding one
and so increase the chances of turning previous defeat to
victory.

3. *Develop an insatiable curiosity about any fear-producing situation.* Let this curiosity lead you to learn more
about the fear stimulus. This has a double advantage.
It takes your attention from your own feelings and thus
diminishes the fear and at the same time enables you to
deal more effectively with the object which caused the fear.

4. *Do not fight your fears. Fight the things which make
you afraid.* The former line of conduct will merely
accentuate the feeling, the latter will help you to get rid
of the occasion for the fear. Fighting fear is a subterfuge
usually adopted to avoid the harder task of fighting the
thing which makes you afraid, but such a subterfuge is
a prelude to inevitable defeat.

5. *Penetrate to the real cause of disguised fears.* A
disguised fear can usually be recognized as such by the
fact that it appears to be silly, does not fit in with the
situation which is its supposed cause, and does not yield
to methods of adjustment which succeed with a straightforward fear. If you conceal from yourself the fear of
losing a loved one and explain your fear reactions as a
fear of poverty, obviously you cannot change your fear
by accumulating wealth. If you tell yourself that you
are afraid of poverty, and if your fear increases the more
money you acquire, you can be assured that it is not
poverty that causes the fear. You must get at the real
cause to enable yourself to adjust with adequacy.

6. *Do not let fear become a habit.* If you find yourself
becoming timorous whenever a certain situation presents

itself, substitute some other reaction for the fear one. Anger is a good substitute, Humor is excellent. Put yourself in an observer's position and notice how funny you look when you are afraid. Whistle, sing, shout, do anything rather than let yourself settle into an habitual fear. Habitual fear is the habit of being ingrown. Fighting is the habit of being outgrown or objective. Always aim to substitute the habit of fighting for the habit of fear.

Dangers that result from fear. When used correctly fear is man's ally in making wholesome adjustments to life. It is only when misapplied, exaggerated, or otherwise perverted that it becomes a threat. Some of these mistakes should now be apparent to the reader, but there are some which need specific mention.

1. *Morality based on fear.* The best type of moral person is the one who is guided by a desire to do the things which would be of direct benefit to his fellows. He has a highly developed social sense and his virtue is a positive endeavor to live up to the conception of service which this implies.

Too often moral behavior is purely negative—consisting of the avoidance of certain acts which are called immoral. If the emphasis is placed upon negative inhibition of behavior the tendency will be to search for some device to check aggressive conduct. One does not have far to seek until he discovers the tremendous negating function of fear. If one is afraid to do a certain thing the action is not likely to be performed. Why not use all the devices at hand to accentuate fear until one becomes terrified at the very contemplation of certain acts?

The value of such morality is very questionable. In the first place, the exaggerated and continuous emotional strain which such fears engender consume so much energy that the victim of them has little left to devote to worthy, positive endeavors. In the second place, the individual may find that the acts in question are not so certain in precipitating the dire consequences as he was first led to believe. His inhibitions are, consequently, likely to weaken as he sees life from a more rational standpoint. If acts are wrong only because one is afraid to do them and the fear is weakened or removed there seems no logical reason for being moral. The only solution is to exaggerate the fear or to become immoral. Certainly this is an undesirable sequel.

The truly moral person is not worrying about how much punishment he will have to suffer for his sins. He is so busy doing worthwhile things that he spends little time contemplating either rewards or punishments.

2. *Discipline is a poor form of control.* Just as the control of one's own conduct by fear is unwise so the control of others through fear is to be deplored. Discipline is the application of fear to other persons in order to force them to do our bidding. So long as the person in power is able to intimidate his subordinates, discipline may be of service to him; but the threats must be made increasingly stronger as the subjects become accustomed to them until a panic follows the very thought of disobedience. Such a state of mind is not conducive to mental health. While the places where discipline is used in this drastic fashion are becoming fewer in modern life, we are still victims of times, not so remote, when fear was given an important place in social control.

If discipline is limited to control by force in order to restrain persons of immature judgment from doing that which would injure themselves or others, it is a justifiable measure. When it is used in place of control by the inculcation of principles of reason in the subject, it can lead eventually only to disastrous results. Discipline is used in too many instances because it seems easier to frighten a person into conformity than it does to give him sound reasons for his behavior. In other instances it is used to force persons to do things for which there is no justification. If people cannot be made to obey our wishes except through intimidation, it is quite likely that our wishes have no merit. It is possible that we should not be obeyed were all the facts known. Obedience that cannot stand the light of reason had better be abandoned.

3. *Attempts to hide fear.* If a person attempts to hide his fear instead of dealing directly with the situation which produced it, he is likely to develop some very harmful types of behavior. One common method of hiding fear is to compensate by bravado. The weakling in the executive's chair is more likely to strut than the man who has a genuine confidence in his ability. The latter does not need to exaggerate and assume any show of importance. The one of limited accomplishments is more likely to tell you about them than the one who has done much. The same thing holds of the person who puts on an exaggerated front of intrepidity. Penetrate his disguise and he goes to pieces in the most pitiable panic.

Here, again, we have an illustration of dealing with the fear itself rather than with the cause of the fear. The man who compensates is trying to hide his fear. If he takes an attitude of bravery in order the better to cope with the threat which faces him, well and good. If he takes such an attitude to convince himself and others that he has no fear he is sure to become more and more timorous at heart and this underlying attitude will eventually manifest itself.

4. *The search for thrills.* There is still another danger, the danger of enjoying fear. Having recovered from a panic with the realization that one is safe, one experiences an exquisite sense of relief and satisfaction. This latter emotion may be so satisfying that the subject of it desires to experience it again. In this quest he does foolhardy and even lawless acts in order to precipitate a fear that will reproduce for him the satisfaction of escape from danger. So long as these endeavors are limited to such things as college pranks, riding roller-coasters, and such sports as ski jumping, they are wholesome. When they take the form of juvenile hold-ups, bank robberies, and the destruction of property, one pays too dearly for his thrill.

Value of fear. We have pointed out some of the pitfalls that result from a misuse of fear, anxiety, and worry. Because fear is misused does not imply that it should be eliminated from life. The knowledge of its abuses should enable us more intelligently to use it effectively and at the right moments. The following excerpt from an editorial states the case for fear very effectively:

"In view of the unjust disrepute of anxiety as a form of mental exercise, an examination of the many good reasons why we should worry is sharply pertinent.

"The best argument for worry is the kind of people who tell you not to. Their smooth foreheads are likely to suggest a corresponding internal blankness. It seems as if even to themselves they must be savorless, these never-worriers. As to achievement, they can never reach the highest; they may jog along complacently either on a mediocre level of success or may, like Mr. Micawber, dance nimbly along the surface of flat failure, but to attain the sure foot that scales the heights one must possess a vivid sense of pitfalls. Poor dullards of optimism, they miss the zest of that success granted only to those who have worried out a course of conduct to meet the most pessimistic forecast of the future.

"As a friend the confirmed optimist is monotonous. You like a few ups and downs in a friend. The never-worrier offers the resilience of a punching-bag to the blows dealt him by his own life, and a corresponding indifference to the blows dealt him by yours. In order to worry well over some one else one has to be thoroughly practiced in worrying over one's self. We all know that when we want sympathy we turn to the best worrier we can find, knowing that he will take our case right on and have a fit over it. When we are choosing a comrade, we find the fact that a person has denied himself the enriching luxuries of worry a positive deterrent. . . .

"But worry, to be genuinely educative, should be systematic and not slipshod. . . . Method with melancholy inclines to have the same result as the proverbial tear-bottle offered to the crying child. In other words, worry is an elusive visitor; welcomed and analyzed, she is as likely as not to go flying out of the window."[1]

QUESTIONS

1. What is meant by an adequate cause for fear?
2. Define fear in terms of conduct.
3. What valuable function does fear perform?
4. Why should fear be temporary?
5. Give the reason why one should not fight the emotion of fear.
6. How can fears be overcome?

[1] *The Outlook*, 1918, *120*, pp. 656–657.

7. Name three allies of fear.

8. Describe some fears that are based on ignorance.

9. Why are superstitions so persistent in their influence upon man?

10. Explain why the supporters of a superstition are so ardent in defending it.

11. What is the double threat that interferes with the advancement of knowledge?

12. How do most persons escape this double threat?

13. Why does martyrdom so often go with advancing knowledge?

14. Why are most modern superstitions related to human conduct?

15. What lesson does the history of the conquest of superstitions about the physical world teach us about the need today?

16. Can you venture a guess as to why we know relatively less about human conduct than we do about physical events?

17. Show how fear may become a habit.

18. How can a specific fear grow into a general fear?

19. Show how diverse fears may combine to make a fearful type of individual.

20. How can we absorb fears from those around us?

21. How can the habit of fear be overcome?

22. What is meant by the habit of success?

23. Why is it harder to overcome a vague fear than it is to overcome a specific fear?

24. Outline the method that might be used to overcome a specific fear.

25. What is meant by a disguised fear?

26. What is the first step that should be taken in dealing with a disguised fear?

27. Name four types of disguised fear.

28. Why are fears which were definite to an infant likely to be indefinite to the same person when he is grown?

29. Describe how Watson taught a child to fear a rabbit.

30. Describe how he overcame that fear.

31. What principle can be stated as a result of these experiments?

32. Show that the "fear of insecurity" is a habit and how it is developed.

33. How could you train a child so that he would not develop the fear of insecurity?

34. Describe some of the devices a person uses to hide his feeling of insecurity.

35. What three different situations may give rise to a feeling of insecurity?

36. How may jealousy be developed in connection with the fear of insecurity?

37. What is a possible explanation why some persons enjoy the conscience pangs of others?

38. Give arguments why the "sense of sin" cannot be a retribution for past conduct.

39. What part does the fear of getting caught play in "conscience"?

40. Show how the fear of guilt is developed.

41. How can the fear of guilt be overcome?

42. Describe the way in which wishes become disguised as fears.

43. Show why exaggeration may signify that a fear is a disguised wish.

44. Name five effects of fear.

45. Name some of the physiological changes that fear causes.

46. What is a good rule to use to overcome self-consciousness?

47. How may fears lead to compulsive acts?

48. State six rules for overcoming fears.

49. Show why morality based on fear is undesirable.

50. What dangers result from discipline based on fear?

51. Under what conditions is discipline a good device to control behavior?

52. What may happen if one attempts to hide his fears instead of attempting to deal with the cause of the fear?

53. What is meant by "enjoying fear"?

54. State in your own words how fear may be of value.

CHAPTER IV

WHAT TO FIGHT FOR

"I just can't seem to concentrate on my studies," complained a freshman student in one of our large universities. "I made good grades in High School, I have mapped out a fine program of work, I need everything I am taking to carry me toward my ambition, which is to become a clergyman, but I simply cannot get interested in my studies. I fritter away my time, gaze vacantly into my textbooks and, if I keep on at the rate I am going, I will surely flunk."

This boy knew that there was something wrong but he could not tell what it was. He had set for himself a definite goal in life, he had mapped out a course designed to enable him to reach that goal, but he lacked the energy to begin traversing that pathway.

Why? If he knew what he wanted, and knew the steps he must take to get it, why should he fritter away his time rather than work toward his ambition?

In high school he had taken a great interest in amateur dramatics, had been given important parts in several plays, and had won some very favorable comments upon his acting. Having finished high school, he apparently gave up his interest in dramatics and registered in an agricultural college with the intention of pursuing the study of horticulture. Here his customary vivacity seemed to wane and he failed in his studies the first year. He was rather unconcerned about this failure but, because of it, decided that he was in the wrong work and the following year entered the university for the purpose of studying for the ministry. Now he became still more listless and indifferent to his work and began to fail from the very start.

He confessed that the only thing which interested him was the theater. He witnessed every play he could afford to attend and made the acquaintance of many of the actors. When telling of this interest he interrupted his flow of conversation several times with the question, "Do you think all actors are bad?"

"Why do you ask that?" he was asked.

"Mother thinks they are all bad, but I don't agree with her. I have met many actors who seem very nice. Do you think all of them are bad?"

The significance of this question is apparent. His secret ambition had been to become an actor. His mother had openly expressed her disapproval, not of his particular ambition, but of the members of the profession he had secretly desired to follow.

At first he had attempted to give up completely his interest in the stage and go into horticulture, the occupation of his father. The conflict between what he wanted to do and what he was trying to make himself do became so acute that it took all his energy and sapped his initiative, leading to failure in his studies.

His second choice was a compromise. He would be able to exercise his histrionic talents in the ministry and, at the same time, measure up to his mother's conception of goodness. But when he began to study the subjects which were prerequisites to his theological work, it looked as though he would get little chance to develop his desire to act and he again became discouraged.

The seriousness of this situation was largely due to the

fact that this boy did not understand the significance of the conflict he was having. He knew he liked the theater, he knew he had no interest in horticulture, he knew he was getting more and more bored with his new plan of work, but he did not know why.

The case of this boy presents a number of important questions that arise in connection with the choice of a vocation and the influence of that choice upon later success. How likely is the stated ambition to be the expression of a genuine desire and how likely is it to be a device to cover some secret wish? If one is to succeed should he not know why he has made the vocational choice he has? Is not emphasis in stating the choice of a vocation sometimes a compensatory device to hide uncertainty as to the wisdom of the choice? Do not young people often make themselves fail so as to convince themselves they are justified in changing to another vocation?

Objectives as incentives. An objective, if properly understood and wisely used, may exert an important influence in bringing success to a person: misunderstood and unwisely used, it may do untold harm.

College students who have a stated ambition do better work, as a rule, than those who have made no vocational selection. The man who schedules his work so that he has a definite assignment to complete in a given time accomplishes more than the one who merely works with no plan to guide him. The one who keeps a record of accomplishment and definitely sets out to beat his former record is more likely to improve than is the one who merely tries to "do his best." The attempt to beat another who is an acknowledged superior is always stimulating. In short, if a person sets out to get somewhere, he is more likely to arrive than if he is merely traveling because he feels he

must be on the go.   To be sure, the drifter often does
arrive at some very desirable locations.   So long as he
keeps moving he is likely to get somewhere, but he increases his chances of a successful journey if he provides
himself with maps and at least keeps track of where he is
and where he is going.

Recognizing the importance of an objective in life, we
are very likely to fall into an error of logic and jump to the
conclusion that the important thing is to get some sort
of goal, to make some sort of vocational selection, no
matter what it may be.   We argue that a poor selection is
better than none.   Quite the reverse may be true.   Would
it not be better to have no goal, to postpone our decision,
rather than to make a poor one?

Back in the teens of the twentieth century it was the
custom to mark highways by painting various colored
emblems on telephone poles and to call these trails by
such names as Jefferson, Lincoln, Yellowstone, and Dixie
Highway.   Maps were printed showing these trails in
beautifully colored lines.   Nothing was said about the
condition of the roads thus represented on the map, the
important thing seemed to be to keep on the trail.   The
one who followed such maps often got into the most
discouraging stretches of mud that have ever been given
the name of highways.   The traveler soon learned that he
could do much better by not adhering too closely to his
maps.   He used them to keep his general orientation but
relied upon local information to guide him as to the best
road to travel.   What consolation is it to the man who is
stuck in the mud to reflect upon the fact that he has a
beautiful map?   Do you suppose he is any happier as the
mules are pulling him out of the mud hole to take out his
map and to gaze at the gorgeous red line he is traveling?

This analogy illustrates an important principle to follow in mapping your future. Certainly it is important to select a vocation, an objective in life, and it is likewise important to map out the course which you plan to follow in your journey to that goal. But it is more important to be critical toward your selection, as well as toward the road you plan to take to realize your ambition, than it is to maintain your course once you have started. There is no virtue in adhering to a road if it is a bad one. Even though it be the best one, a rough journey may be inevitable and, in such a situation, one should not let roughness deter him; but it is foolhardy to adhere to a bad course when the only reason for doing so is that one has made a decision and feels morally obligated to stick to it for no other reason than that a choice has been made.

Vocational advice. The theory that one should adhere to the choice of a vocation, once it has been made, has been associated with another fallacy; namely "the fatalistic implication that in the grand cosmic scheme there is but one task that can be accomplished by a single person. It implies that if one finds his niche, success is assured. It further implies that the failures made by 'misfits' are due solely to the fact that they did not find the right avenue for their talents."[1]

No person can ever expect to make such an ideal choice of vocation that he will fit into it exactly with no attempt at adjustment on his part. It is better to attempt to adjust than to excuse one's mistakes by continual talk about being a square peg in a round hole.

No matter how well you choose you will find that you do not fit exactly; life is a matter of adjusting as you go

[1] Kitson, H. D., "Suggestions toward a Tenable Theory of Vocational Guidance," *Manual Train. and Voc. Educ.*, 1915, *16*, p. 267.

along.   Besides, each vocation has a great variety of specialized branches so that the vocation has the possibility of adjusting to the individual as well as the individual adjusting to his vocation.   There must be a continual process of interaction which should lead to a more and more harmonious relationship as time goes on.

Nevertheless, one wishes to make as good a choice as it is possible to make.   Is there a definite procedure that one may follow to insure the best selection?   There has been much selling propaganda for vocational guidance. The impression has been circulated that one may submit to a series of tests, interviews, and personality analyses which can be used to indicate precisely what field of endeavor he should follow.   Nothing could be farther from the truth.   There is no combination of tests of intelligence and personality traits that can inform you precisely what you are best fitted to do in life and any person who makes the claim that he can guide you in your vocational choice with such precision is grossly misrepresenting the facts.

The vocational adviser can give advice, but both he and the person he is advising should recognize that it is merely *advice* that is being given.   Advice is always an inaccurate guide because of the personal prejudices of the adviser and because of the limitation of knowledge. If accepted with these reservations, vocational advice may be of value.   If its significance is overestimated it may do untold harm.   The more emphasis the adviser places upon the certainty of his recommendations the greater the degree of skepticism the advisee should exercise in following it.   Beware of the person who tells you he knows exactly what vocation you should follow!   He is either a charlatan or a misguided enthusiast.

How to select a vocation. Keeping in mind the futility of attempting to find the one vocation for which one is preëminently fitted, and remembering that any help contributed by an adviser in this connection is nothing more than advice, how should one go about making a tentative choice in order to gain the benefits which accrue from having a definite objective even though that objective may later be changed?

1. *Investigate before you select a vocation.* This seems so obvious that it should not necessitate statement and yet it is failure to follow this simple rule which leads to most of the trouble in connection with vocational selection.

Do not let anyone "sell you" on a vocation. When one has been sold he has yielded to distorted influence, usually from some one who is prejudiced for his own personal reasons. It is bad enough to buy such things as tooth-paste, books, foods, clothing, and the like in a slip-shod fashion, without investigating what competing products are on the market. If the misrepresentation has been too gross you can easily change when the article is one which is being constantly consumed and must, in any event, be replaced; but it is unfortunate if you permit such lazy behavior to dominate you in the choice of such an important commodity as a life's work. Many a middle-aged man has found himself inextricably lodged in a vocation which was urged upon him by some well-meaning but prejudiced friend. The probabilities that a man will remain in an occupation depend (according to statistical studies) much more on the financial and domestic responsibilities which he must meet than upon his success in or fitness for his job. If a man likes his work he welcomes additional responsibilities—they act as incentives to greater and greater successes. Hating his work, he begins to hate the incumbrances which force him to remain in work he does not enjoy. Such an outcome is usually the result of sheer laziness in making the original selection.

Investigate before you select a vocation. Do not select in a hurry.

2. *Make your own choice.* Taking your time in making a selection should not deteriorate into mere passive waiting. Nobody makes a better victim for an aggressive salesman than a slow but passive buyer. If you were in the market for a car, for example, the sensible procedure would be to investigate, as thoroughly as you could, all the cars in your price range. You would have to listen to sales talks; but you would try to evaluate them all, and you would discount what the more aggressive salesmen told you. You would not wait to have the different cars brought to you, you would go out and hunt for every possible buy. If you buy before you do this you are foolish. What distinguishes buying from being sold is active investigation instead of passive waiting for advice.

Do not wait to be sold. Make an active study of the whole situation; get all the advice and help you can; but reserve the final decision for yourself and attempt to make it as unemotionally and rationally as possible.

3. *Use reliable sources of information.* How can you get the information you wish?

a. Read books about vocations. There are a number of books which describe the various vocations. Any librarian will assist you in locating these. Make as complete a list as you can of vocations which are within the limits of your personality and abilities and then compare them in the following respects: (1) the amount of preparation required, (2) the means of getting established upon the completion of preparation, (3) the opportunities for progress within the field, (4) the compensations, both monetary and in satisfactions inherent in the work itself, and (5) the intellectual, emotional, and physical desirability of the work.

The information you may be able to gain from a library will answer these questions only tentatively. It will not enable you to come to a final decision but will permit you to eliminate those vocations which are totally out of the question. With your range of selection narrowed by this preliminary survey, you will be in a position for more intensive study. The next step is to make a thorough study of this limited group.

b. Talk with people who know. The best way to proceed from this point is to get first-hand information by talking to men actually engaged in the various vocations on your list. Do not ask them to advise you as to whether you should enter their field. They do not know how to advise you. Merely get them to talk about their work. You will find most of them willing to do this if you will but listen. Talk to a number of persons in each field. Talk to disgruntled ones as well as contented ones. Let them tell the unpleasant as well as the pleasant features so that you can make an impartial judgment.

c. Try your hand at the most promising vocations. Having sifted down your range of selection to a few alternatives by the foregoing methods, give each of these a trial to see how you like them and how well adapted to them you are. Get a job during the summer or during your spare time in each of the fields. You certainly cannot consider that you have chosen wisely if you have not had a taste of the sort of thing you will have to do in that vocation.

The object of these various procedures is, let us repeat,

not to enable you to select the one vocation for which
you are best suited; it is to give you a perspective of the
field, to enable you to know just what the possibilities
are, and to give you the satisfaction, when you have made
a choice, of feeling that it has not been a blind choice.

Are vocational interests accurate guides?   Certainly
it is apparent to the most casual observer that a person
will work with more energy and effectiveness and for
longer periods at an occupation which stimulates his
interest than he will at one which has a superficial appeal
for him.   Should a person work along the line of his interest for a considerable period of time, he would doubtless develop proficiency in that work.   Why not depend
upon interests, then, as a guide in the selection of a vocation?

A difficulty arises from the fact that interests may
change much more quickly and much more radically
than abilities and skills.   A girl may change her interests
from office practice to housekeeping almost overnight
but it takes her some time to develop skill at housekeeping.   A boy can change his interest from medicine to law
but the training taken in medicine cannot be readily
shifted to law.   In brief, the situation is this: Interests
affect proficiencies—we do better work when we are interested in our jobs; but interests are very volatile and
shifting and may play havoc with our abilities.   A person
with shifting interests cannot hope to change his skills
rapidly enough to keep up with these interest changes.

Should we then devote our energies to maintaining
stable interests?   Can we force an interest in a job we
hate?   Only serious mental disruption and unhappiness
can result from such attempts.   We do not need to look
far to observe many instances of men and women who,

because of social and economic conditions, have been forced to do work which they hate. Such persons do mediocre work, watching the clock to see how quickly they can rush off to a golf course, to a movie show, or a night club. They may become rounders and drinkers in a vain attempt to secure a little fun from an otherwise intolerable existence. They may learn to hate the social order which has enslaved them, become cynics who hate and despise those who seem to be happy in their work. Their only consolation may be that some day they will be able to leave this "vale of tears" and enter a more tolerable existence in the life to come.

Let it be clearly understood that such pessimism results not from the actual work one is doing but from the attitude which one has developed toward that work. It is well known that two men may be working side by side at the same occupation, one hating his work and the other obtaining the keenest enjoyment from it. But all preachments to the disgruntled worker, admonishing him to learn to love his work, are usually vain.

Source of vocational interests. If interests are of such vital importance in vocational success, it is well to understand pretty clearly the nature of these interests. Where do they come from? What makes them shift from one objective to another? Are we forced to spend our lives as victims of changing interests or can we, through knowing their essential nature, exercise some sort of control over them?

1. *Early vocational interests are likely to be a reflection of family interests.* The little boy has a strong tendency to be influenced by the likes and dislikes of his mother and father. If the father likes his vocation very much and if this is seconded by the approval of the mother

the child is very likely to think his father's vocation is very desirable and may choose it for himself. If his father hates his work, continually talks about its difficulties, the boy is very likely to adopt the same attitude. If the mother complains about the father's work and is continually upbraiding the husband or shows in any way that she dislikes his work the child may react against this work. One boy, when asked what he would like to do, replied that he did not care much what he did but added that he would prefer anything except the work of the father. In this case the father was so engrossed in his work that the mother continually complained that he neglected his family for it. The boy looked on his father's vocation as an enemy of family harmony. He would avoid this outcome in his own life by selecting anything but the work his father was following. Interests resulting from these and similar situations should not be relied upon for the selection of a vocation.

2. *Heroic romancing is likely to color the preferences of the young child.* A boy would like to be a locomotive engineer because it seemingly offers thrills. He reads a detective story and decides he would like to be a detective. He sees a movie starring an aëroplane pilot and decides he will take up aviation. A girl sees a romantic movie, projects herself into the rôle of the star actress and decides she wants to go on the stage.

3. *Some childhood ambitions express an attempt to compensate for some real or fancied inferiority.* A boy with a poor physique will picture himself as an athlete or a director of physical education. A boy who has few friends will dream of becoming a Napoleon, will strut in his imagination before great armies of followers. One who has a speech defect will desire to be a criminal lawyer or a

William Jennings Bryan. A boy who has been impressed with his naughtiness will look forward to the priesthood or the ministry.

Sometimes these childhood interests persist throughout life with no apparent disadvantage to the individual. Sometimes the results are disastrous. The value or the threat of these interests lies not in the interests themselves, nor even in the cause behind them but in the fact that the possessor is ignorant of the basis of his interests. It would pay each person repeatedly and continually to examine the possible causes of his interests and evaluate these causes rather than to consider the interests in isolation or to hunt for rational explanations to justify the interests themselves.

Critical attitude toward interests is essential. The value of an interest to a person cannot be determined by the age of the person when it first appeared, by the length of time it has persisted, or even by the means by which it first came to the life of the owner. It might easily be possible that a chance meeting with an interest turns out to be a fortunate one. Its retention should not depend upon this early chance, but more upon later rational examination and decision. The danger lies in premature narrowing of interests or blind and unthinking persistence in an interest instead of rational interpretation and control. As a person reaches maturity, and throughout later life, there is a narrowing of interests, but this narrowing should not be permitted to operate too early in life. Maintaining a wide range of interests as long as possible is good insurance against unhappiness both in relation to vocations and the general conduct of life.

To be sure, at the other extreme we have individuals

who will never choose because of their fear of making a wrong choice. They are the chronic misfits, sure of but one thing, and that is that they are doing the wrong work. They have no interest in anything and drift from one job to another. This attitude should not be confused with the maintenance of a breadth of interests which we have just advocated. The person with a breadth of interests is attracted by many things with more or less equal force and withholds specialization for a time. The drifter lacks interest in anything. He is using his lack of interests as an excuse for failure or for a lack of application. It is not a poor sign for a young person to have too many interests; it is a bad sign when he has none. A complete lack of interests probably denotes a failure in insight, a conflict with some unconscious attitude which it would be well for the victim to uncover and deal with directly and consciously.

Can a person direct his interests? If you discover that it would be to your advantage to become interested in something which is relatively distasteful to you, must you bow to your interests? No. You can direct your interests by putting into practice the following simple rules:

1. *Think about the job instead of how you feel about it.* Activity breeds enthusiasm, but thinking about your interest in a job without being actively engaged in the job breeds monotony and discontent. Get busy and you will find your interest growing.

2. *Make a game of the job.* The attitude of a game is that of putting all your energies into it to beat your own former record, some competitor, or to learn to do it in some new way. The true contestant in a game is never satisfied and this dissatisfaction drives him on to better performance. The one who contends that he lacks in-

terest is often merely defending a weak complacency. He has a false sense of superiority that a contestant in a game can never adopt.

3. *Hunt for new elements in the job.* The more you learn about it the more interest it will gain for you. When you lack interest you are virtually bragging that you know all about it. You do not. If you will but look for them, you can find new meanings in what appears to be the most monotonous task. Interest is merely finding new meanings.

4. *See the relation of what you are doing to broader lines of activity.* Thus you can appreciate the significance of an apparently trivial task as related to exceedingly complex activities. You will cease to regard yourself as a useless appendage to society, but will see yourself as a useful link in an endless chain of related performances.

Understand and guide your interests and they will furnish the energizing influence to take you to your objective in life. Let every little whim control you and you will find your energies dissipated and your ambitions shattered. Finally, be master of your own interests and do not let others take the reins for you and dictate to you what you should do and in what you should be interested. Take their advice and learn from what they can tell you, but do not confuse these advantages with the submission to their commands. Eventually, your interests, if they are real interests, must be your own and can only come by activity in the task itself.

Making ambitions effective. What can be done to make ambitions function most effectively? Some persons voice very noble objectives but make no effective moves to reach the goal which they have set for themselves. Others seem to be inspired to tireless endeavor in their efforts to reach the object of their ambitions. Must one wait for inspiration to light upon him in some mysterious fashion, or can one take active steps to make his ambitions effective?

In the final analysis, the only reason why a person does anything is because he is dissatisfied. The result of perfect satisfaction is inertness. Dissatisfaction produces tension and provides an urge to activity of some sort. However, dissatisfaction is not enough. If it operates exclusively and extremely the result may be such a vivid sense of discouragement and hopelessness that one does nothing. The thoroughly discouraged person feels that there is no use trying, and gives up. Dissatisfaction must be accompanied by some assurance that the tension can be relieved in some manner. Consequently, an ambition, to be valuable, must make the person dissatisfied and at the same time open up to him the possibility of some hope of satisfaction.

The greater the contrast between one's goal and one's present status, the more poignant the dissatisfaction is likely to be. Therefore, if a person seems to lack incentive it has been found advantageous to make his goal higher in order to increase the contrast. The danger in this procedure is that the goal may be so far removed from reality that it ceases to be effective. To have a vague longing for something which is admittedly beyond reach may increase dissatisfaction but there is the danger of ultimate discouragement.

In order to inspire hope in a person the goal must be near enough to reality to make the person feel that he can bridge the gap. What is needed is immediate action, and the hope of getting some benefit in a relatively short time is the strongest incentive to undelayed activity. If a mistake must be made in either direction, it seems better to make it by getting an objective which is too near rather than one which is too remote.

If, because one has a near objective, he actually reaches it, what happens? Is he likely to congratulate himself upon having reached his goal and to desist from further endeavors? Quite the contrary. He is likely to experience such a feeling of exhilaration at having accomplished something that he immediately sets another objective to be reached. He has taken one step toward acquiring the habit of success, and sets about to make himself dissatisfied again so that he can repeat the thrill. If objectives are so high that they induce feelings of failure, they are failing in their purpose, and lower ones should be adopted. If they are so low that they lead to a false sense of pride, they should be raised. The proper function of ambition is to produce enough dissatisfaction to stimulate effort and enough success to create a sense of achievement.

An important conclusion which follows from these considerations is that ambitions and ideals should be changeable instead of static. The important thing is accomplishment of some sort rather than the amount of progress made toward some fixed goal. The questions to ask yourself are: Am I getting somewhere? Am I having a good time playing the game? Have the experiences of today prepared me to be even more successful tomorrow? The questions to avoid are: Have I maintained in its original form the goal I set for myself? How much farther do I have to go? What shall I do when I get there? How long will it be until I can retire?

Daydreams or ambitions. Why does an ambition stir you to activity? Why does it make you do better work and incite you to work harder than you would if you had no ambition? It does so because you vividly imagine how you will feel when you achieve your desires, when you attain the heights of achievement which you have set for yourself. Suppose you see a successful man gaining the plaudits of his friends. You project yourself in imagination into his position and get a thrill similar to the one you would get if it were you who was being praised. At the same time you realize that this imagined thrill is not as great as the one you would get were you actually being praised by your friends.

If this glow of imaginary achievement, when contrasted with the real facts—that you have not done anything to merit praise—stimulates you to attempt to bridge the gap, you have a motive for work. You work because you have a hope, an expectation, that some day, if you work hard enough, you will experience in reality the thrill you now feel with your imagination. The element which makes the ambition effective is the expectation of accomplishment. The most important question is: Do I really expect to be able to become the sort of person I imagine myself to be? It is not enough to say: I would like to be; I hope to be; or I wish I were.

Furthermore, you must have some sort of clear conception as to how and why you are to achieve your expectation. How much schooling do you need? How many years of training are required? Have you the required personality and intellectual qualifications? If you do not look over the whole situation in such a realistic fashion; if you think that achievement is dependent upon fate, some chance circumstances, or the gift of the gods; if your vision does not inspire you to work, you are a daydreamer instead of a person who is wholesomely inspired to accomplishment. Let your daydreams rule you and you will become a useless visionary—or worse—but if you let your imagination stimulate you to rule your environment you will accomplish something, even though it may be different from the goal you pictured to yourself.

Substitutes for achievement. The person who dwells upon his dreams without being stimulated to make them real may adopt various devices to relieve the pain thus produced.

1. *Turning ambitions to "sour grapes."* One method is to diminish the lure of one's visions by adopting a cynical attitude toward them. If a person can convince himself that his daydreams are sheer nonsense, the pain will be diminished. Consequently, he may set out to prove to himself that a man is a fool to hope for anything better. He tells himself that an objective looks inviting so long as it is at a distance, but that when one achieves something it loses its attraction. Why strive for something so evanescent? One is doomed to disappointment, he argues, so why make a fool of himself striving for something whose only charm lies in its remoteness? He strives to get confessions from those who have succeeded to the effect that their thrill of anticipation was keener than the thrill of accomplishment and then gloats over his superior wisdom in avoiding such an elusive quest. Like the fox, who found he could not get the grapes he desired, he says the grapes are sour anyway. He gets comfort from such an aphorism as: "Blessed is he who expects nothing, for he will not be disappointed."

He begins by setting his goal too high and ends by disparaging that goal and laughing at others who are foolish enough to attempt to improve themselves.

2. *Overemphasis on self-sacrifice.* Do you ever hear a really successful man dwelling upon the things he had to

give up in order to attain his position? Rarely. Yet this procedure is very common with young people who are just starting out to work toward their goal, especially if the stakes are very high and the goal seems very remote. To be sure, one must forego certain pleasures if he wishes to accomplish anything in this life; but when a person is completely absorbed in his work, interferences, even though they might in themselves be pleasurable, simply become unimportant because of the contrast with the greater interest. If you find yourself too much distracted from your work by trivial affairs it is a sign that you are not enough interested in your work. You cannot build up interest by fighting the distractions; you can only do it by using any device you can discover to increase your absorption in your work.

To the outsider, looking on, an architect who is absorbed in designing a skyscraper may be making a sacrifice when he gives up golf, the opera, picnics, and other pleasures that the observer holds dear; but the architect is so engrossed in his project that he does not want to play golf, go to the theater, or go picnicking. He is not making a sacrifice; he is doing the thing he wants most to do. He is not pitying himself and he wants no pity from outsiders. He is happy—he has found real happiness in a constructive occupation.

You will find, if you begin to give up pleasurable activities in order to increase your interest in a vocation, that such renunciations, instead of increasing your interest in the vocation, will make the repudiated pleasures appear more desirable and will eventually make you hate your work. You will have to give up more and more—you will go out of your way to find some sacrifice to make and your only reward for this will be a false sense of virtue for having done so. But your imagined virtue will not have the desired effect of stimulating interest. Such emphasis on the negative aspect of interests is wrong and the sooner in life you discover it the better it will be for you.

After hearing a concert by a famous unmarried opera singer, a young girl was heard to remark, "She deserves great credit for having renounced romance for her art." As a matter of fact, the singer never had a romantic nature, she had not renounced anything, but had devoted her life to the thing that interested her, her singing, and felt no sacrifice in the procedure. The auditor, the young unsophisticated girl, was merely giving voice to a conflict which she herself was experiencing. She had a strong romantic nature, but felt it her duty to devote her life to a "career" which she thought was incompatible with matrimony. When such a conflict arises, emphasis upon what one is missing when he undertakes to achieve some ambition is usually fatal. It makes for unhappiness, and will detract from the sort of zeal which success demands. A person who is devoted to his vocation certainly has time to fulfill other interests. History is filled with examples of successful persons who have had satisfactory romances as well.

3. *Habitual daydreaming.* The main task of life is adaptation. Life is a continual adjustment and readjustment to an ever changing environment. The man with an active imagination is much better able to effect these adjustments than is the man who cannot visualize the various possible situations which may lie ahead of him. In a sense the ambitious man is a dreamer. He builds the future in his imagination, usually with great vividness. But he does more than daydream—he sets about to make

his dreams come true. The dream makes him more dissatisfied with reality and he sets about to change reality. This is the wholesome way to use one's imaginary processes.

At this point a paradox comes in. Daydreams in and of themselves are likely to be pleasant. They give us a taste of imaginary success; we get a temporary realization of our wishes; we increase temporarily our feeling of self-esteem; we become indifferent to the disagreeableness of reality; we may be even deaf and blind to the facts of life which we do not wish to observe. All these aspects of the daydream are pleasurable and incite us to continue living in an imaginary world for the sheer pleasure we derive therefrom. On the other hand, we have seen that the only way in which these dreams can be of any value to us is to provide a contrast with the unpleasant aspects of real life and thereby make us unhappy and discontented. The contentment derived from the daydream should increase our discontent with reality and incite us to work toward the fulfillment in reality of the contentment which we dreamed about.

Furthermore, it is a fundamental law of mental life that we tend to repeat and make into a habit, through such repetition, those forms of activity which bring us pleasure. Why do not we all become happy dreamers? Why come back to reality at all? Mostly because we cannot escape. The realities of life force themselves upon us and awaken us rudely from our daydreams, just as morning wakes us from the sleep and dreams of the previous night. We *must* face life. The temporary daydream, or lapse from reality, has given us a taste of something better, it has made us hate some things in life even more cordially than we did before. What shall we do about it?

How daydreams become abnormal. As we have said, the normal man sets about to make his dreams come true. The first step in the direction of abnormality comes in *wishing* one could live always in the land of dreams, that one could avoid the hard devious tasks involved in transforming reality so that it approximates his dreams. The next step comes in the attempt to escape from reality into the land of dreams. The last step is where one actually accomplishes this; where one lives within himself and severs his relationship with his environment. He becomes a dissociated individual. Most of us at times have wished we could live in the land of dreams; some of us have tried to do so with little success; few persons reach the last stage, fortunately, that of losing their contact with reality.

But why, you may ask, this insistence upon adjusting to reality? If life is sordid why not escape from it? If daydreams provide happiness and reality provides unhappiness, if one can achieve the habit of living in fantasy and gain uninterrupted pleasure therefrom, why come back to reality? If most persons cannot achieve happiness through daydreaming because they cannot make their dreams continuous, why condemn as pathological the few who can? The answer is that we are animal organisms who are subject to all the influences of a physical world. We may be beset by the evils of wind and storm, the ravages of other animals, large and small, the pangs of hunger, the agony of suffering from disease, and all the other things which torment the human body. The few who isolate themselves to live in contemplation, in the world of imagination, can do so only because some of their fellows, who are facing the realities of life, are kindhearted enough to provide for their physical welfare. Let the individual who has achieved the habit of living in

the world of fantasy dwell alone on an isolated island—
alone with the wild elements and carnivorous animals—
and he will either awaken to the realities of life or find
his bones decorating the parched sands. Have I any right
to demand that hundreds of other mortals devote their
lives to providing the means whereby I may achieve
happiness in daydreams?

Bring the issue vividly to your own case. If some one
is kind enough to tolerate you and to support you, you
might live in your fantasies. But you cannot do it in
isolation. You either raise the food to eat or buy it with
money provided by others, and money means the results
of some person's grappling with the realities of life. You
either sleep in the open or under a roof erected by some
one who faced life as it is. You wear clothes produced by
yourself or by the labor of others.

The daydreamer is a person who is living "his own life"
to the n*th* degree, but when viewed in any sensible light
the insistence upon one's right to "live his own life" becomes mere idle chatter. It is the defense of one who is
failing in life and who expects all his friends to rally to his
support and provide for him. A man who is making an
attempt to adjust deserves the support of his more successful fellows, but when a man retires from the struggle
and takes on a "holier than thou" attitude, claiming his
life of "contemplation" is nobler than the life involved
in facing life as it is, he deserves little help. He needs the
jolt that reality can give him, he needs to be made unhappy enough to get into the death grapple with life.
Happiness achieved through daydreaming is socially an
unfair form of adjustment. It is usually begun early in
life and each of us needs to be on our guard against it.

An illustration will show the extremes to which a person

may go in escaping from the realities of life into the world
of his imagination. In one of our mental hospitals, for
several years, lived a woman who won the sympathetic
interest of all who saw her. She was only twenty-five,
charming in appearance, of good education and intelligence. Throughout her stay at the hospital her entire
time was taken in caring for a pet rag doll. She had made
the doll herself out of old rags, had stuffed it with anything she could find. She had made a complete wardrobe
for him, consisting of shirts, suits, underwear, pajamas,
and everything a little boy would need. She would wake
him in the morning, give him an imaginary bath, dress
him, feed him, give him his lessons, take him walking,
undress him and put him to bed every night. She watched
his health, took him to imaginary doctors, and nursed
him through imaginary illnesses. It was all done with
pathetic realism. One day, for example, she displayed a
bandage on his arm and, being asked the reason for it,
she said, "His arm looks somewhat emaciated so the
doctor gave him a hypodermic injection of goat gland."

One can easily imagine the misfortunes which precipitated this mental upset. The woman had lost her son
when he was eight months of age, just one month after
the death of her husband. Life had become too hard for
her, she could not face it. Instead, she retired into a
world of her own creation. The normal person does otherwise. He accepts any event in life, no matter how calamitous, resolutely clears up the débris, and starts all over
again. We are likely to give our sympathy to this be-
nighted woman but she really deserves less consideration
than the one who sets out to acquire another husband and
child or reconciles herself to a changed existence. Far
from being an heroic thing, the retirement into the world

of fantasy is a cowardly thing. It is a failure to face real life.

"It cannot be insisted too strongly that all fantasies are egoistic in character. There is displayed in them a complete absence of any lofty moral purpose, even though the modes of action they depict may appear blameless. The central figure is invariably the dreamer, and the end that is striven for is invariably a personal and selfish end." [1]

Does this mean that every time a person retires into the world of imagination he is performing a function which is dangerous or which will lead to disastrous consequences? By no means. The ambitious person, the one who accomplishes things, is a dreamer; he must be able to foresee the future or he is very likely to lack incentive to work. What, then, is the distinguishing mark by means of which we can discriminate between dangerous fantasies and normal and helpful imaginings? The distinction is not in the amount, in the intensity, or in the nature of the daydreams. It is in the outcome. If the daydream incites to active adjustment with the real environment, it is wholesome; if it leads to a greater separation from the objective and real world, then it is a dangerous activity.

Types of distorted behavior that result from daydreaming. The dangerous nature of daydreams will be more apparent when we consider some of the unusual forms that they may assume.

1. *Absences.* In the midst of a conversation, at a play, at dinner, on the train, almost anywhere or at any time, the victim of absences will go off into a semi-trance. He will stare into space, will fail to hear or see what is going

---

[1] Green, George H., *Psychanalysis in the Classroom*, G. P. Putnam's Sons, 1922, p. 45.

on around him, and will assume a fairly rigid posture. Usually the slightest extra disturbance will bring him out of it. He will give a little jump, or take on a bland smile, awake to the fact that he has not been aware of the events immediately preceding. Usually he will assert that he does not know what the content of the daydream was.

The intensity, the length of time involved, the degree of insensitivity to the outside world, and the blocking of memory for the content of the dream vary with individuals and with the different dreams. Some are very mild and some so deep that they resemble a real sleep.

In moderate degree and amount, absences should not be taken too seriously. The little boy is likely to lose himself in the thought of Christmas as the day approaches. The adolescent youth is likely to ignore his surroundings in the contemplation of his mental picture of the loved one. In such cases, however, the subject usually knows pretty clearly the content of his reverie. The young lover will probably blush and deny knowledge of the content of his fantasy, but his blushes belie his denial and he is usually only too well aware of the nature of his thoughts.

Where absences are frequent, and where the subject really does not remember the subject of the dream when he is brought back to life, the implication is that there has been too great a preoccupation with internal mental pictures. When carried thus far, they should not be viewed complacently.

2. *Obsessions.* More suggestive of danger for the one who entertains them are obsessions. Obsessions are obtrusive, unwelcome, and unreasonably persistent ideas. Whereas the daydreamer will admit that his daydreams are pleasurable in content, and that he encourages them

because they offer an escape from unpleasant realities, the victim of obsessions is besieged by thoughts from which he would gladly escape but which continually hound him. Whereas hope infuses daydreams, fear is the characteristic note of obsessions.

Why do unpleasant, unwelcome thoughts keep recurring and interfering with other more wholesome ideas? In simple cases it is easy to see the reason. If you have been in a very spectacular accident, it is hard to shake off the memory of the experience. You continue to picture the various incidents to yourself, often elaborating upon them and imagining what might have happened in addition to what did happen. An emotion persists after the immediate situation has passed.

In some obsessions, however, the ideas seem silly and totally irrelevant. For example, the following obsession was reported by a normal individual:

"I have had and still have a fixed idea that causes me any amount of discomfort. I don't remember ever being seriously injured with a knife wherefore I should feel great fear toward one. I can't remember where I ever developed such a feeling of perfect terror for that object. The thought of it comes at most inopportune times when there is no occasion at all for its appearance. I can be talking on an apparently interesting topic of conversation when all at once, without any warning whatever, I shudder as I feel the blade of a knife hurting me. I know it is ridiculous to imagine that I am being cut, but I cannot help being frightened. The knife seems to wound me in various places at different times. Sometimes I can feel the sharp blade in my mouth and I am perfectly certain that in real life it never was there."

Another individual reported: "For three years whenever I allowed myself to be idle I was obsessed by the idea that I saw a large roll of carpet which rolled or unrolled itself eternally."

Still another says: "When I was about eight years of age I had a fixed idea. I thought I was going to cut my throat from ear to ear with a certain large butcher-knife in my grandmother's kitchen. I couldn't throw off the idea. I was afraid to go near the knife. This persisted about two weeks, then gradually wore off." [1]

Whether the obtruding idea is simple, as in the case of the automobile accident, or whether it is bizarre, as in the case of the knives, roll of carpet, or the idea of suicide, the nature of this type of disturbance is essentially the same. There is an unpleasant emotion in the background which the victim would gladly evade if he could. The most probable explanation of the obsessions whose meaning is not apparent is that the subject has repressed, that is, has made intense efforts to prevent the recall of, the initiating circumstances. In spite of these efforts the emotion continues to dominate as though it were recalled. The ideas which would naturally accompany the emotion are not recalled, however, and in their place comes the idea which is present in the obsession as a symbol for the original experience. What the real cause is the subject does not know, and the outsider could only guess.

Where such repressions (active attempts to forget) are present it is quite likely that the forgotten event has some moral implications. In other words, an obsession is quite similar to what we ordinarily refer to as conscience, or the sense of sin. In the latter the actual cause of the emotional upset is known to the individual and his feel-

[1] Berry, Charles S., "Obsessions of Normal Minds," *Jour. Abn. Psychol.*, 1916, *11*, pp. 19–22.

ing of guilt, which is obsessional in nature, is quite conscious. In the typical bizarre obsession the unpleasant part is forgotten and the emotion of fear of guilt attaches itself to some symbol or substitute.

How should one deal with an obsession? Since the important element in the obsession is the emotional tone of fear which is behind the obsessive idea, the plan of procedure should be to discover, if possible, the real foundation of that emotion. The obsessive idea is merely a disguise to hide the real significance of the emotion and this disguise should be penetrated. A disguise is usually designed to hide something unpleasant, so we should expect to find the disguised ideas undesirable but, even so, it is better to face the unpleasant than to waste an endless amount of time tormented with ideas which, on the surface, are silly.

Having discovered the real cause for the emotion, the next step is to acquire a new attitude toward it. Even sinful and hateful things must be dealt with directly if they are to be mastered. The obsession, in other words, is merely an indication that one has run from an issue in real life and that, in spite of this flight, the emotion has caught up with him, and remains to torment him in disguised form. An obsession is like a ghost, it terrifies only when we are afraid to investigate its nature. Turn about and face the ghost and you find it to be merely a shadow, a tree trunk glowing in the moonlight, or some person enclosed in a sheet bent on a practical joke. Face an obsession and you will often find the emotional situation hidden behind its terrifying disguise will shrink in importance when exposed to daylight.

3. *Hallucinations.* When a person perceives things, such as voices and visions, when there is nothing in the

environment to stimulate such perceptions, we say he is having hallucinations. These experiences can come as a direct result of excessive habitual daydreaming.

At times we discover an individual who is working with great zeal, who makes the claim that he is inspired by some outside influence and who, as evidence in support of this claim, describes the visions he has seen or the voices he has heard urging him to go forth on some great mission. He himself, as well as his auditors, is likely to be filled with awe and to assume that success is assured because of the outside help which the presence of such voices or visions seems to guarantee.

The confidence which faith in such mysterious support engenders in the one who possesses it is, to be sure, of some value in giving zest to his endeavors. Having faith that one is "destined" to do a certain thing, that one has a "mission" to fulfill, that the "spiritual world" is behind one; all these are sources of inspiration and thus have a value in boosting courage in an otherwise fearful creature. But their influence is a treacherous one and if we had a record of all the individuals who were so "inspired" we should find only a small proportion who have been permanently helped by voices and visions. The majority are to be found in institutions for the care of the mentally ill.

There is nothing particularly unwholesome in the fact that a person has had a "vision" or has heard a "voice." Normal persons have such experiences as well as those who have serious mental difficulties. The effect they have upon the subject determines their wholesomeness or morbidness.

Where do they come from? They do not come from the outside. They come from the internal mental life of the one who experiences them and are very likely to be the picturing forth of the wishes of the subject. A person who is very anxious to communicate with an absent friend, either dead or alive, may work himself up to such a peak of excitement that he actually sees his friend or hears his voice. One who wishes he could get approval for some project may, through the intensity of this anxiety, hear approval from what he conceives to be a divine source.

It is very easy to have one's preceptions distorted by one's emotions. For example, a person who is sitting alone in a large house, fearing marauders, is very likely to interpret every squeak of the floor, every whistling of the wind, every scratching of a mouse, every banging of a curtain as the approach of the anticipated assault.

In such situations there are two possible ways to overcome the tendency to misinterpret every little noise. One way is to investigate and thus to reassure oneself that the sound is not a warning of impending calamity. The other method is to take steps to build up confidence. For example, when one is alone in a big house the presence of a companion would induce courage. When the fear is eliminated the sounds are not even heard, much less misinterpreted. The latter method, of course, is the most effective and only permanent method of dealing with the situation. If one is afraid, it will do little good to trace down each tiny suggestion of danger and prove to oneself that it is harmless. While one is being thus uprooted a dozen others will arise.

The same principle applies when dealing with "voices" and "visions." They are evidences of some sort of emotional stress. Investigation will show that they are unreal and this unreality substantiates the conclusion that their cause is in the internal mental processes of the one who experiences them and not in the outside world. Hunt for the wish or the fear which lies behind them, deal with these and the "voices" and "visions" will disappear.

4. *Delusions.* It is an easy step from daydreaming to delusion. A delusion is a false belief, while a daydream is largely a picturing of things as we wish they were. A persistent wish that a thing were so may easily end in a conviction that it is so.

In extreme cases we easily recognize a delusion. When a man proclaims that he is Napoleon, the Messiah, or a great inventor, while his life shows that he is a very ordinary person, we laugh at him. But all of us tend to wish we were different from what we are and some of us believe that we are. Most of us do not make these claims openly, but the content of our daydreams reveals it. The joy we get from stories, movies, and novels illustrates this.

For example, we get pleasure from "Cinderella" and "Ugly Duckling" stories because we imagine ourselves in situations similar to those in which the heroines of these stories found themselves. The plot of these stories is very similar to the fantasies indulged in by many people. The typical structure of these tales is somewhat as follows:

"(1) The hero is born of people of exalted rank—gods, heroes, emperors or kings. Sometimes one parent is a god, and the mother a specially selected person, *e.g.*, Remus and Romulus were born of Mars and a vestal virgin. Heroes were born as a result of the union of a god with a nymph or a mortal.

"(2) The hero is abandoned or persecuted by his real parents, or by his father.

"(3) The hero is adopted by people of low origin, whom he regards as his real parents.

" (4) The hero distinguishes himself above his play-fellows by stature, beauty or dignified bearing; or by deeds or bravery, by his conversation or by miracles.

" (5) The hero meets his real father, and so impresses himself upon him that the latter acknowledges him, and places him in his rightful position. Alternatively, the hero meets and slays his father, unwittingly.

" (6) The hero rewards those who treated him well when he was unknown, and revenges himself upon those who treated him badly. Sometimes there is a great deal of forgiveness of the latter, provided they acknowledge his present rank." [1]

The child may read one of these stories and imagine how grand it would be were he some noble person who would some day be discovered. He may wish he were a great person but he does not let his wish slip into a belief if he cares to remain normal. The one who develops pathological delusions does not stop with the wish, he believes that he is a great personage and sets out to prove to the world that he is. It is much easier to believe that one has been born great, even though others do not know about it, than it is to go about achieving greatness by the devious route of hard work.

Obviously one who dwells on such fantasies, or adopts false beliefs about himself, does so because he has failed to adjust satisfactorily. The wholesome policy is to deal with these tendencies in their early stages. We should not wait until we believe that we are some great personage be-fore we recognize the tendency to delusional development. If we take too much delight in stories and dramas which follow such plots as the one just outlined we should re-

[1] Green, George H., *Psychanalysis in the Classroom*, G. P. Putnam's Sons, 1922, pp. 70–71.

gard this undue interest as a warning that we need to come down to earth and recognize our limitations instead of distorting facts to suit our fancy.

How to cure daydreaming. Daydreams are symptoms, indicators that the person who uses them is not adjusted to his environment. They are valuable indicators because they are signs which appear in early stages of maladjustment and point the way to a remedy before much damage has been done. The daydreams themselves should not be regarded with great seriousness but they should be recognized as indicators of some need on the part of the subject.

1. *See that daydreams lead to activity.* If they stimulate a person, they are wholesome. If they are adopted as a substitute for endeavor, they are unwholesome.

2. *See that more fun is derived from real achievements than from imaginary success.* A person does eventually what furnishes him the most pleasure. If he gets a real taste of success, imaginary success will become insipid.

3. *Search for the underlying cause of bizarre fantasies.* If the daydreams tend to become queer fantasies, search for the emotional disturbance which the fantasy symbolizes and deal with this underlying factor rather than attempt to suppress the fantasy. If the real cause is dealt with rationally the fantasy will disappear of itself.

4. *Do not be afraid of daydreams.* Use them as indicators of your attitudes toward life. Evaluate and improve upon these attitudes and you will have made your daydreams serve a useful function. View calmly your imaginings as ambitions. Instead of fearing them, let them encourage you to transform reality so that it will more nearly conform to your dreams. Thus you will have converted a potential enemy into a valuable ally.

QUESTIONS

1. In general, what effect does an objective have on work?
2. Show how a stated ambition may be a disguise to cover a mental conflict.
3. Can you defend the statement: It may be better to have no specific objective than to have a poor one?
4. To what extent should one adhere to an objective after he has stated it?
5. Criticise the statement: It is extremely important that each person find the one task for which he is best fitted.
6. Show how vocational choice and vocational adjustment supplement each other.
7. To what extent can a person be guided in his choice of a vocation by tests and measurements?
8. Outline the procedure for choosing a vocation.
9. Why should a person not wait to be sold upon a vocation?
10. Three sources of information about vocations are mentioned. How significant is the order in which they are given?
11. What effect does interest in a job have upon the character of the work done?
12. How important is it to stabilize our interests?
13. Describe the different ways in which childhood experiences may determine adult interests.
14. Upon what should the retention of an interest be based?
15. What values may result from maintaining a wide range of interests?
16. What danger must the person with a breadth of interests avoid?
17. Give four rules for controlling and directing interests.
18. What is the place of dissatisfaction in relation to ambition?
19. What is the usual effect upon an individual when he reaches an objective?
20. Why should ideals be changeable?
21. Explain how an ambition stimulates a person to activity.
22. Distinguish between a daydream and an ambition.

23. Describe how cynicism develops.
24. What effect does emphasis upon sacrifice have upon interest in a vocation?
25. Show how denying oneself in order to work may result in hatred of the work.
26. What feature of daydreams may tempt us to substitute them for actual achievement?
27. Why do we not all live in the world of dreams?
28. Show how daydreaming is a "selfish" adjustment.
29. What treatment should be accorded to a daydreamer?
30. What is the characteristic mark which indicates that a daydream is dangerous?
31. Describe what is meant by an "absence."
32. Show how an absence may be a normal activity.
33. What is an obsession?
34. Distinguish the daydream from the obsession.
35. Describe how an obsession is produced.
36. Describe some typical obsessions of normal people.
37. What part does repression play in an obsession?
38. What should be done to escape from an obsession?
39. What is the characteristic emotion of an obsession?
40. What is an hallucination?
41. Under what circumstances are hallucinations normal?
42. Show how an hallucination may stimulate a person to great exploits.
43. What two methods may be used to overcome hallucinations?
44. What is a delusion?
45. How is a delusion related to an ambition?
46. Show how a delusion may be regarded as a "grown-up" fairy tale.
47. Why is it important to deal with a delusion in its early stages?
48. Give four rules for the cure of daydreams.

CHAPTER V

HOW TO FIGHT

"A large bottle of cream, two-thirds full, was left one night in a farmer's shed. Two mice investigated the situation. By vigorous jumping they succeeded in gaining the top of the bottle and jumped in for the cream. They were then in danger of drowning. Mouse Number One had been trained by the modern method of constant failure and he cried out, 'Help, help,' and when no help came, gradually lost strength and fell to the bottom. Mouse Number Two had been trained by the constant stimulus of success and had become so habituated to facing difficult situations that he had, even in a practical way, gained the insight that doing is itself worth while for its own sake. So he cried out lustily, 'Hustle, hustle,' and suiting the action to the word, kept trying to jump out of the bottle. At first he improved by practice and jumped higher and higher, but soon the effect of practice was overcome by fatigue, and gradually as he became exhausted, his jumps were lower and lower, but he nevertheless kept struggling; and gradually as exhaustion came on, the cream became harder and harder. In the morning mouse Number One was found dead at the bottom of the bottle; mouse Number Two was serenely asleep on a lump of butter."[1]

What is your reaction to this fable? Do you feel proud of mouse Number Two? Does his refusal to give up

[1] Burnham, W. H., "Success and Failure as Conditions of Mental Health," *Mental Hygiene*, 1919, *3*, p. 395.

illustrate the type of conduct you wish you had shown in a similar situation? Or do you feel that he was foolish to labor to get out of one difficulty only to get into another and probably worse one, the menace of the farmer or a cat who should find him trapped in the bottle? You will be able to discover something about your own attitude toward life by your response to this fable.

There are some very serious problems which a tale, so manifestly absurd, raises in our minds. The mouse certainly did not know that his lashing about would churn up some butter; he could not see the outcome of his activity. To what extent should a person fight even in the face of apparent opposing odds with no possible foresight into a successful termination of his struggles? In the preceding chapter we discussed the importance as well as the dangers of getting a clear view of the future to guide us in the present. When we cannot see ahead are we justified in blind fighting? Suppose the jar had been filled with skimmed milk or with water? Mouse Number Two would have died in spite of his fighting. "Well, he would have died fighting," you might answer with a feeling that he had done something virtuous in fighting, even if he lost. Why do you respect more a man who dies fighting than one who gives up easily? Is there any virtue in fighting in itself, or is it because you have been taught that it is a sign of weakness to surrender, no matter what the difficulty may be? Suppose we grant that it is well to fight wisely; if one lacks wisdom, should he fight anyway?

Again, this fable implies that, if you work hard enough, you will eventually win. Is that so? The most casual observation of life demonstrates that it is not so. Many people put up a heroic struggle and lose. In fact, so many people lose that, if the only justification for fighting is the

victory that lies ahead, one is forced to admit that fighting
is rather unfruitful. Perhaps, if we study the motives
which lie behind the fighting of various persons, if we can
discover the effect that fighting has upon them, if we can
point out the dangers of fighting as well as the advantages,
we may arrive at some sort of satisfactory estimate of the
value of fighting and may be able to give it a suitable place
in our own lives.

Faith in the future. While the child, or an animal,
struggles merely because he is uncomfortable, and lashes
around with random movements and with no realization
of the outcome of his endeavors, the mature individual
has learned to expect some favorable outcome from his
struggles. Experience has taught him that inertness can
bring him little else than failure while exertion on his
part may bring a change of circumstances. Faith in the
future comes to him because his strivings in the past have
been followed by a cessation of the discomfort which
initiated his fighting.

This faith in the future may take two forms. In some
instances he may expect a specific result to follow his
efforts. When he is hungry, for example, a grown man
does not yell and throw himself around; he obtains food
and eats, fully expecting that the hunger will disappear.
When he is cold he builds a fire, knowing that he will
obtain comfort from its warmth. In such a complex
situation as treating an enemy with kindness, he may
not be so sure of the outcome, but he has a reasonable
expectation that his treatment may effect a change in the
behavior of his enemy.

In other cases, because of his lack of experience or his
ignorance of the laws which control a situation, he may be
unable to foresee the outcome of his efforts, he may not

even know that he should exert himself at all. All he knows is that things are not to his liking and he has no knowledge of the procedure he should follow to modify them. Lacking any vision of what the future has in store for him, does he assume that things will remain as they are? By no means. He knows not what will happen, but he can be sure of one thing, and that is that circumstances will be different. A person does not have to live very long to learn that everything in life is continually changing. They may become better or worse, he cannot tell which, but he may know with certainty that they will be different from what they now are.

Faith that life will change is very reassuring to us when circumstances are unfavorable. We know that there will be some change and, if everything is extremely unfavorable, we argue that the chances favor a change for the better. If things cannot get much worse they may get better. Such optimism is warranted and is wholesome. We do not need to predict when and how the change will come, we may not know enough to make any such prediction; but we can be certain that the turn will come.

The writer has had persons lay before him a set of unfortunate circumstances which made the future look absolutely hopeless. These poor creatures could not see a ray of light ahead of them; all was utter blackness and there seemed nothing specific upon which to pin the slightest hope. The only help that could be given in such cases was to encourage the unfortunates to "sit tight" and wait. Later events proved the value of this procedure.

When we cannot see clearly ahead we need not assume that there is nothing ahead. There *is* something and we can be absolutely certain that it will not be a continuation of existing conditions. *If there is one thing that you can be certain about in life, it is that things will change.*

While it is relatively easy to adopt this attitude and to stress this faith in the future when we are in unpleasant circumstances, we are not so ready to do so when we are prospering. At such times we hope that the law of change will be inoperative or, if change must come, it will keep its present direction. This is a form of wishful thinking which can only end in disappointment. It is just as foolish to expect permanency of conditions when we are happy as to fear impending doom when we are depressed. Knowledge of this law of change should give rise neither to chronic optimism nor to chronic pessimism. We are all familiar with the chronic growler who cannot enjoy a sunny day because he complains that it is a weather breeder and that tomorrow will be cloudy. The wholesome individual enjoys the sunshine when it is here, but at the same time prepares for the rain; he makes the best of bad weather but knows that it will not last forever.

Another fact to bear in mind is that no event is wholly dependent upon our own endeavors. "The outcome of every human venture is determined by the interplay of factors, only a few of which are under our control. We may do our best in a given situation and emphatically deserve success. But the uncontrollable factors in that situation may conspire against us and eventually bring about a stinging defeat. Conversely, we may find success literally given to us, pushed into our hands by forces which we did not set in motion and the operations of which actually eluded our attention."[1]

Our future is determined by the operation of inexorable

[1] Gilkey, J. G., "Getting a Perspective on Success," *Rice Institute Pamphlet,* 1930, *17,* pp. 162–174.

laws, most of which are beyond our control. Does the knowledge of this fact lead to a fatalistic attitude? Instead, it should warn us against taking too much credit to ourselves when we are successful and against placing too much blame upon outside factors when we fail. We do not know enough to guarantee to ourselves that strenuous endeavor will bring success; but we do know enough about the laws of life to warrant continuing to struggle instead of abandoning ourselves to fate. At any rate, the man who is succeeding can easily take this position and contend that it pays to struggle, even though the man who is failing does not find it so easy to persist in working when he sees no resulting success.

Looking at the issue broadly, it would appear that struggling should not be rated very high if its sole value is the success which it brings; it too often fails to do so. But struggling is not justified solely because of the possibility of success; it may exert a tremendous influence upon the worker and play a big part in promoting mental health. We should, for this reason, be less concerned with the evaluation of endeavor in terms of resultant success or failure, and stress, instead, its effect upon the individual.

Values of work. No matter what effects fighting may have upon the objective environment, it certainly effects changes in the fighter. These changes are, from the point of view of mental health, the more important. If fighting leaves the fighter a more virile, happier, more knowing man, it merits a high rating on the scale of human values, regardless of whether the fighter won or lost in the battle. We question the value of an objective victory which leaves the fighter a moral and physical wreck.

Ordinarily when we speak of a fight we think of a spasmodic affair, a rare occurrence which suggests an emergency which must be met by drastic means. A milder type of fighting is the struggle that a person makes each day of his life. Life, to be successful, must be a continuous struggle, even though it does not involve a threat against the very existence of the fighter. This daily, habitual form of fighting we call work, and it is an extremely important element in the mental balance of each one of us.

The notion that work is undesirable, a punishment meted out to man for his sins, is no longer tenable. Modern researches have demonstrated that work is man's best friend. It is a means of prophylaxis against mental disease and a therapeutic agent for effecting cures. Let us examine some of the specific advantages of work.

1. *The zestful individual becomes more knowing.* In the psychological laboratory the intelligence of animals is measured by the ease with which they can learn to extricate themselves from puzzle boxes and mazes of various sorts. The active animal does much better in these experiments than does the listless animal. In fact, animals are never tested unless they are hungry or are impressed in some manner with the undesirability of being confined in the test contrivance. Should the animal lie down in a corner and sleep it is obvious he would learn nothing about the maze nor be able to extricate himself.

The same principle holds with children. The active child gets acquainted with life merely because his activity throws him into contact with so many aspects of existence. To be sure, he annoys his elders, because of the successive predicaments into which he gets himself, but these very crises provide the materials for learning. If, upon discovering himself fastened in a pen, he calmly sits down and makes no effort to extricate himself, he is losing golden opportunities. Whether he succeeds in getting out or not, his activities enable him to get some insight into his objective world.

So with grown persons. The zestful person learns as he goes through life while the unobserving, listless person loses most of what is going on around him. One woman, for example, made an extensive tour through Europe and saw nothing of interest except the weather. Some persons close their eyes and ears to persons and objects around them unless they are convinced that they are essential to some immediate purpose. What a waste of good opportunities!

Intelligence is largely alertness. Learn to keep your eyes and ears open, to discriminate between different events and persons, to understand the significance of seemingly trivial circumstances, and to vary the way in which you respond to your daily routine, and life will take on new meanings. Exploration will get you into predicaments; but getting out of predicaments is what gives zest to life.

It is this willingness to get into predicaments which staid, older individuals find so hard to understand in young persons. They have no confidence in the ability of the younger generation to solve their own problems, they feel that they must step into the picture and govern the lives of youngsters, and reason that it is necessary to do so in order to keep them out of trouble. The energetic youngster, thus guarded, realizes that he is being robbed of the fun of living and exerts even more energy in contriving predicaments to get into as a result of this protection.

If a child has been protected carefully throughout his younger years, he is much more likely to lack judgment

in the creation of these stimulating dilemmas when he
gets older, and as a result often goes to extremes in the
rashness of his behavior. This does not vitiate the principle we are advocating. It merely indicates that the
child has not been given the opportunity of solving his
own problems early enough in life and thus learning by
his own experience. As an illustration, when two girls
don overalls and hold up a bank for the thrill involved,
it demonstrates the results of too much restraint with a
consequent lack of stimulating situations earlier in their
lives. Had they been footloose earlier, experience would
have taught them to be more discreet.

The energetic worker, the alert individual, the strenuous
fighter gets a great amount of benefit and pleasure from
life, even though he may not gain the immediate and
apparent end toward which his energies are directed. He
gains knowledge of life from sheer activity.

2. *Work brings personal satisfaction.* Does this sound
like a paradox? Can work be a pleasure? Certainly it
can and should be satisfying. If endowed with a fair
amount of intelligence, a man is never contented with
idleness. Only the feebleminded person can be happy in
continuous inactivity, and the more intelligent one is,
the more idleness irks him.

On the other hand, some persons complain that they
hate to work, they protest that they work because they
must do so and look forward to the time when they can
desist, when they can rest or play. This dislike is not due
to the nature of the work itself, for you may observe one
person taking keen delight in the very activities which
another detests. The difference is wholly in the attitude
of the worker. Whence comes this attitude?

In the first place, it may come from the false teach-

ings of a group of ascetics who believe that enjoyment is
sinful and that one must devote himself to undesirable
activities. They look askance at anyone who enjoys his
work and tell him that he is sinful because he does not
take life seriously enough. Seriousness is synonymous
with unhappiness with these people. They have erroneously given up all pleasure in life, are jealous of anyone
who apparently is happy, and set out to make him unhappy if they can.

Again, work may be unpleasant because we feel that
we must do what we do not want to do. This may come
about because we happen to be associated with persons
whose ambition in life is to dominate others. The "bossy"
person is not content to make his victims work but he
must make them unhappy in the doing. But why let
your life be ruined by a domineering creature? You can
outwit him by changing your attitude and doing the work
because you want to do so. You do not have to defy him.
That is just what he would like because that would increase his feeling of exhilaration, he would then be sure
that you did hate to obey him and he would take even
more drastic steps to enforce obedience. Let him think
you are working because he is forcing you but, at the same
time, do your task because you want to do so.

3. *Work dissipates emotional tensions.* When you
have suffered some great loss, when you have been un-
bearably irritated, when loved ones have disappointed
you, when you are tormented with fears, and even when
you are unbelievably happy, nothing provides so good a
safety valve as work. Inactivity in the face of situations
which tend to arouse violent emotions of any sort merely
accentuates the emotional tension until some activity is
inevitable. If no legitimate or valuable energy outlet is

available, you will be very likely to "blow off" in some
bizarre and unfortunate manner. Work serves the dual
function of giving an outlet to pent-up emotional energy
and at the same time accomplishes the useful functions
which are usually inherent in work.

When emotionally aroused, do something of an active
nature. A walk, a game, a swim, setting-up exercises—
any active outlet is good; but work is one of the best
outlets.

4. *Work is a good distraction from unpleasant thoughts.*
If a problem confronts us, we should face it, study it in
all its aspects, and never evade it until it is solved. While
we grant the truth of this principle, we must admit that,
at times, we are troubled with undesirable thoughts which
cannot be helped by thinking. If a friend is at sea during
a great storm, our thoughts about the storm will not have
any effect upon his safety. If I have taken an examination and have handed in my paper, further thoughts
about the examination will not help my grade. If I have
made a mistake and have made all the amends I can
make, it does no good to torment myself with thoughts of
"what might have been." Life is full of instances where
one needs to forget, to let bygones be bygones.

One does not forget by telling himself he will not remember. To reiterate: "I will not remember, I will
forget," is merely to remind oneself of the unpleasant
condition. Find something more thrilling, more vital to
think about and the unpleasant memory will be crowded
out. While work is not the only distraction device that
can be found, it is an excellent one to use.

5. *Work has therapeutic value.* For most mental ills
work has been found to be a better therapeutic agent
than is rest. At one time in the history of medicine the

"rest cure" was in vogue. Expensive sanitaria were organized in which patients were made to rest in bed or in invalid chairs, with nothing to do but to brood on their troubles and to become more and more "introspective." The same treatment was used in many state hospitals for mental diseases.

This method has been largely superseded by the "work cure." Modern hospitals are equipped with "occupational therapy" departments where the patients make rugs, baskets, furniture, toys, lace, brooms, and other useful articles. Other patients work on farms, do landscape gardening, masonry, plumbing, carpentry, and the like. The modern state hospital for the mentally ill is really an industrial community where everybody who is at all capable of working is given a useful occupation.

The busy life is the wholesome life, the idle life is unwholesome. The greatest harm of an industrial depression is not the loss of money that is involved but the loss of work that it brings.

Kinds of workers. If all persons were alike, the general prescription of work might be sufficient. But there are great differences between individuals, differences in the way they work, in the kind of work which appeals to them, in the motives for working, as well as in the effects which the work has upon them. Work which would be beneficial to one person might be detrimental to another. A glance at some of these differences will enable us to discern the beneficial effects of work in a clearer light.

1. *The bubbling energy worker.* The most wholesome type of worker is the one with exuberant physical energy who works as an outlet for his abundant vitality. When this vitality is accompanied by superior intelligence the work is very likely to be very significant and such an

individual is inevitably successful in anything he undertakes. Work is no task for such a man, it is a sheer joy to
him to be doing something and the harder the job the
greater the thrill he derives from it. If he has any spare
time it is consumed in devising something new to do. He
rests, not by being idle, but by finding something different in which to engage. He works until physically tired,
gets a thrill from such healthful fatigue, relaxes, sleeps
well, and awakes full of energy for another fling at the
fascinating game of life. He works best under pressure
and you never hear him making such remarks as: "I
am going to take on a lighter load so that I can do it
better." Such a statement is likely to come from one
who lacks vitality.

When work turns sour and the tedium of life over-
takes you, it would pay to take a lesson from such vital
personalities. Build up your physical reserve by physical exercise, sunlight, and good food; then work will become thrilling to you and life will have new zest.

2. *The fearful worker.* Work which is motivated by
fear is an unwholesome type of work. The fearful type
of worker is likely to work as hard as the energetic type,
he may even accomplish some worthy results, but he is
more likely to break at the critical moment.

In some cases the cause of the fear is fairly obvious.
He is afraid of losing his job, of incurring the displeasure
of his superiors, of making some mistake, of being sur-
passed by his fellows, of what people will say about him.
He whips himself unmercifully, is never happy in his
work, continually feeling he should have done more or
better work. Because of this self-criticism he cannot
be spontaneous in his activities; at the point where he
should throw all his energies into a task, his fear is likely

to dominate, and he holds back. If he could exercise the same amount of energy, and at the same time be dominated by self-confidence, he would accomplish wonders. Motivated by fear, his work is always faulty, lacking the final punch which is so essential for successful accomplishment.

In other cases, the fear is not so apparent. It may be the result of some hidden conflict, may be more or less unconscious, and the activity in work may be a distraction device to enable the worker to forget or to escape from himself. These persons are literally running away from themselves into work. They are always undertaking more than they can accomplish because more work and more obligations mean a better chance to escape. Furthermore, they hate to complete any job because completion means the removal of one avenue of escape. Hence, they are always starting things and never completing them. They do not want success so much as they want work. Consequently they miss the joy of accomplishment, which is so essential if one is to enjoy his work.

3. *The dutiful worker.* Doing a task because one feels that it is his duty to do so always detracts from the joy of work. If we have been overimpressed with the seriousness of life, if we have been made to feel that anything which brings pleasure must, for that reason, be of inferior value, and have been convinced that the serious business of life is work, we are in a fair way to becoming unhappy drudges.

The dutiful worker may derive some moral exhilaration, he may keep his conscience subdued, but work has for him never more than a negative value. He works to pay off a moral obligation and, having paid his debt, he feels free from any further urge to work. If he is sinful he must work harder to pay off the debt; if he is good he has little need to work.

Why work, in and of itself, should have any moral value is hard to conceive. Work is a natural activity, a biological function like eating and breathing, and an energetic man can no more refrain from work than he can from performing other biological functions. To argue that he deserves credit for doing what he cannot help doing, provided he is a normal human being, is certainly a trick of logic, a trick devised by those who wish to keep the worker subservient.

The dutiful worker seldom gets anywhere. He acquires a hangdog attitude, keeps at his work because he must do so, becomes a mere human machine whose only objective is to keep at it till death calls him.

4. *The pioneer.* For some persons an important charm of life is the uncertainty which the future holds for them. Behind the curtain which hides the future from their eyes lie all sorts of unpredictable possibilities which immensely intrigue them. They want not stability but wish only to experience the unforeseen events which each day offers to them. Life is a series of surprise packages and they delight in gambling on the possibilities of tomorrow. In the pioneer days of America these persons were found in covered wagons traveling west to the land of opportunity. They will leave a steady job to prospect for gold. News of a new oil strike finds them flocking around to get into the area of "good luck." They are inveterate gamblers. Life is a sporting proposition and the thrill which comes with uncertainty is much more important than the actual winnings or losses. All they want is a new stake to bet again and again on the future.

5. *The applause seeker.* The applause seeker keeps his eye upon the reactions which other people make to his work rather than upon the work itself. He notes the slightest sign of approval or disapproval and continually "plays to the galleries." This type of behavior may be observed in some children in school. They give a hesitating reply to any question and determine by the facial expression of the teacher whether they are on the right track, changing with lightning speed and with remarkable frequency until they see the coveted sign of approval. They become the "yes-men" in business and industry. They make good lieutenants but seldom independent executives.

6. *The compensating worker.* The person with a dominant feeling of inferiority, whether it is based on a real or imagined defect, may be motivated in his work by an urge to prove to himself and to others that he can overcome the defect or can make up for it by proficiency in another realm. The person who is weak physically may attempt to become an athlete, to achieve some distinction in work requiring a strong body; or he may try to make up for his physical weakness by intellectual prowess. The girl with little personal charm may devote all her energies toward making herself seductive or may become enthusiastic in mapping out for herself a career as a substitute for her lack of personal charm.

The inferiority motive is a very potent one in the lives of many people. It has its values but, at the same time, has some dangerous elements. When dominated by the inferiority motive the person is never contented with mediocrity, he must excel. He is excessively ambitious. On the other hand, if he is not able to overcome the feeling of inferiority through his efforts at compensation

he becomes more and more discouraged and loses all
incentive to do any work. He must either be a great success or he regards himself as a total failure. He can never
take an average position in life. If forced to be an ordinary personage, as is usually the case, he is thoroughly
unhappy.

7. *The domineering worker.* If, as a child, a person
has been too well cared for or has been dominated by
adults, he is very likely to be driven by an insatiable
impulse to gain his freedom. According to his way of
thinking, the most convincing evidence that he has
achieved this independence is his ability to dominate
others. He measures his own freedom by the subservience of others. If he becomes even a minor executive
he uses his office to demonstrate the fact that he is "the
boss." The true executive should win the coöperation
of his subordinates with the view of effecting an efficient
organization. The domineering person is less concerned
with efficient production than he is with procuring submission to his every whim. The sillier the whim and the
more unquestioning the obedience of his subordinates
the happier he becomes.

Such persons make successful army officers where unquestioned obedience is the order of the day. They
become atrocious mothers and fathers because parenthood offers too ready an opportunity to dominate helpless children. If they are able to establish themselves
in an executive position in industry they are likely to
spread discontent throughout the organization. Most
persons resent being forced to obey the commands of
these persons because they sense the motive behind them.
When a worker and his superior are both dominated
by this same motive, the results are truly volcanic.

8. *The intelligent worker.* An intelligent fighter makes a study of the entire situation, selects a key objective— the immediate end to be accomplished—and then concentrates upon reaching that objective. Having done so, he takes another survey of the new situation and repeats the procedure. This process he continues indefinitely.

The worker who is an habitual fighter uses his intelligence in a similar fashion. He cannot settle down to a task merely because he has done so before. He is continually asking himself what it is all about. What does his work accomplish? Could it be done more efficiently? What is the immediate end to be achieved by his task? How does it fit into the complete industrial, business, or professional scheme of which it is a part?

This intellectual curiosity concerning even a prosaic task not only makes the work more interesting but makes for creative changes in procedure, and consequent improved efficiency, as nothing else can do. It is really the determining factor which decides whether a man is to become a mere cog in a complex social and industrial order, or whether he is to play a vital part in the development of civilization.

Can a person decide the type of worker he will become? How can you best make use of the above classification? First, determine which types apply to you. You may find one which fits fairly well but you are more likely to find yourself to be a combination of several types. If such a personal survey is to be of any value it must be made impartially and without reference to the merit of the type which seems to fit. You cannot effect any worthy change unless it is preceded by absolute honesty in evaluating existing conditions.

Each type has some merit, some have more than others.

Arrange them in order from the one you consider most
worthy to the one you deem least worthy. If you find
that those at the lower end of the scale fit you, attempt
to substitute those at the upper end by changing your
methods of work and your attitudes toward your work.
It is well not to attempt to conform rigidly to any one
type. The types as outlined are not mutually exclusive
and to attempt to conform literally to one or another
would merely narrow you. Because you use your intelligence in your work is no reason why you should not
take a chance at times. You might pioneer and at the
same time overcome some handicap. Your work will
have more spice if you vary your approach rather than
if you try to specialize in any one type of attitude.

Effect of work upon the worker. What effect does
your work have upon you? Work does not affect all
persons alike; even the same work may influence different people in quite diverse ways. The effect depends
largely upon the motive of the worker in performing the
work, in his attitude toward it.

How often "overwork" is given the blame for mental
breaks! To hear some persons talk one would be inclined to believe that work is a dangerous thing, that
one needed always to be on his guard lest he work too
much, too hard, or too long. Those who generalize in
this fashion seldom take into consideration the nature
of the work that is done, the reasons that the person
has for working hard, or any other circumstance in his
life. Furthermore, they must admit that there are many
people who work prodigiously throughout their lives
with no ill-effects, whereas the one who breaks, presumably from overwork, has not, in reality, worked so
very hard. Work is a sort of scapegoat upon which to

hurl the blame when things go wrong. In short, work
has been maligned by those who are too ignorant or too
much afraid to put the blame where it belongs.

Some persons who overwork also break down, others
who overwork thrive upon it. Where overwork and a
break go together it can usually be found that the work
was an incidental factor, often a device used by the individual to escape some difficulty and is a minor factor
in the total picture. Overwork may be a symptom that
something is wrong with the individual, but the trouble
is not in the work; it is something else. The subject may
be trying to compensate for some inferiority, may be trying to distract his attention from some difficulty, may be
trying to outdo some rival because of jealousy, or the like.
If he breaks, it is more likely to be the result of failure to
accomplish these ends than it is to be due to overwork.

Instead of being harmful in and of itself, work is extremely beneficial and the busy man is much more likely
to be happy than is the idle man. This is true even
though the work may be motivated by some underlying
conflict. Nor is the beneficial effect of work dependent
upon the outcome of the work. Even though the work
may accomplish little of objective value the worker will
be benefited because of his activity. Even if the busy
man can boast of no more results than the idle man he
will have been happier while working than the idle man
will have been while loafing.

If you wish to get the utmost benefit from working
the first thing you must do is to rid yourself forever of
the erroneous notion that work is unpleasant, distasteful, or an undesirable means to a desirable end. If you
would benefit from your work, enjoy it. And this is possible no matter what the job may be. If you wish to

learn this lesson watch children at play. They will do dirty jobs, persist at such a seemingly undesirable task as digging a hole in the ground, perspiring and straining with every ounce of energy in them until they are completely exhausted, and yet with unbounded enthusiasm and pleasure. It is not the work which he is doing which inspires this enthusiasm, it is the attitude of the child toward the work. Furthermore, the child will approach almost any activity with this spirit until some disgruntled adult tries to make him unhappy by instilling in him the fallacy that the pleasant things in life are useless while the necessary things are unpleasant. Take a lesson from these youngsters and learn to play your way through life. Play is not doing useless things, it is enjoying the things you do. You can enjoy anything if you set out to do so.

Get rid of the notion that work is a punishment to man for his sinfulness. Work is a blessing to man, it is his salvation from many ills, his escape from life's sorrows. The man who works till death will be happy till death. The man who retires will immediately begin to get old and death will overtake him more quickly and relieve him of the unhappiness of a life of uselessness.

Causes for laziness. No person is "born" lazy. Young children are spontaneously energetic, actively interested in almost everything they see and hear; the world about them is continually offering surprises to them, and they are perpetually engaged in exploring and probing into all sorts of fascinating mysteries. If a child becomes lazy it is because he learns to be so. He learns to become lazy usually because adults interfere with his natural zest. Those who thwart him in this fashion may not know that they are teaching the child to be lazy but their teaching is effective nevertheless. What are some of the ways in which laziness is learned?

1. *Too much supervision.* Over-solicitous adults may minister to the every need of the children in their care so that no opportunity is offered them to learn to express their energies. Over-anxious adults may fear that the children may make mistakes, and to forestall such eventualities do everything in their power to prevent them from attacking a problem in their own way. Some children, to be sure, fight against such solicitude and become even more energetic because of such treatment. Some find their efforts at independence useless and give up. Such children have all the appearances of being lazy, but it is inactivity based on a sense of failure and the futility of effort. If caught in time such laziness may be easily overcome. What over-supervised children need is an opportunity to be themselves.

2. *A device to enslave parents.* Other children discover that they can enslave their parents by laziness. If their own activity results in withdrawal of affection by their parents, and if inactivity prolongs attention, they may remain lazy, helpless, and listless in order to provide themselves with an instrument to make older people do their bidding.

In a number of instances, children have not learned to read because their parents read to them. When their parents stopped reading to them they learned readily enough.

If a child wins love and attention when he is lazy, and receives indifference and scolding when he is active, is it strange that he should learn to be lazy?

3. *Dislike for particular tasks.* A mother once complained that her child was lazy, that he shirked all duties

around the home, and that he used all sorts of devices to get out of work. She was asked to name some particular task which her child was too lazy to perform. Her reply was that he would not wash the dishes.

"Do you like to wash dishes?" the mother was asked.

"Certainly not. Who could enjoy washing dishes?" was her reply.

Is it any wonder that the child tried to get out of doing a task that his mother manifestly hated? His laziness was merely a reflection of her own attitude.

When parents attempt to make a young child do tasks which they themselves hate to do, the child will naturally and rightly get the idea that he is being exploited. Why should he do the work his parents hate to do? Why should he not revolt against doing anything he is told to do by persons who obviously impose upon him? Much so-called laziness starts in exactly this fashion.

When we are not successful in exploiting the other fellow, when he will not enter with zeal into the performance of a task we hate and which we have tried to pass off to him, we become moralizers and chide him for being lazy and preach him a little sermon on industry. His laziness is merely a defense against our trickery. He has found a useful tool to beat us at our own game and our moralizing is a weak attempt on our part to deprive him of his weapon.

The same principle applies when we become our own taskmaster and attempt to force ourselves to do some undesirable work. We refuse to admit that the reason we lack initiative is dislike for the work, and take on an attitude of inertia. It is easier to call ourselves lazy than to admit that we dislike a particular job which we have told ourselves it is our duty to perform.

The answer to laziness of this type is to learn to enjoy the task we should perform. Once a person, be he young or old, wants to do a thing, he will do it. In proportion as you develop a desire to perform a job, laziness will take wings. You cannot fight laziness directly, by saying you will not be lazy; but you can rout it by learning to like to do the things you find at hand to be done.

4. *Physical fatigue pains.* Physical fatigue pains will cause laziness only when such discomfort becomes chronic. Laziness developing from overwork is the exception rather than the rule. The indolent person is likely to show a history of lack of physical exertion rather than an excess of it. One learns to loaf by loafing and he learns to be energetic by exerting himself. An overdose of hard work may result in a temporary swing to extreme inactivity but this is likely to be shortlived. The one who is accustomed to hard work seldom wants a prolonged vacation.

When a person who works hard develops laziness, the cause is to be found in his attitude toward his tasks rather than in the fatigue and consequent physical pain which his work involves. Hard physical work, fatigue, and rest are sequences which are enjoyable to the healthy individual. The joy of resting when one is thoroughly tired is a reward for which anyone is willing to pay the price of hard work and fatigue. One who has experienced this sequence is not likely to develop laziness.

5. *False social standards.* Probably the most potent cause for laziness is the absurd notion that there is something degrading in hard work. The bloated, wheezy, big-paunched individual, whose only remnant of a virile youth is his bellowing voice, is mute evidence of the folly of rest without work and fatigue. Rest is pleasant when

it is bought by work; but let one try to steal rest without paying the price and he finds that it has lost its lure. The meal which brought satisfaction to the vigorous youth brings only discomfort to that same person after he has developed a fifty-inch waist line. What a contrast between the duty sleep of the fat "sitter" and the exhilaration which comes to the boy who has won his sleep by healthful exertion!

Dangers from work. The normal, healthy person need have no fear of work. He begins his tasks with zest, glad because he has a job and because he has the vitality to engage the job; he works energetically until he is thoroughly tired or until he feels he has accomplished something, and then relaxes and rests. He is not bored with his work; he is intrigued by it. His holidays are merely diversions which heighten the joy of work by contrast and in turn are made more delightful because of the work with which they alternate. The sequence of fatigue and rest is thoroughly wholesome and there is no danger either in fatigue or in rest provided the sequence is maintained and there is a fair degree of balance between them. It is when this normal cycle is upset by untoward circumstances that danger follows. What are some of these disturbing factors?

1. *Chronic fatigue.* Physical labor, when greatly overdone, becomes torture and shortens life. Peasant women may be worn out at thirty because of incessant toil. Sweat shops may ruin the health of children and bring about premature deaths. In our modern machine age instances of this nature are becoming more and more rare and the average man has little to fear in the way of harm from excessive physical toil. Nevertheless, the fear which began in earlier stages of civilization seems to have carried

over to our present age and we find persons who, while taking not enough exercise to keep their bodies trim, prate about the dangers of excessive fatigue and their need for rest. The chronic fatigue which threatens the modern man is not the result of excessive physical toil but of other factors—fear, worry, and other emotional tensions.

Fears should stimulate us to make adequate reactions to the fear-producing situation. Such reactions may produce fatigue, but such fatigue is no more unwholesome than fatigue produced by any type of work. The fear cause removed, the subject may relax and recover his accustomed vitality. The reason fears deplete our energies is the fact that we make inadequate reactions and permit the fears thus to become chronic.

Suppose you have a fear of failing in a course of study. Use your intelligence, develop a more effective method of studying, and bend your energies to passing the course instead of nursing your fear and feeling sorry for yourself. Suppose you are afraid of financial ruin. Make a complete survey of the situation and get yourself out of your difficulties the best way you can instead of going around in circles in your thinking. In short, if you let fear stimulate you to be more efficient, you will forestall chronic fatigue. If you tear your hair and cry, "What shall I do? What shall I do?" expecting the answer to come from the blue sky, you are simply dissipating your energies and will eventually break under the strain, as well as reach no wise plan of action. Having stormed in an inefficient manner until the break comes, you will then blame the crash on the fact that you worked too hard. The trouble lies not with overwork but with the inefficient manner of dealing with the fear.

"The wise man thinks about his troubles only when there is some purpose in doing so; at other times he thinks about other things. . . . It is amazing how much of both happiness and efficiency can be increased by the cultivation of an orderly mind, which thinks about a matter adequately at the right time rather than inadequately at all times." [1]

It is safe to say that the so-called "nervous breakdown" is never the result of overwork, although it is often attributed to this cause by its victim; but rather it is due to chronic tension which results from a refusal to meet emotional situations squarely and adequately. What the victims of this malady need is not rest, but training in meeting life adequately. To prescribe rest for these persons is to add one more inadequacy to their repertoire and to fix their attention on themselves rather than on the objective facts which need adjusting. Chronic fatigue in modern civilization, whether it reaches the breaking point or not, is due to emotional strain and not to overwork. Do not let well-meaning, sympathetic friends lead you into the pernicious form of self-deception which hides an emotional conflict behind the excuse of overwork.

2. *Working out a rage.* People can be very irritating. One who is in authority over us can badger us without mercy and, while we should like to fight back, we realize that it is inexpedient to do so. The boss can criticise us, not because our work merits criticism, but in order to convince us that he is boss. Our comrades may cast sly insinuations in our direction in order to increase their own self-esteem at our expense. Tact makes us forbear direct retaliation until we can contain ourselves no longer.

[1] Russell, Bertrand, *The Conquest of Happiness*, Horace Liveright, 1930, pp. 71–72.

Work may provide an excellent outlet in such circumstances. We expend the pent-up energy in an explosive attack upon our tasks. But there is a danger in this sort of outlet. If it is temporary, it does no harm; but when long continued it makes for inefficiency and we transfer to the work the irritability we feel toward our human aggressor. The work, which was in the first place an outlet, is blamed for the irritability. It may become so hateful to us that it becomes intolerable and we either break under the load or must quit. It is a mistake to change your vocation because you are irritated by some one with whom you are forced to work.

3. *Working to reduce your energy.* Unfortunately, some young people are taught that exuberant energy is a dangerous thing, that restraint and decorum require extreme inhibitions that are quite difficult for the energetic type of youth. When they express themselves too energetically to suit the taste of their self-constituted moral guides, they bring disapproval upon themselves with such force that they actually become afraid of themselves. They discover that when they are extremely tired from physical exertion they are less likely to act with the violence which their elders dislike. Consequently, they court the things which will deplete their energy. When they are energetic they are condemned, when listless they are commended. Why not do the things which make them listless?

Work should be undertaken from no such perverted motive. We should work to get an opportunity to increase our skill, to get satisfaction from constructive endeavor, to gain the thrill of accomplishment.

The boy or girl who runs to the gymnasium because he is afraid of himself, afraid of the energy which he feels surging up within him, is manifesting evidences of perverted teaching. Instead, he should exercise to build up his body so that he will gain more vitality; he should practice games so that his skill will increase and he will be proud of his prowess; he should compete in a game with all the energy he possesses so as to win if possible, or, if he fails, to have the satisfaction of knowing he did his best—never should fear of his own vitality incite him to wear himself out.

4. *Working to get sympathy.* Another misapplication of work is its use to gain sympathy from other persons. This reaction is the outgrowth of the misconception that work is undesirable, that it is a punishment meted out to man for his sins, that one is to be pitied if he is forced to exert himself. If a child has parents who voice this attitude, what better way to gain their pity than to pose before them as an abused, overworked creature? If, in addition to this attitude, the parents have tried to pawn off undesirable tasks on their children, emphasis upon how hard they are worked is a subtle way of punishing their parents for their supposed abuse.

"How hard I have worked! How tired I am!" is what they say. What they imply is: "How cruel you are to make me work so hard! See how you have made me suffer! Now, aren't you sorry?"

Soon the attitude changes into a greater perversion, the perversion of self-pity. They feel so sorry for themselves that they hunt for all sorts of evidence of the abuse they are suffering and develop pains, aches, and actual disease symptoms to convince themselves and others that they are living a hard life. Physicians' offices are filled with persons of this sort who want to be told that they have been working too hard. With what glee they receive the prescription of a rest!

5. *Working to escape a mental conflict.* We have described how work may be used as a distraction device to enable us to forget some undesirable situation. When used in moderation this procedure is justifiable, but there is danger when it is carried to an extreme degree. Its use is justifiable only when one has faced the issue at hand and, after surveying all the factors involved, has arrived at the conclusion that there is nothing he can do about the situation but to await eventualities which time will bring. Having arrived at such a conclusion it would be foolish to continue to think about the matter. Some distraction is needed to make the time pass more quickly, and surely work is an admirable form of such distraction.

The danger comes when one employs the distraction before he has faced the issue. He is not justified in running away from his own responsibilities; he has no business to forget a problem which he knows he should solve. Consequently, the harder he works the more insistently the problem will come up to torment him. He works harder in his attempt to escape, but the harder he works the greater becomes his torment until his work turns into a wild mania.

Work is a game. It should now be fully apparent that any harm that may come from work is not an inherent feature of work itself, but develops solely from a wrong attitude on the part of the worker.

Study the man who is living an efficient and happy life and what do you find? You will discover that he has carried through his life the same attitude that the child has toward his play.

"It is just as easy to enjoy your work and life as it is to hate it and be miserable. The man who hates his work does so not because the work is necessarily hateful but because he has failed to learn a few simple devices which will change his attitude.

"Your birth means that you have been selected as a player in the greatest game ever devised—the game of living. What a game it is! What thrills you will experience if you will let yourself enter into it! Each dawn is a new challenge to enter a new contest. What if you did lose yesterday? Today is another chance to make good. Look upon life, each day of your life, as an opportunity to overcome challenging obstacles. Each day you will have a better chance to win than you had the day before. Each morning, when you open your eyes, you are opening them on new opportunities, new chances to win, new prizes to gain, new rules to learn, and new competitors to play with.

"You may choose between enjoying life or enduring life as a drudge.

"Decide to enjoy the things you have to do and you will get along faster. You will win by playing to your utmost capacity in your present position, taking advantage of every opportunity as it comes, and playing your way into better positions as they arise." [1]

QUESTIONS

1. Which of the three following propositions do you favor?
   a. Fighting is virtuous in and of itself.
   b. If one fights long enough and vigorously enough, he will win.
   c. The only justification for fighting is the fun you get from fighting.
2. State the two forms that "faith in the future" may take.
3. Show how each form develops.

[1] Morgan, John J. B., and Webb, Ewing T., *Making the Most of Your Life*, Long and Smith, 1932, pp. 4–5.

4. Under what circumstances is it most advantageous to adopt an attitude of "faith in the future"?

5. Under what conditions do we tend to hope that things will remain static?

6. What is the wholesome view to take toward changing conditions?

7. What is the significance of the fact that our future is "determined by the operation of inexorable laws"?

8. What is the most significant effect of struggle?

9. Name five beneficial effects of work.

10. Why is zeal an aid in learning?

11. What are the relative advantages of getting into predicaments and being guarded from trouble?

12. To what extent is a person justified in getting into predicaments purposely?

13. What is wrong with this statement made by a mother: "I will protect my child when he is little; then when he grows up he will be better able to take care of himself"?

14. Describe two ways in which a person may learn to hate work.

15. What effect does activity have on emotional tensions?

16. Compare the benefits of work and rest for mental ills.

17. Describe the most wholesome type of worker.

18. Point out the dangers of work which is motivated by fear.

19. What effect may hidden conflicts have upon work?

20. Why should work not be considered a moral exercise?

21. Point out the advantages as well as the dangers of pioneering.

22. Why is it difficult for an "applause seeker" to become an independent executive?

23. Show how compensation may provide a dominant urge to work.

24. Why is success so important to the person who compensates?

25. What difficulties are likely to be encountered by the one who has the urge to dominate others?

26. Describe the way an intelligent man works.

27. Select the type of worker which appeals most to you and defend that selection.

28. Give some reasons why work should not be too strongly blamed when a mental break occurs.

29. What is essential if you would get the most benefit from your work?

30. What is the thing which distinguishes work from play?

31. What harm comes from the notion that work is a form of punishment?

32. Name five causes for laziness.

33. How can laziness which is caused by too much supervision be overcome?

34. Describe how laziness can be used to enslave parents.

35. Show how laziness can grow from dislike of particular tasks.

36. To what extent can physical fatigue cause laziness?

37. Can you refute the statement that work is degrading?

38. What conditions should surround work to make it thoroughly wholesome?

39. Where did our fear of chronic fatigue have its origin?

40. What is the underlying cause of many "nervous breakdowns" which are so often blamed on fatigue and overwork?

41. Describe how work may be used to rid ourselves of irritations.

42. What dangers are involved in this use of work?

43. Show how excessive exercise may be adopted because of the teaching that inertness is synonymous with goodness.

44. Show how the complaint of fatigue may be used to hide self-pity.

45. Show how work may be used to disguise a mental conflict.

CHAPTER VI

EMOTIONAL MATURITY

"If you look back to when you were happy and then come to the now when you're not, it seems a most terrible and tremendous gulf—and you see yourself just floating—drifting farther and farther away from the happy years and just being taken along, taken along, to God knows where, God knows to what. . . . That's very frightening." [1]

Is it really terrifying to realize that there is a great gulf between your present position and your infancy, a gulf so great that you can never retrace your steps? Would you run back to infancy if there were no gulf? We all have to grow up physically, we must act like adults in our conversation, in our dress, in our ordinary occupations; but many of us are not so mature emotionally. We are afraid to forego the childish ways we learned of enjoying ourselves, we have developed no adult emotional outlets to take their place, we are little more than grown-up babies having little or no fun, except when we can pretend we are infants again, and make sorry spectacles of ourselves trying to catch a bit of the pleasure we imagine we had years ago.

Does it pay to look back? It may be natural for a person who is not yet weaned from his childhood to attempt to be a child again. It may be harmless for a grown man to have temporary spells when the memory of his childhood accentuates the troubles he is having as a

[1] Hutchinson, A. S. M., *If Winter Comes*, Little Brown, 1921, p. 168.

169

man. But whether it be immaturity or weakness that
impels him to look backward, his glances should be temporary and should stimulate him to make more of the
present. If he is too much disturbed by the memory of
his past, too much enamored by the past to face the
future, he is headed for serious trouble.

The fundamental trend of life is forward. Forward a
man must go if he is to fulfill the essential purpose of his
life and be a happy individual. Any less important trend
which destroys this forward movement, or any reversal
of trend which carries him backward, unless it be purely
temporary, is hostile to his best interests and should be
fought vigorously.   Any such counter trend is called
regression.

A temporary regression, a brief spell when we return
to the emotions of childhood and live once more in their
influence may be a valuable stimulus in enabling us to
face the critical hardships of the present. A staid banker,
who would not dare appear in an undignified attitude
lest he undermine the confidence of his clientele, habitually
takes a fishing trip for relaxation. When on this trip he
does not take a bath, seldom shaves, wears the most
disreputable garments, carries with him the odor of a
veteran fisherman, eats the most abominable food, and
puts up with hardships that would seem intolerable in the
winter. Should his friends see him they would not recognize him, but he takes good care that they do not. He
goes into a wild country and severs communication with
the outside world. He completely relaxes in this primitive
condition and returns to his work a new man, able to
bear up under the burdens of another year. His temporary
regression is valuable because it is a rest from strain and
a preparation to take up the battle where he left off.

Contrast with this the case of a man who found life too hard and decided he would "get back to nature." He bought a little land in a sparsely settled district and lived entirely alone. He tried as nearly as he could to bring back scenes similar to his boyhood days, but could not. He grew more and more morose, would have nothing to do with the few neighbors he had, and soon grew to be more useless than one of the cows on his farm.

Indeed, if the mind is flexible, there may be a positive value in a temporary regression. The professional man is better able to engage in his profession after a sojourn in the woods; the laborer is stimulated to work harder because of a day at the circus or the county fair; to be a kid again at Christmas instills new life into our veins; a trip through our memory book will make us proud of the distance we have traveled in our journey through life. It is the rebound again to the present that makes regression normal and wholesome, it is unwholesome only when we go back and stay back.

Varied aspects of maturity. Progress toward maturity involves development along a large number of different fundamental trends with no assurance that speed of development keep the same pace in all of them. Some lines of development take place spontaneously with little need for supervision from the individual or from others and with little chance for trouble along the way. In other directions development is a hazardous undertaking, needing all the wisdom we can gather to help us, and offering all sorts of threats of failure.

1. *Physiological maturity*. Physiological maturity, for example, illustrates a form of development which follows a fixed pattern with little control on our part. As years pass our physical organism grows, matures, and decays

and there is little we can do about it. To be sure, we have
learned certain rules of hygiene which are valuable, but
even though we may break all the known rules of diet,
exercise, relaxation, and the like, we will probably become
physically mature. Disease of some sort, or gross mal-
functioning of some organs of the body are about the only
things which will stop this progress.

2. *Motor maturity*. More control is required for the
maturing of motor habits but, in this field, the requirements of maturity are well known, the plan of progress
well defined, and development is, consequently, relatively
smooth and uninterrupted. Regression is not very likely
to occur in the realm of motor habits. We do not need to
warn adolescents against the danger of regressing to the
infantile motor level—against crawling upon their hands
and knees, for example, instead of walking. Unless we
develop an organic paralysis we are not likely to demand
that we be spoon fed, that some one clothe us and tie our
shoe laces, or that some one write our name for us. Only
in extreme degrees of mental disease does a person regress
in his speech performance and return to the babbling
stage of the infant.

3. *Emotional maturity*. Emotional maturity presents
quite a different picture. It does not come spontaneously
but requires careful supervision. Emotional education
is difficult because we know so little about the objectives
to be reached, and so little about how emotions may be
changed that progress is likely to be most haphazard.
It is no rare sight to behold some grown, educated, cultured man with the emotional behavior of an infant. We
would be highly entertained to behold a grown woman
spilling her food all over her dress, babbling like an infant,
and crawling on her hands and knees; but we take seriously

the infantile temper tantrums that this same woman displays in order to induce her husband to purchase for her an expensive garment. Why should we laugh at her drooling and take seriously her tears?

Importance of emotional maturity. It is a serious matter when a grown person has the emotional behavior of a child. Most of the patients in mental hospitals are people whose bodies are mature but whose emotions are infantile. They are there because they have never grown up emotionally, or, if they have grown, they have regressed to an infantile level. Sanity depends upon emotional maturity more than upon any other one thing.

In almost all cases of extreme mental disorder it is possible to find manifestations of childish emotions. One patient is an extreme pouter; he will sit alone for days and will draw away from anyone who makes overtures to him, apparently doing nothing but nurse a grudge of years' standing. A woman will have a temper tantrum, yelling oaths at the top of her lungs at the least restraint upon her freedom. Another will shed bitter tears because she has been denied some trivial article such as a hairpin. Another grown woman will tear off her clothing as an act of spite to embarrass her attendant. Others will laugh without restraint one moment and cry with the utmost abandon the next. A man will strut and brag about his prowess with all the naïveté of a little boy. The ward of an ordinary mental hospital is a grotesque caricature of childhood emotions.

Most criminals have never grown up emotionally. Crime takes a great many forms but even with the wide diversity in the expression of criminal trends there is usually the common factor of childish emotions. Criminals are self-centered, want what they want when they want it, think that the world owes them a living, and set out to collect it with little or no consideration for others. An emotionally mature person would have a hard time being a criminal of any variety.

For example, a child seems to have no emotional appreciation of the sufferings of others. It was said that Hickman, the man who committed the brutal child murder in California, displayed absolute indifference to the most lurid references to his crime. On the other hand, some criminal acts display the most extreme emotional abandon. One woman tells with delight how she plunged a knife into another who made fun of her lameness.

Again, most social upheavals—wars, political aggressions, race riots, lynchings, feuds, and the vast number of social ills to which we are all subject—are due primarily to emotional infantilism. Even the social reformer who presumably steps in to correct such ills is often as immature as those he is trying to help, and as a result, he merely adds another set of ills to the ones he presumes to correct.

Society has been grossly negligent of this problem. We have instituted agencies to train us to take care of our physical health so that we can mature physically into perfect manhood and womanhood. We have organized a great educational system to train our intellects so that we may be able to think clearly and rationally on all problems. But we have no organized system to enable us to educate our emotions. We let our emotions take care of themselves, let them develop in a hit-or-miss fashion, and then organize drastic means to punish or isolate those who make too great mistakes in adjusting their emotional lives. We set up standards of emotional behavior, moralize about them, have elaborate devices to get square with those who do not conform, but we have no adequate system for training people to meet our moral requirements.

To make matters worse, we have been taught to take a hypocritical attitude toward our emotions. We try to make ourselves believe that they are unimportant, that we are not actuated by any emotional drives at all, or, if we are, that our emotions are of a particularly noble sort. As a young college student it will pay you to examine your emotional life critically in the light of what we are about to describe as the normal progress of emotional development. If you can maintain a wholesome emotional life you need have little fear of any serious mental disruption.

How emotions act. An emotion is a stirred up state of the individual. When one is stirred up, his muscles are tense, he feels that he must do something, and usually does do things. He manifests this "stirred up" condition to an outside observer by bulging eyes, tremors, jerky movements, a pallor or blushing, a choking voice, tears in the eyes, facial tensions, and like signs. In addition to these external indicators, the subject of emotions feels queer feelings in his internal organs, a ball in his throat, cold chills, and the like. Sometimes the emotional feelings are pleasant and sometimes unpleasant, but the essential thing is that they drive their subject to activity. To be emotional and to do nothing are incompatible situations. If one is emotional he must do something. The important thing is what he does.

Some persons have erroneously taught that training of the emotions is training in restraint; that one must learn to be inactive when he becomes "stirred up." Such a method usually brings only disaster. It causes a piling

up of the tensions involved until activity breaks out in
some unexpected quarter. We shall try to show that
emotional growth does not involve emotional restraint
but direction of emotional behavior into adult forms of
activity.

Emotional arousal presupposes some conflict. It results when the person has been thwarted in some fashion, when the ordinary course of his life has been interfered
with. Without conflict and thwarting there could be no
emotion; with thwarting or stimulation more violent than
the immediate outlets can take care of, there must be
some resulting emotion.

First stages of emotional life. Let us first begin with
an examination of the characteristics of the emotions of
children. Having become familiar with these we will be
in a position to trace the development from these early
forms to the wholesome emotions of adult life.

1. *Intolerance of discomfort.* A child is particularly
intolerant of any form of discomfort. Hunger pains, the
prick of a pin, a bath that is too cold or too hot, an unusually loud sound, restraint of the freedom of movement,
a violent movement produced by some outside force; all
these will arouse the emotions of the tiny child. Stimulated
in any of these ways it is normal for the child to show his
discomfort. He has not learned enough to understand
why these unpleasant feelings operate so he must become
very vigorous in his protests against them. To be sure,
we have no way of knowing how the child actually feels;
but we can judge by his behavior that he dislikes any
intense stimulus, and if his protests do not lead to a modification of the unpleasant situation his emotional activity
will become more and more vigorous. It will subside only
when conditions change. All this is normal for an infant.

He should not be expected to be tolerant of unpleasant situations.

2. *Demands for immediate relief.* Not only does the child show intolerance of any discomforts but he shows little patience in dealing with them. He wants relief and he wants it immediately. When he is hungry he is unwilling to wait until he is fed. He will protest until he is fed or worn out with the exertion his protests produce. Having rested he will renew his struggles for relief.

3. *Egocentricity.* Naturally the child cannot be anything but egocentric. At birth his knowledge of the external world is nil, he is interested only in his own comfort and, not understanding how the external world bears on his well-being he can have little interest in it. Childhood is the time when it is normal to be self-centered.

4. *Explosiveness in behavior.* The intensity of reaction of a child is largely proportional to the degree of emotional excitement. Restraint is totally foreign to him. Give him an emotional stimulus and he will react as inevitably as a charge of gunpowder will explode at the pull of the trigger.

These four characteristics of emotional behavior should change radically as the individual advances from childhood to adult life. They may not be entirely superseded but should be changed so completely that they are not readily apparent. If you are intolerant of discomfort, if you demand immediate gratification of your every whim, if you are primarily self-centered, or if you are explosive in your behavior, then you are immature emotionally. Of course, everyone would be loath to admit that he has these evidences of immaturity. We easily deceive ourselves and, after having acted in a certain manner, work out an elaborate explanation of our conduct. The best way to determine whether or not you are immature is to take the judgment of others, preferably those who are not overly friendly toward you.

Development of tolerance. How much pain can a normal adult stand? A little observation will show that there are great individual differences. Some persons have suffered an excessive amount of physical illness and have learned to bear up under it with remarkable fortitude. There are many tales of the way in which certain individuals have borne up in emergencies under the necessity for intense suffering. Men have had bones set or limbs amputated without anesthetics; some have been known to perform operations upon themselves, and, in the days of the Inquisition, others have endured having their bodies torn apart, limb by limb, rather than recant or betray a friend.

Most of us have the most profound admiration for such heroic persons because we realize that we would be unable to perform as well. Between the total intolerance of childhood and these extremes of endurance, we have all degrees, depending upon the training in each case.

Endurance is learned. A person who has suffered very little pain will be more likely to go to pieces under slight provocation than one who has had to suffer much. This learning takes place not because one sets out to train himself to suffer but because he finds himself in a situation which produces inevitable pain and, instead of continuing to bewail his fate, as a little child might do, he finds that he gets more ultimate satisfaction by deciding to endure his lot in silence. Usually he tries to distract his attention from the actual pain by interest in something else. He learns that attention to the pain increases its intensity, while attention to other activities will decrease the suffering. It is well known, as an illustration of this principle, that an athlete may injure himself in a game, but may be totally unaware of the pain as long as the game continues. When the game is over and he attends to his injury the pain mounts by leaps and bounds. In brief, we learn to endure because we discover that we suffer less in this manner than if we keep our attention fixed on the pain itself.

In the dark ages of our civilization certain persons had a perverse idea of the value of suffering. They lost sight of the fact that the only reason one should learn to endure pain was that he might actually suffer less, and thought there was some specific virtue in suffering itself. For this reason, they instituted all sorts of devices to torture themselves, starved themselves, slept on nails, whipped themselves, and poured acids into their wounds. They thought that their holiness increased with such physical torture.

We see similar spectacles in our insane hospitals today, the only difference being that the mentally deranged who practice self-torture give no reason for their conduct.

Other persons will go to all sorts of extremes to avoid pain of any sort. Some take bromides, such as cocaine or morphine, in order to alleviate their suffering, and become drug addicts.

In the face of all these differences, ranging from one extreme to the other, is there any definite standard of normality? Probably there is not. All we can say is that the normal man should avoid physical pain as much as possible, but, when the occasion arises when he must endure suffering he should learn to take it without acting like a child. The man who yells with pain until the whole neighborhood is disturbed gains little respect from us no matter how much he may be suffering. We expect a child to yell but we expect a grown man to contain himself. On the other hand we do not expect him to go to the opposite extreme and gloat over his suffering or beg the physician to do something to make it hurt worse.

Let us apply this principle to other aspects of life. We all have to do things which we do not want to do. Some of us complain loudly continuously while others go at the job and get it over with. Some freshmen "yell" about taking certain subjects they do not like. Granted they do not want them, their dislike is no reason for failing in them nor an excuse for leniency if they do. Suppose you do not like some persons with whom you must work or live. The mature adult is able to keep some of his feelings to himself and treat such persons with some consideration. If you are on a pleasure trip or witnessing a play, you may feel like laughing or crying and may actually do so, but it is not necessary to disturb all around you with your emotional outbursts in the way an infant would do. Have you ever had a pleasure trip ruined by being forced to listen to some physically mature, but emotionally immature woman crying out in ecstasy: "Oh, isn't this grand! I'm so glad I came. Did you ever see anything so beautiful?" Whether it is pleasure or pain you are experiencing, learn to contain yourself if you would be emotionally mature.

Learning to wait for your rewards. Working for a distant goal, foregoing the pleasures of the moment in order to gain a greater but more remote reward is a sign of emotional maturity. Children and adults of lesser intelligence require immediate rewards if they are to be motivated to "carry on." The greater the intelligence of the individual and the higher he goes on the professional scale the longer will a person work for a goal, with its concomitant pleasures, gladly relinquishing what the lesser mortal deems essential in the way of comfort from day to day. Witness the students who will live in a poorly furnished room, with little heat, restricting themselves to the most sparing diet, taking little sleep and no recreation, all because they expect some day to reap the reward of their labors.

But it takes more than a vision of the distant goal to enable a person to make such sacrifices; he must learn the lesson of waiting for his gratification when he is young if it is to be effective. The spoiled, pampered child finds it very hard to forego personal comfort for an evanescent distant reward. How does he learn thus to postpone gratification?

"He has to learn through painful experiences. It is a very hard lesson and few people make a final, completely satisfactory adjustment in this respect. At first it appears in very simple states; the child must not grasp every article of food that appears on the table as soon as he is seated. At first he does so; but as he is restrained and finally punished if he does not refrain and eat in due form, he learns that he gets more to eat and more social approval if he eats with reserve than if he eats like an animal.

"Again, he finds that immediate gratification of a desire often prevents him from enjoying something that would have given him satisfaction had he foregone the first pleasure. He, for instance, omits his afternoon nap so that he can continue his play, and learns to his chagrin that his afternoon's indulgence has cost him a trip to the movies. He learns that his failure to consider the future made him pay too big a price for the small pleasure of the omitted nap. Thus he has to learn the lesson of fore-going pleasure for future gratification.

"Moralists misleadingly elaborate upon this phase of development and hold up ideals which the individual can achieve only by long periods of prolonged abstinence from certain immediate pleasures. As a result many persons tend to feel, quite erroneously, that their future happiness is in direct proportion to their present sacrifice. For instance, a man saves his money so that he will have plenty to enjoy himself with when he gets older; but unfortunately when he gets older, he has acquired the habit of doing without the pleasures that money will buy, so that he cannot enjoy his money when the planned-for future arrives. Take another and equally familiar example. In a still further elaboration we build an ideal picture of a future life filled with pleasures to compensate for our failure to receive pleasures in this world. This may be merely a form of consolation for disappointments, but it can also be so exaggerated that one denies himself all sorts of innocent pleasures so as to increase the amount in store for him. It takes an exceptional individual to attain the proper balance between delayed gratification, that is, the withholding of gratification, and present indulgence." [1]

Mistaken learning in this field is due to placing the emphasis on the wrong factor. The important thing is not the sacrifice but the pleasure that one earns as a result of the sacrifice. One is not paid literally for sacrificing any pleasure; the sacrifice is a device to be used to gain more pleasure in the end. If it does not lead to a greater amount it is foolish to make the sacrifice.

[1] Morgan, John J. B., *The Psychology of the Unadjusted School Child*, Macmillan, 1926, pp. 36–38.

Learning to care for others. The need for love is, in the last analysis, a need of help and protection from another. There is no love between fishes. When the fish is hatched from the fertilized egg, both the mother and father are totally indifferent to the infant fish; they may be miles away. The infant fish is never protected or nurtured by his parents and his continued existence and his growth to maturity are determined purely by chance and his own activities.

In marked contrast, the human infant is born in utter helplessness and will never mature unless he is cared for by some interested adult. The child must have love or he will die.

This first love situation is a totally one-sided affair. The child receives the attention of his mother, nurse, or whoever happens to have undertaken the responsibility, without giving anything in return. Nobody expects him to give anything. He cannot do so. But we do not expect this situation to continue and if we find an adult who continues to receive from others and gives nothing in return we know that we have a person who is still in the infant stage of love. We expect him to grow up and to have reached the stage where he will take the responsibility of loving another who needs his ministrations with no hope of return on his part. In other words each person should traverse the pathway from getting everything and giving nothing to the place where he gives everything and gets nothing. There is no particular virtue in making this progress; it is merely a biological necessity which is inherent in the human race.

To say that a child is egocentric is no condemnation of the child. It is merely another way of saying that he is helpless, that he is dependent upon the love of other

persons, that he must take from them, and that he is
incapable of reciprocating. To say that an adult is egocentric is saying that he has not learned, that he is emotionally immature. If a person has not learned, the
corrective procedure is to teach him. Teaching is not
accomplished by condemnation but by giving the essential
training which has somehow been missed.

Stages in the development of love. The steps in this
learning usually follow a rather definite course and we
shall outline these in order.

1. *Love for parents.* The mother usually provides the
first lessons in the child's love development. When you
were hungry, your mother fed you; when you were cold
or hot, she changed conditions to make you more comfortable; when you hurt yourself, she alleviated the pain;
when you were sick, she nursed you. In brief, she was an
essential feature in making life happy for you. She
became an important part of the world for you; there
was no happening in which she did not play a part. You
soon learned that with mother present you were happy
and comfortable, with mother absent you were likely to
be uncomfortable. She was *the* important part of your
surroundings.

After a time you learned another important fact about
your mother which distinguished her from the inanimate
part of your environment. She did so many different
things in so many different ways that she was not so
easily understood as your blocks, your toy train, your
doll, and the like. You discovered that if you wanted her
to do your bidding you had to study her more closely.
You had to learn her moods, what pleased her and what
displeased her. You learned when she would caress you
and when she would punish you. You discovered certain

tricks which would make her do your bidding; whether
you should laugh, cry, throw things, hold your breath,
pout, or run away. You learned these things by studying
her every movement and facial expression.

The beginning of your love for your mother, in other
words, showed itself through your interest in her, your
study of her, which had as its object exploiting her for
your own interest. Your object was not to do things to
make your mother happy but to understand how to
make her act so that you would be happy.

Please keep in mind the essential feature of this first
stage in the development of love. It is essentially a study
of the other person, an interest in him, which is motivated
by a desire to make him act according to your wishes.
Any love for another which has exploitation as its main
object is merely an extension of infantile love. This is
true even when it appears in older persons.

2. *Beginnings of reciprocity.* Should the child be unfortunate enough to have his social environment limited
to his mother or to persons who are as solicitous of his
welfare as is his mother, he will be deprived of the opportunity of developing beyond the receiving stage of
love. Usually this is not the case. He comes into contact with brothers and sisters, and others of his own age
outside his family. They have, like himself, developed
very little beyond the stage of receptive love and are
just about as selfish as he is.

When a group of young children get together, each
member of the group being interested solely in getting
what he wants without consideration for the wishes of
the others, the result is confusion and discomfort for all.
Through numerous group contacts, through coöperative
games, and the like, the child learns that he gets more

genuine pleasure when he is considerate of the rights of others than when he thinks only of his own wishes. He considers others not through any sacrificial impulse, nor from any moralistic concepts, but because he gets more when he acts in this manner.

This forms an important stage in the development of love, and persons who do not fully learn this lesson never mature emotionally. This stage of love has sometimes been called the gang stage; it might also be called the co-operative game stage. The give and take relationships that grow at this time should run all through the remainder of the love life of the individual.

At first the only satisfaction from such a changed attitude toward others is that the child gets more, in a very objective sense, from his considerate treatment of them. It is a sheer business proposition. Later he gets, in addition, a feeling of personal satisfaction through seeing that the others are happy as well as himself. The infant cares little whether his mother is happy. As he develops to the stage of reciprocity he sees that his happiness need not be at the sacrifice of another's comfort. When others are happy they in turn make him feel better. Consequently, he learns to get an internal glow when he has been the means of bringing a display of pleasure to the face of another.

3. *Romantic love.* At adolescence, because of the maturation of the physiological organism, a new element is injected into the emotional life. In the lower animals such maturation leads almost reflexly into physiological mating. As we advance on the animal scale, and especially when we come to man, more is involved than the physiological processes which we see in the lower animals. Normally, in man, there is an emotional interaction between the sexes which is vastly more important

than the simple biological elements, and which makes romance the most significant part of human life.

This romantic element does not come to life suddenly or in any miraculous fashion. It is a direct outgrowth of the emotional development of the boy or girl prior to adolescence.

Unless a person has developed in his social life to the stage of reciprocity he is in no condition to enter into any romantic attachment. The love of a boy for a girl or a girl for a boy, if it is to be successful, cannot be based on infantile emotions.

Suppose, for example, a girl has not developed beyond the stage of an intense love for herself. She cannot love a boy in any real sense. She may be thrilled when he bestows a gift upon her because of the fact that she is being gratified in her selfish whims. She may enjoy his adoration because it is an extension of her own love for herself. The boy may be ignorant of the true state of affairs and derive some pleasure from the companionship of such a girl, but in a short time he tires of adoring a girl who cares not a whit for anyone except herself.

Mythology has represented this dilemma in a very interesting and instructive story of Echo and Narcissus. Narcissus was a young man who, upon seeing his image in a clear pool, fell in love with it and spent the remainder of his life trying in vain to bestow his affections upon his own reflection. As a punishment Echo was condemned to love Narcissus, but lived a life of torment because she could get no response from a man who thought of no one but himself. This situation is duplicated in thousands of instances and, of course, the romance is blighted.

Nor can romance be successful if the girl or boy has not advanced beyond the stage where he still expects to be waited upon by his parents. If a boy's sweetheart is merely a substitute for his mother, if he expects her to wait upon him with the same interest that his mother devoted to him, he is likely to be disappointed, and the girl is likely to react against such abject slavery.

In short, romance should follow in due course after both individuals concerned have learned thoroughly the lesson of reciprocity. The real preparation for romance is not isolation, it is not the building of fanciful pictures of an accidental meeting with a Prince Charming, or a beautiful girl of your dreams; it is wholesome association with numbers of persons of both sexes until you learn to know personalities as such.

4. *Social maturity.* The socially mature person is more interested in other persons than he is in himself. As he matures he studies other persons more and himself less. He gains more happiness through bringing happiness to others than he does by seeking his own satisfaction directly. As he matures he gains more pleasure by giving and less by means of receiving from others. He sees the world as an opportunity to do things and less and less as an opportunity to have things done for him. In short, he becomes socially more objective, and less and less egocentric. He becomes more and more outgrown, and less and less ingrown.

Parenthood provides the ultimate opportunity to become emotionally mature. The socially mature parent studies his child, watches the growth of his personality, and contributes to it rather than absorbs it.

This does not mean that all parents are socially mature. Some parents take a possessive attitude toward their children. In poorer homes children may be looked upon as means of support when the improvident parents become incapable of taking care of themselves. In other instances it may take the form of emotional bondage which is much more insidious and vastly more harmful than any economic bondage could ever be. Such a parent appears to be extremely devoted to his child. He showers her with gifts, gives her abundance of affection, gratifies her every whim, warns her against the wiles of young men, thus making her afraid of the attentions of any possible suitor, criticises any particular individual who seems to be interested in her, and virtually surrounds her with barriers beyond which she cannot go. All this is done under the guise of parental devotion, and the poor child does not realize she is enslaved until it is too late for her to free herself. A typical illustration of such a situation was that of Elizabeth Barrett Browning. Under the guise of conventional morality, her stern father virtually enslaved her, attempting to keep her for himself, until the tremendous love which she developed for Robert Browning finally gave her the courage to defy him and to escape with her lover.

The altruistic parent gives to his children, but it is not the selfish type of giving. Its purpose is not to place the recipient under obligation to the donor but to enable him to be a more happy, more free, and more autonomous individual.

The altruist is not more moral than the selfish person, he is merely more mature; he has learned one of the important lessons of life. Furthermore, he does not give with any sacrificial feeling. He is not giving up his own happiness by contributing to the happiness of others; he gains more in happiness himself by this means than he could in any other way. The one who brags about his unselfishness has not learned his lesson; he only thinks he has, and is deceiving himself more than he is deceiving anyone else.

Maturity in emotional expression. The infant's reaction to an intense emotion is random activity. He is emotional because he has no ready solution, so he tries first one response and then another, increasing the energy of his activity the longer his random activity proves fruitless. It is normal for an infant to thrash around without rhyme or reason as soon as he is thwarted or antagonized in any manner. The adult should have learned better ways of meeting difficulties.

The adult has poise. He appears to be calm in the face of emotional disturbances; his comrades cannot discern whether he is upset or not. They think that he has no emotional response because they cannot see it. But the poised man is not necessarily unemotional; he is merely refraining from those forms of emotional expression which will enable his friends to discern their significance. He has learned through his past experience that, if an outsider can know the exact nature of his emotions, this knowledge can be used to control his conduct. He knows that he can keep the upper hand in a social situation only so far as he can hide or disguise his emotions. This means that the effect of emotional behavior on the other person is the guiding principle in the emotional life of the mature person. The infant is ignorant of the effect of his emotions upon others, or at least he discounts this effect, and is concerned wholly with his own feelings. The mature person who is always making the claim that he must "express himself," who gives vent to his feelings no matter whether his comrades show signs of approval or disapproval, or whether it exposes him to ridicule or manipulation, is really an emotional baby.

Most of the thwarting which we experience is at the hands of other persons. People get in our way more than things. The mature man knows that he must handle people if he is to get along. Consequently, his emotional behavior is designed to influence others. Let us illustrate by anger. The infant shows his anger regardless of whether the persons who are interfering with his comfort will be influenced favorably or unfavorably by his angry behavior. The mature person studies the people who annoy him, decides whether they are best influenced by anger or some other reaction on his part, and acts accordingly. If he decides that anger is an effective instrument which may bring his opponent to terms, he uses it, gauging all the time its effect upon the other person. If he sees it is succeeding he can continue or accentuate his angry behavior. If it fails he can change to something else.

Take another illustration. A child is very likely to seek the approval of others by boasting or showing off. When he is small such behavior may bring him a certain amount of approval. But when he becomes a man and tries to entertain the office force with the story of the big fish he caught, the wonderful golf game he played, the way he cleaned up on the stock market, the way he forced a prospect to buy a skyscraper, what happens? He is at first listened to with tolerance, then with bored expressions, then with painful silences, and finally, if he has not learned the wisdom of modesty in the meantime, with ribald comments as soon as he begins, "That reminds me of the terrible fight I had with that fifty-pounder in Pelican Lake."

But we soon learn that others are not permanently intrigued by our exhibitions of prowess. We gain more by refraining from making our accomplishments too apparent and, instead, by showing appreciation of those of others. The adult who complains that he is not appreciated, that others do not recognize his ability, is acting like a child. His attempts to make them honor him bring nothing but indifference or innuendoes.

In short, the emotional behavior of a mature person is controlled by the reactions of other persons and is directed toward influencing them. The immature person seeks only to satisfy his own feelings, is indifferent to the outcome of his emotional behavior, and consequently accomplishes little of value by expressing his emotions.

Emotional regression. We have drawn a sketch of the normal progress of emotional life from infancy to maturity. It sounds very simple and it appears as though it should be easy to traverse this pathway. But there are many pitfalls along the way, unexpected dangers meet everyone who attempts to make the journey and many are tempted to give up any attempt to progress or are prone to turn back and be content with childish emotions rather than press on toward emotional maturity.

Every young person should know the enemies which are likely to make his emotional progress difficult so that he can recognize them when they do appear instead of being deceived as to their true nature. He should, moreover, know how to deal with them when he does meet them. If he is able to recognize them and knows how to deal with them he should have no fear. We shall, for this reason, point out some of the dangers which threaten emotional development, not to frighten the reader, but to give him assurance.

Causes for emotional immaturity. Why does a person fail to make normal progress in his emotional learning or why does he revert to a childhood level?

1. *Present failure.* If you are thoroughly unhappy, if your attempts to remove the cause of unhappiness are futile, if you see no opportunity for betterment in the near future, you are very likely, as a result of such failure, to wish you were back at an earlier stage of your career when you were happy. If you are thoroughly miserable you are apt to recall a time when you were happy. If your present associates are unkind to you, you are likely to wish for the presence of some one who, you recall, was kind to you in the past.

Failure may do one of two things to you. It may incite you to go ahead, to fight harder, to work for better conditions, or it may so discourage you that you retreat. Regression is primarily a withdrawal reaction; it is a giving up of the fight. If it is but temporary, if it is a breathing spell during which time courage is built up for renewal of the fight, it may be and often is valuable. If prolonged, on the other hand, the renewal of fighting becomes harder and harder and fear grows stronger and stronger until one becomes totally whipped.

2. *Memory distortion.* The tendency to revert to the past is accentuated by a distortion in our memory of what has passed. We compare our present discomfort with a distorted picture of the glories of the past. Could we avoid such distortion there would be much less likelihood of regression.

"The unsatisfied married man only remembers that when unmarried he was free and that his earnings were his own and forgets all the unsatisfied longings he had as a single man. The girl who awakens to some of the vices of the world, instead of using such knowledge to fortify herself for the future, vainly wishes for the period when she was innocent of all such knowledge. The

young man who is jilted by a girl scorns all women except
his mother, into whose sheltering arms he runs, if not
actually, at least in desire. They all run back in an endeavor to find things as they recall them in the distant
past.

"This tendency to see only the glowing part of the
past has been very aptly called by Dr. Frederic Knight
the Old Oaken Bucket delusion. When we were children
we hated to get water with the old well-sweep. It hurt
our backs; we skinned our knuckles; we almost froze in
winter. Heavy! The thing weighed a ton even when it
was empty! We simply loathed the moss that added to
its weight. We just ached to get away from the farm
and to see life. The future distant scene was the thing
that looked pleasant to us then. Now, after we have
seen the rough part of life the gold age lies in the past,
because we have distorted the whole thing and see only
the pleasant parts. Even the old heavy bucket that we
hated so much looks pleasant in contrast to the hardships
of the present. So, tired of life, and seeing nothing but
trouble ahead, we go back to the 'good old days,' and sing:

> "'How dear to my heart are the scenes of my childhood
> When fond recollection presents them to view!'" [1]

3. *Habit of shirking difficulties.* A difficulty is merely
a name to indicate that something new has arisen which
makes our accustomed way of acting ineffective. We
should do something different. Usually we are stimulated
by each difficulty to emotional excitement, and through
this excitement we do act in a different manner. We
make progress through difficulties and emotional arousal.
But we can let the whole situation rest with a mere emo-

[1] Morgan, John J. B., *The Psychology of the Unadjusted School Child*, Macmillan, 1926, pp. 144–145.

tional upheaval, the repetition of the sort of thing we did as an infant, and moan our bad luck when such behavior brings no result. In short, we may have developed the habit of failure and shirk difficulties, instead of developing the habit of fighting and solving problems when they arise.

The combination of these three forces is usually back of every case of regression.

How far can a person regress? Life is never static for any prolonged period. One is either going forward or slipping backward. Seldom do we move forward with smooth consistent progress. Ahead we go one day only to slip the next. If, in spite of this halting progress, our advances exceed our regressions, we can consider ourselves normal and fortunate.

The real danger comes when instead of being fairly consistent in our gains we are consistent in our losses and succeeding periods of time find us reverting nearer and nearer to infancy in our emotional life.

Once started on the regression pathway, the victim finds it more simple to continue to slip than he does to fight against the tendency, so that it takes a violent counter force to stop him. Usually those who have to live with him do not realize what is going on. They see a person who was formerly active becoming inert, interested only in sitting alone, either doing nothing or reading. His reading and other solitary activities are often mistaken for scholarly interests, and in the early stages he may be given credit for becoming a wonderful student. Perhaps he is a student, but he keeps all he learns (if anything) to himself, and his reputation as a profound student, who is too deep in knowledge to be understood by others, grows with the depth of his regression.

When he approaches too near to infantile emotions he is totally incapable of adjusting to others. He will sit by the hour doing nothing; questions will elicit no answers from him; he will engage in no social activities; he will spend endless time ruminating. He is fit to live only in an institution for the mentally diseased and is usually committed there. Here he continues his backward course and in a period of years may become as immobile as a living organism can become. He must be tube-fed in order to be kept alive. You may slap him, prick him with a pin, make insulting remarks about him, and to all these stimuli, which to an ordinary man would be extremely irritating, you get no more of a response than you would from a telephone pole. He may live for years in such a condition until finally he dies. About twenty-five per cent of the population of our mental hospitals are made up of persons of this type, whose main trouble is emotional regression.

Regression begins gradually. The reason why regression operates in this way can be clearly seen. Having met a difficulty, the victim of this process reverts to an infantile method of meeting it. Finding that this infantile reaction is ineffective the next step is to do nothing. Doing nothing is fatal. We were given our emotions so that we would be stimulated to fight when things go wrong. The fighter gets into trouble, of course, but it is much better to get into trouble than to end up an inert mass of organic matter which has no more vitality than a withering potato in a dark cellar.

The early symptoms of regression are often mistaken for goodness or studiousness. The truly good child is the one who coöperates in social schemes because he has learned that it is the best thing to do. He is actively good and will revolt when taken advantage of. The regressive child is negatively "good" in that he does nothing. His goodness is unintelligent, a mere failure to be bad. It is unfortunate that teachers and parents are so willing to mistake inertness for goodness merely because it does not cause them annoyance; but such is the case.

Regarded as good, these cases go on for a number of years until their situation becomes almost beyond repair. For example, a boy about twelve, who was not as strong as his comrades, was bullied by them; he was called a sissy whenever he tried to enter into their games, and in despair he developed the habit of staying at home working at his studies, instead of trying to "horn in" where he was obviously unwelcome. His parents, not appreciating the real cause of this manifestation of studiousness, encouraged him in this course, and he became the leader of his class in scholastic attainments. But in the third year of high school a change seemed to come. Instead of doing good work he merely sat in the class room and did nothing. He would not recite, would sit with a book before him staring at the page for an hour at a time—looking intently but seeing not a word. Physicians diagnosed him as an advanced case of regression and he was sent to a mental hospital. His relatives said that this disorder came suddenly during the third year of his high school work. Instead, it had been developing for years, but they had failed to see the significance of his failure to fight his difficulties actively. The real student works hard, but because he is interested in his studies, not in order to run away from the more difficult job of adjusting to bullying comrades. There is great danger in identifying as virtue what is really a cowardly flight from reality.

How to guard against regression. Regression provides a real threat to a wholesome emotional maturity. It is a real mental illness and should be guarded against as one would guard against a plague. It starts insidiously and creeps up on one in a most subtle fashion. Do not wait until it has gotten a grip on you. Avoid the very first indications of its presence.

1. *Be afraid of the tendency to live in the past.* If you must be afraid either of the past or the future be afraid of the past. There is really no reason to be afraid of the future; in it lies hope. Living in the past is the retreat of cowards no matter how one may attempt to defend such a procedure.

2. *Let backward looks be but temporary.* If you are discouraged and tend to look to the past, use such a backward glance only to stimulate you to renew your struggle, and go ahead. Even a losing fight is better than a permanent retreat, and the chances are, if you keep fighting, that you will not continue to lose indefinitely. If you quit you can do nothing but lose.

3. *Keep before you the goal of altruism.* Failure in love life is the prime cause for regression. The reason for this is a childish conception of love. When you regard love as an agent through which you can receive benefits you are taking a childish and impossible view of the situation. When you see love as an opportunity to give of yourself you will be on the way to genuine and lasting happiness and the chances of regression to an infantile level will be relatively remote. The altruist should not be regarded as a martyr for he is not relinquishing his right to happiness. He has merely learned an adult means of gaining happiness in place of the ego-centric ways practiced by a child.

QUESTIONS

1. What is implied in the term emotional immaturity?
2. What is meant by regression?
3. What is it that makes regression dangerous?
4. How can temporary regression be made an asset?
5. Give some instances of temporary regressions which benefit those who make use of them.
6. What phase of maturing requires the least care and supervision?
7. Why is motor regression quite unlikely?
8. Give some reasons why emotional maturity requires careful supervision.
9. Point out the part that emotional maturity plays in mental disease.
10. What bearing has emotional immaturity on criminality?
11. Show how social maladjustments may be explained on the basis of emotional immaturity.
12. Why is it we have so little understanding of our emotional lives?
13. What are some of the things a person does when he is emotionally excited?
14. What harm results when one attempts to restrain his emotions?
15. What is the relation between emotions and conflict?
16. State four characteristics of the emotional life of children.
17. What is a good procedure to follow to determine whether we are emotionally mature?
18. Contrast the endurance that some people have developed with the tolerance of infancy.
19. Describe the manner in which one learns endurance.
20. What perverse practices grew from the conception that there was virtue in suffering?
21. What artificial means do some persons adopt to avoid pain?
22. How does the normal man react to physical pain?
23. Epitomize the reactions of the mature man to intense emotions.

24. Distinguish between a child and a mature person in respect to waiting for rewards for his efforts.

25. Outline the steps that are essential if one is to learn to wait for his rewards.

26. What danger must be avoided in learning to wait for rewards?

27. Show how the necessity for protection provides a foundation for love.

28. Contrast the love of an infant with that of an emotionally mature adult.

29. Outline the steps in the development of love.

30. Why does a child love his mother?

31. What incentive has the child for desiring to understand his mother?

32. How is reciprocity learned?

33. In what sense is romantic love the gradual outgrowth of lessons learned before adolescence?

34. What happens to romance if an individual has not progressed beyond the stage of love for himself?

35. How is a person's romantic life affected if he has never advanced beyond the stage of love for his mother or father?

36. How does reciprocity lead naturally into romantic love?

37. How would you characterize the love reactions of the socially mature person?

38. Why does parenthood offer the best opportunity to demonstrate complete emotional maturity?

39. Show how moralizing about love interferes with a true understanding of its nature.

40. What characterizes maturity of emotional expression?

41. What is the adult attitude toward "self-expression"?

42. What is it that controls the emotional reactions of an adult?

43. Name three prominent causes of emotional immaturity.

44. Show how failure may cause regression in emotional life.

45. Explain how memory distortion facilitates regression.

46. Normally, what should an emotion make one do when he meets a new situation?

47. How much can a person regress and remain normal?
48. Describe the behavior of the person who has regressed to a pathological degree.
49. What characteristic of regressive behavior makes it easily misunderstood?
50. Give three rules for guarding against regression.

CHAPTER VII

CORRECT THINKING

Two is less than four. You believe that, do you not? Now, let me prove to you that two is equal to four.

Let $x = 2$. If you multiply equals by the same factor the results will be equal. So let us multiply each side of our equation by 2.

We now have $2x = 4$. If you subtract the same quantity from equals the remainders will be equal. So let us subtract x^2 from each side of our equation, and we will have: $2x - x^2 = 4 - x^2$.

Factoring we have: $x(2-x) = (2-x)(2+x)$.

If we divide equals by equals the results are equal. So we divide each side of the equation by $(2-x)$ and then the equation stands: $x = 2 + x$.

Since the original value of x was 2, by substituting this value, we have $2 = 4$. Q.E.D.

Do you now believe that $2 = 4$? Certainly not. I may have tricked you in this demonstration, but I have not changed your beliefs. You are certain you have been tricked, although you may not know the precise point where the deceit occurred. You believe certain things so strongly that I could not change your beliefs no matter how much evidence I bring to bear to convince you that you were wrong.

Relation of truth to beliefs. In what way are belief and truth related? A belief is my feeling about a fact and has little to do with the truth or falsity of the fact. If I believe a fact, that belief does not have anything to do with making the fact true. If a fact is true, my belief or disbelief has nothing to do with the truth of it. If you assert that $2+2=4$, your assertion does not make it any truer than it was before you made it.

Even though there is no direct causal relationship between truth and belief, does not firmness in belief imply that the fact is likely to be true because of this certainty? By no means can we argue in this fashion. Over and over again, we find our faith shaken in some belief of which we have felt very certain, or we find a fact true of which we, at one time, were very skeptical. At one time we may have believed in Santa Claus. Most of us have doubted the ability of man to fly. Now our beliefs in these two fields are completely reversed. We do not believe in Santa Claus and we are convinced that man can fly.

Again, the fact that large numbers of persons believe a certain thing has little to do with its truth. At one time all thinking men believed that the sun moved around the earth. Now we are certain that the earth moves around the sun. Astronomical verities are entirely independent of the number of adherents of any theory relating to them. The same thing may be said of beliefs in any realm. You cannot prove the truth of any proposition by gaining supporters for that truth.

2 **Importance of clear thinking.** If our beliefs are to be sound we must learn to think clearly. Certainly, if our reasoning processes are all confused we cannot expect to arrive at valid conclusions. We must learn the rules of clear thinking and apply them rigidly. However, even when we do this we fall into errors and find ourselves arriving at conclusions which are false, as when we prove that $2=4$. If we can make such mistakes in simple

problems of this sort, how much more likely are we to
fall into logical errors where the factors are much more
complicated.

Man is engaging in a constant search for ultimate truths
and it is through his rational processes that he makes
progress in this direction. Beliefs arrived at through this
method express the result of man's reasoning to date.
As his investigations increase, his beliefs are changing in
line with his new findings and progress comes only through
the continual modification of beliefs. In other words,
beliefs should grow out of reason and should follow the
logical processes in which man engages. As he corrects
past errors in his reasoning he approaches nearer and
nearer to the ultimate truth.

The difficulties in the way of clear thinking are en-
hanced by a little trick we play upon ourselves. Instead
of waiting until reason brings to light a belief which we
should accept, we adopt the belief first and then try to
support that belief by reasons. The belief may suit our
tastes, it may have been suggested by a trusted friend,
or it may serve some selfish end. For example, if we start
a business venture we want to believe that it will succeed.
We start off with the conviction that it must succeed
because we want it to and then dig up arguments to prove
that it must. If we like a person we want to believe that
he is friendly toward us. We observe only the parts
of his behavior which confirm this belief and close our
eyes to any evidence to the contrary. These illustrations
could be multiplied indefinitely. They represent the
greatest danger in thinking; we tend to select the beliefs
that we like, we accept them as part of our creed, and
then hunt for evidence that they are true, usually ignoring
or distorting any evidence to the contrary. Beware of the

belief that gives you personal satisfaction. You can hardly imagine a person getting any great personal enjoyment from believing that $2+2=4$; but what a thrill he gets from believing that "Mary loves me." If by chance he should discover some evidence that $2+2$ did not equal 4 he would view the evidence with calm intelligence. Let some one give him evidence that Mary really loves another and he cannot view the evidence with equanimity. It is extremely difficult to handle in a rational manner a belief which is based on emotional preference.

What is involved in clear thinking? There are some very simple rules which, if followed, will enable us to avoid the traps which lie in the way of clear thinking.

1. *Freedom from emotional prejudice.* We are all aware of the fact that we cannot reason clearly when we are thoroughly angry. We know that we cannot evaluate the personal traits of a person whom we love ardently or whom we hate violently. What we fail to recognize is that every emotion affects rational thinking in some degree. If you have recently purchased a house you are prejudiced in favor of arguments that it is a valuable property and against any evidence that it is not worth the sum you paid for it. If you have recently lost a position you can hardly be expected to hunt for arguments to justify your employer in releasing you.

Does this mean we must get rid of our emotions if we are to think clearly? We can hardly do this for the simple reason that emotions are with us always. We can, however, adopt methods to enable us to escape the influence of emotional prejudice on our thinking. We can attempt to see clearly what our emotions are and how they may prejudice our thinking. Then we can discount the conclusions which are favorable to our emotional bias and give extra weight to the opposite views. A great scientist once said that when he discovered some fact that went against his theories he carefully recorded it and gave it great weight in his thinking because he knew that he was emotionally prejudiced against it. When he found things which favored his views he knew that he would not forget them, nor would he slight their influence in his thinking. It would pay all of us to follow the example of this man.

2. *Willingness to accept any conclusion.* Are you willing to go anywhere your reason takes you? If your rational conclusions contradict your cherished beliefs, which must go, the belief or the results of reason? In answer to these questions you may counter, "Why should I give up a cherished belief for a rational conclusion when I know that that rational conclusion may be wrong? When you proved to me that $2 = 4$ should I throw away the belief that $2 = 2$?"

The answer to this is that my little trick has contradicted a logical belief and not an emotional one. When a logical process brings you to an intellectual contradiction, the next step is to hunt for error and to persist until a reconciliation has been reached. The danger comes when you find your faith shaken in some belief which you want to hold, but for which you have little logical evidence. If you can follow your reason when your favorite theories are threatened thereby, you are on the road to clear thinking.

3. *Criticism of beliefs.* We are all likely to fall into the silly and conceited error of thinking that our acceptance of a theory somehow enhances that theory. Then, once having taken the step, we cannot go back, we must be loyal to the cause we have espoused. We develop it into a creed or code, devise some slogans to express our position

cryptly, and force ourselves into a loyalty that will brook
no criticism or opposition from ourselves or others. Such
loyalty may be commendable in certain fields but it has
no place in the realm of thinking. In fact you should
be more critical of a belief you have accepted than one
you have rejected in order to counteract the natural
tendency to do exactly the opposite.

4. *Willingness to change your beliefs.* All great thinkers
have had to admit over and over again that they were
wrong. It is this willingness to change beliefs which
marks off the versatile man from the old fogy. Look back
and if you cannot see where you have changed you can
rest assured that you have already stagnated no matter
what your chronological age may be.

It is a bad sign when the young child rigidly adheres to
the belief that there is a Santa Claus, and fights against
evidence to the contrary. Resistance to change is a mortal
enemy to clear thinking.

The wish to believe. But do not beliefs have value?
Has it not been said that man's beliefs are his most cherished possessions? Do not beliefs furnish an anchor to
keep us from drifting in the world of thought, and should
we not cling to that anchor? Should we not try to get a
fixed system of beliefs and maintain them unchanged?
This might be desirable were our beliefs sound ones. In
so far as our beliefs depict realities they provide a safe
anchor, but beliefs are often false. To adhere tenaciously
to a false belief is certainly unwise.

Doubt is an irritating state of mind. In doubt we
are torn between two or more solutions; we cannot decide which one deserves our support and wish that we
could decide to adopt one of the possibilities and discard
the others. Our impelling motive is to gain rest from the

tension of indecision; we find ourselves less concerned with divining the real truth and more interested in arriving at a satisfying belief. We ask ourselves which belief would give us more comfort. But comfort derived from anchoring to an erroneous belief is likely to be shortlived. Doubts assail us anew and we cling to the belief all the more tenaciously.

For example, suppose a woman has a hard time selecting a hat. She tries them on one after another and becomes more and more uncertain which one she should purchase. Finally, feeling that she must make some choice, she takes one. But she is by no means certain that she has chosen wisely. To eliminate this uncertainty she tells herself that she has made a wise choice, ceases to look at any more for fear her doubts will be renewed, and goes home. If she can believe implicitly in her choice she is happy. Therefore she hunts for corroborative evidence that she has the most perfect hat. She asks her husband what he thinks of it. If he raves about its beauty she is made happier; her faith is substantiated. If he shows indifference she gets angry, and complains to him of his lack of appreciativeness or condemns his esthetic taste. She is angry not because of his tastes but because his indifference has renewed her doubt. She wants him to agree. If she had no qualms in her own mind she would not care what he said.

This illustrates the way in which we react in other situations where belief is involved. The less solid support we have for a belief the more we seek to force ourselves to believe, the more we hunt for others to corroborate our belief, and the more intolerance we have for those who differ from us.

If a belief results from intellectual analysis we accept

it coolly and take it as an inevitable conclusion. We have no need to urge ourselves to believe, and we are not irritated when others do not agree. When belief comes as an escape from indecision it becomes a mere symbol of intellectual laziness. We believe because we are tired with the strain of indecision. Belief becomes a form of complacency, a substitute for clear thinking.

Our lives are filled with instances of beliefs of this sort. We defend vigorously our choice of a car, a typewriter, a suit, or a home. We believe we are right because we want to believe we are right. Our reasoning becomes perverted. We argue to convince ourselves and others that we are right; we will not be changed. This type of reasoning has been called rationalization. It is the mustering of arguments to support a decision we have already accepted or to support a line of conduct we have already adopted. The greater the zeal with which we argue, in such cases, the greater is the reason for us to infer that we are doubtful of the correctness of our beliefs.

Beliefs which are adopted to give us complacency may do no particular harm so long as we do not take them too seriously or so long as we do not confuse them with beliefs based on rational thinking. A good way to measure the validity of a belief is to determine how much you wish to believe it. The more you wish to believe a thing the more you should suspect it of being untrue. Most insane delusions are built upon the wish to believe.

There is just one way to avoid the errors we have been considering and that is a clear understanding of the way to think, a mastery of the technique of clear thinking.

The technique of clear thinking. In order to avoid the pitfall of wishful thinking, rules of logic have been devised to guide us in our rational processes and to enable us to detect fallacies when they occur. These are too elaborate and technical to enumerate here, but we can give some of the essential principles which underlie these techniques.

1. *Maintain a questioning attitude.* How, why, when, where, and what should be dominant in the vocabulary of the thinking man?

"You cannot solve a problem if you do not even know that a problem exists and you will not know a problem exists if you do not keep alive the faculty of asking questions. If you take in things just as they come and store them away in your mind, it becomes a mere warehouse. You will have to keep a card index of what is there and dispense it when the demand arises. A lot of it will never be used if your mind is simply a place for storage. . . .

"The observation which led Galileo to his great discovery was nothing spectacular. It was a simple little thing that many others had observed but which had been taken for granted with no questions asked. Galileo asked questions of himself which led to his great discovery.

"'One day when seventeen years old he wandered into the cathedral of his native town. In the midst of his reverie he looked up at the lamps hanging by long chains from the high ceiling of the church. Then something very difficult to explain occurred. He found himself no longer thinking of the building, worshippers, or the services. . . . As he watched the swinging lamps he was suddenly wondering if mayhap their oscillations, whether long or short, did not occupy the same time. Then he tested this hypothesis by counting his pulse, for that was the only timepiece he had with him. . . . The highly accurate pendulum clock was one of the later results of Galileo's discovery.' He learned that if a pendulum is of a definite length, the time of its swing, no matter what its extent, will be the same.

"It pays to ask questions. What if some of them lead nowhere? If you ask them continually and ask enough of them, eventually you may ask one that will lead to some highly important problem. If you never ask them you will not see problems and if you never see them you certainly cannot answer them. Every discovery is an answer to some question." [1]

2. *Learn to make your questions specific.* "If you do not know the answer to a question it is very likely to be because you have not stated it clearly. Play with the question; state it in all the different ways you can. In the final form the answer should be a simple *yes* or *no*.

"General Gorgas, surgeon general of the Army, was assigned the task of discovering the cause of malaria. To ask: 'What causes malaria?' is too vague a question to be answered. He set out to simplify it.

"He knew enough about diseases to assume that some micro-organism was responsible.

"'Where does this organism come from?'

"This was still too vague. So he asked: 'Does it come from dampness?' 'Is it carried by ants?' 'Is it carried by bedbugs?' 'Is it carried by mosquitoes?' Each of these questions could be answered by a simple 'yes' or 'no' after suitable experiments. He performed experiments designed to answer each question and found the answer. Malaria is carried by the mosquito.

"The successful thinker is the one who reduces his thinking to simple terms. The unsuccessful one is satisfied with vague questions. Since vague questions cannot

[1] Morgan, John J. B., and Webb, Ewing T., *Making the Most of Your Life*, Long and Smith, 1932, pp. 74–75.

be answered, such a person is sure to fail. Reduce your thinking to 'yes' or 'no' simplicity if you would find the solution to any problem." [1]

3. *Hunt for data to help you answer your question.* Some persons ask questions merely to annoy others. One little boy, discovering that his mother was disturbed by historical questions, made a special study of history in order to discover questions that would irritate her. Some students delight in humiliating teachers in this fashion. Others ask questions, whose answers they think they know, so that they can display their erudition.

The best use of questions is to stimulate you quietly and unobtrusively to go about discovering the answer to them. Do not expect others to answer them or for the answers to drop from the blue into your lap. Hunt for evidence bearing on your questions until you discover the solution for yourself. In this way you get the intellectual value that questioning should produce. The purpose of questions is not essentially to get answers but to teach you to think, to give you the fun of finding the answers. To permit others to answer your queries spoils that fun.

4. *Keep your eyes open for contradictions.* In ancient times, when an answer was found to a problem it was very likely to be stated in the form of a proverb, and such a proverb was regarded as a guiding principle in seemingly applicable situations. Even today proverbs seem to retain the force of unquestioned authority. For example: "Make hay while the sun shines." "Dropping water wears away the stone." "Store away for a rainy day." "Prosperity rewards the industrious." "Early to bed and early to rise makes a man healthy, wealthy, and wise." "Honesty is the best policy."

[1] *Ibid.*, p. 90.

The very fact that such statements are codified and stated clearly makes them take on an air of authority which places them beyond the realm of questioning. Nevertheless many contradictions can be found even in this elementary statement of principles. How can you reconcile "Haste makes waste" with "The early bird catches the worm"? "Nothing venture, nothing have" contradicts "A bird in the hand is worth two in the bush." How can one live up to the adage "Look before you leap" if he recognizes that "He who hesitates is lost"?

These proverbs are very similar to and are derived in the same manner as scientific principles. They are generalizations derived from a number of specific and concrete experiences. Science attempts to derive a general principle from a number of life situations and to state that principle in a form which will make it applicable to similar situations. Hence, scientific principles and proverbs are merely tentative explanations, subject to revocation, change, or revision as new experiences are added. The scientist has to keep this fact in mind and be ever ready to modify his so-called laws. The thinking man and the scientist can never rest content with the feeling that they have attained knowledge of ultimate truth. Belief for them is no retreat from doubt; it is their habit to doubt. Belief for them is a tentative formulation of their findings to date.

5. *Experiment rationally.* An experiment is a question put to nature. For example, Gorgas was led to believe that the mosquito carried malaria micro-organisms. He then reasoned: "If this is so, men exposed to mosquito bites should develop malaria, while those not so exposed should not develop it." How could he be sure? He exposed one group of men to mosquitoes and protected

another group from mosquitoes. This was an experiment. The former group did get malaria while the latter did not. Nature in reply to his experimental question had answered him.

Experiment is more than tinkering. It should be preceded by definite reasoning. This reasoning starts with a general principle. If this principle is true, the reasoning goes, then, under such and such conditions, certain results should obtain. Do they? They do or they do not, and the question is answered.

Reasoning is a wholesome exercise. This outline merely portrays the processes that any intelligent and normal man will follow in using his intellectual abilities. To be sure, there are all degrees of skill in following these techniques. A man like Galileo is an excellent example of one who was an expert in reasoning. We cannot all equal him and most of us will make mistakes.

What are the consequences when one makes a mistake in his reasoning? He will be confronted with evidence that he is wrong, will retrace his steps and endeavor to discover in what particulars he has erred. Mistakes in reasoning are normal for the simple reason that intellectual processes in man are so varied and complicated that no one can ever hope for perfection in his thinking. He should regard reasoning as a game, a game requiring time and training, a game in which there are all sorts of hazards to make it stimulating and exciting, a game in which one may approach nearer and nearer expert skill, but where improvement is always possible.

Perversions of reasoning. What do we mean when we say a person has lost his reason? The reasoning of some persons becomes so distorted and twisted that it follows neither rhyme nor reason, and no one can follow them. It appears on the surface that their disorder is primarily a disorder of their rational processes, that they have lost their power to think clearly.

Study of such individuals has revealed the significant fact that their trouble is not primarily with their rational processes, but that they have used their reasoning to hide some other difficulty. Their distorted reasoning is a defense mechanism which they use to disguise from themselves and from others their main difficulty. This distinction is important because, if anything is to be done for such persons, the real trouble must be treated rather than the rational processes. In other words, you cannot argue with these irrational persons; they will give you counter arguments *ad infinitum* and you will get nowhere. Get the real trouble ironed out and reasoning will take care of itself.

For example, a graduate student thought that he was being unjustly discriminated against by faculty and student body. The real reason for this feeling was that he felt a fear of incapacity and a desire to excel in his studies which grew into a consuming passion. The slightest evidence of poor work he exaggerated tremendously, but always explained it as a scheme on the part of his enemies. Whenever a class discussion arose he took as a personal affront any argument opposed to his opinions, and took much time telling others how the person who opposed him was scheming to discredit his work. If any two persons laughed and gave each other a knowing look he was sure that he was the subject of discussion. He compiled ten pages of evidence of mistreatment on the part of his teachers and fellow students, and presented this document to the dean with the request that these persons should be dealt with summarily and a special committee be appointed to examine his work so that he would be given a fair deal. An elaborate hearing was arranged, all involved were given an opportunity to state their case, and it all ended in a series of charges and counter charges with no headway in any direction. It seemed illogical, but the exact truth could not be ascertained by any weighing of evidence or examination of logic. Finally a specialist in mental diseases was summoned, and it was discovered that this young student was suffering from a fear of failure which he did not recognize but which led him to conclude that others were intent upon securing his downfall. How foolish all the testifying and argument in such a case!

Most of the trouble which reason is adopted to disguise lies in the emotional field. The reasoning of those who are deluded is dominated by their emotions, and is used merely to justify perverted emotions. They wish to believe and then use their rational processes to justify these beliefs. Let us examine some ways in which this takes place.

1. *Distortion of evidence.* Accuracy in reasoning depends, in the first place, upon the truth of the facts which one gathers about which to reason. If these facts are distorted, obviously the reasoning based upon them will be in error. The truth of an argument depends upon the truth of the premises with which one starts.

Facts may be distorted in two ways. One may actually perceive facts incorrectly or he may make a biased selection of facts, ignoring those which he does not wish to consider, which might spoil his argument, and emphasizing others which support his beliefs. Both of these lead to vicious results although the latter may be more insidious in its operations.

Let us see how some facts may be perceived incorrectly. It will pay to begin with some very simple illustrations and then go on to some more complex situations in which such distortion takes place.

If a teacher is convinced that a certain pupil is bad, everything he does gives support to that opinion. Without trying she watches every movement he makes, sees evidence of malicious intent in every facial expression, and exaggerates the importance of minor infractions. On the contrary, the boy in love can see no flaw in the object of his affections. What appears to other boys as clumsiness is to him manifest grace; her crude impudence is clever repartee to him. Love and hate so distort our vision that they make us blind in the judgment of our unbiased friends.

The scratch of a mouse, if it is heard in the middle of the day, will pass almost unnoticed or will be taken at its true value—a harmless tiny noise. Let that same sound occur at night, when we are all alone, after we have witnessed a mystery play, and we are sure that we are to be the victim of some sinister plot. The boy who has just heard a frightful ghost story cannot walk through a cemetery at night with equanimity. The adolescent girl who has read in the papers the account of an abduction sees the harmless man who happens to be walking up the street behind her as a potential assailant.

In a very real sense, we see in the world about us the very things we expect to see or the things we are afraid we might see. There is really no such thing as purely objective observation; we can only see through colored glasses, the coloring of the glass being the product of our own emotional attitude. We recognize this in others; we discount the fish stories of our friends, we laugh up our sleeves when they tell us how they worsted an opponent in an argument, or we put our tongues in our cheek when a lover orates about his sweetheart. Yet we take ourselves seriously when we distort facts in precisely the same fashion. We discount the statements of others and expect our descriptions to be taken seriously.

The scientist makes an heroic attempt to overcome this well-known human weakness. He does it by developing instruments of precision; he devises machines to record facts as they are, so that his judgment and his bias will be eliminated. Where he cannot measure facts with instruments he obtains the reports of various persons with opposing biases and attempts to get at the truth by combining these diverse observations. For example, if a sociologist wants to get an estimate of the behavior of a certain individual he takes the reports of several persons who love the individual and weighs it against the reports of an equal number of persons who hate him; or better yet, gets the reports of a number of persons who apparently have no pre-formed opinion of any sort.

The second method of distorting facts, that of weighing heavily evidence on one side while ignoring contrary facts, works in a much more subtle fashion. Even though the evidence is gathered by instruments of precision, false weighting of such evidence may wholly misrepresent the true situation. The searcher for truth cannot go out to find evidence to support his contention, he must go out to find contrary evidence—a thing which is very hard to do if one is emotionally biased, and most of us are biased in spite of our attempts to be unprejudiced.

For example, it would be possible for you to prove by this method either that thirteen is for you a lucky number or an unlucky number. Record faithfully every time some unfortunate event is accompanied by the number thirteen, and you will find such events. Record all those situations where thirteen is connected with lucky events and ignore the others, and you will find support for the luckiness of the number thirteen.

Witness the number of favorable testimonials that can be gathered for any patent nostrum, any cigarette, any tooth-paste, and you will have convincing evidence of the operation of this fallacy. In brief, you can prove anything you set out to prove by the proper selection of evidence.

The rule that applies here may be stated as follows: Doubt the evidence presented to support any proposition which is advanced by one who favors that proposition; doubt the evidence which is opposed to any proposition when that evidence is advanced by one who is against the proposition. This is easy to do when others are doing the arguing; it is even more important to do it when you yourself are involved.

An illustration may make clear the extent to which such errors may go. A woman who had lost her husband through death tried to escape her grief by all sorts of devices—traveling, study, club work, and the like, all to no avail. One day, with her niece, she visited a spiritualist and asked the medium to communicate with her husband. Her intense desire to commune with him made her believe that she actually had talked with him. After the séance she was so much more happy that her niece conceived a plan to bring her solace. She communicated in secret with the medium and gave her a great number of facts about the deceased husband. On the next visit to the medium the woman had her last doubt removed that she was actually talking with the dear departed husband. She continued to attend the meetings until she learned to communicate with him—in her imagination, of course—

without the help of the medium. The husband informed
her that he was happy, that he wished her to return to
the old homestead and take up her life where she had
left it off and promised to continue to commune with her
if she would do so. She is now living in daily communion
with him, happy, and thoroughly convinced of the reality
of all this. The niece at times feels somewhat guilty for
having perpetrated this trick upon her aunt; she justifies
it on the grounds of increased happiness for her, but
lives in constant dread that the aunt may awake to what
has happened. This is not likely to happen because of
the intense desire of the woman to believe in the reality
of the communications. She would ignore any evidence
that it was all a fiction of her imagination.

2. *Unwise generalizations.* Another source of fallacious
reasoning is the tendency to make broad generalizations
from a few facts. Science proceeds on the basis of generalizations from concrete experiences and states these generalizations in the form of principles which have a wider
application than the facts upon which it is based would
warrant. But science protects itself from error by never
taking too seriously these principles. They are regarded
as hypotheses—that is, guesses—which are subject to
further verification or modification with accumulating
facts.

Most slogans get their following, not because they have
ever been tested, but because they are repeated so often
that we begin to accept them. We have all been the victims of such sweeping statements as: "Make the world
safe for democracy." "Save and prosper." "Buy and
bring prosperity." "Spare the rod and spoil the child."
"Your best friend won't tell you."

The great danger which arises from generalizations lies

in the fact that there is always some truth in them. They are true in some instances and because of this fact we are led to believe that they are true in every case. Perhaps the world should be made safe for democracy; it does not follow that war was the only way to bring that about or even that it was the best way. Some persons who save prosper and some who buy prosper; it is a question of buying or saving at the right time. Some persons may need to be whipped but that does not prove the wisdom of the indiscriminate use of punishment.

3. *Misuse of analogies.* An analogy proceeds on the unsound assumption that if two or more things agree with one another in some respect, they will probably agree in other respects. When we define an analogy in this manner, its limitations and dangers are apparent and few of us would be deceived by it. In actual use, however, it is usually disguised so subtly that its distortions are not apparent and it provides one of the most insidious forms of deceiving ourselves and others.

For example, we might say that the eyes are the windows of the soul. We can get a very clear picture of what a window is and what its functions are, but we have little knowledge of what the soul is or of the actual way in which the eye functions. We immediately see the eyes in a very concrete way embodying all the characteristics of a window. We picture the soul as a miniature man sitting behind the window, looking out on the world and trying to gain knowledge of it. When we do not see clearly we imagine a dirty window or one with defective glass which distorts the picture. Instead of clarifying our notion of the function of the eye and the nervous process of vision we only confuse ourselves by such a device.

The force of illustrations to carry a point with an audience is based largely on this form of deception. The auditors are able to visualize the illustration and because of this clarity of the illustration they think that they understand the abstract principle which the illustration represents. An analogy makes a point clear but it never proves anything. Yet if you want to convince people of a fact you may do it more easily by a forceful illustration than by any other device.

The development of delusions. Man's superiority is largely centered in his rational processes. Through reasoning, man has been able to discover many of the secrets of the universe; he has discovered laws and through knowledge of these laws he has gained control of his environment in a superlative fashion. But this progress toward a rational understanding of life in all its aspects has been a halting affair. Whole generations have labored under false beliefs; men have slain others because their beliefs did not agree with their own, only for later generations to discover that the martyrs were correct and their murderers were in error.

The reasons for these mistakes have been twofold, as we have pointed out in our discussion to this point, errors inherent in the reasoning process itself, and errors due to the fact that beliefs are often based on our emotional attitudes.

The rule that should be followed to avoid such errors is to survey each rational process with cool objectivity in a constant attempt to discover errors and to discredit any belief which has more emotional backing than rational support.

Stated in another way we may say that delusions are largely emotional distortions which bring to their defense rational processes to make these distortions appear to be truths. A delusion is distinguished by the wish to believe; it is an error of emotion and not an error of reason. It is built upon emotions and must be corrected by changing the underlying emotion. To do this, the true emotion behind the delusion must be discovered. This is not easy, for usually the emotion is concealed behind a barrier of apparently rational arguments, and listeners are more inclined to argue in retort than to study the motives behind the arguments.

The delusion is most likely to develop in the person who has learned to value reason most highly. He begins by wishing certain things were so when obviously they are not. As we have seen, some persons develop a vivid imaginary picture and visualize events as they would like them. The man who depends upon reason cannot do this; he cannot make a wild jump from reality to fancy by route of imagination; instead he argues that they are as he wishes them.

Here again, let us remind the reader that the only way to keep sane is to face reality frankly and, when it does not conform to our wishes, to attempt to change it by the process of hard work and in conformity with the laws of life as we have learned them. Any short cut is sure to lead to disaster and the short cut of distorting reason is no exception.

Delusions of persecution. The young man who was coming into the office made a very fine impression. His hair was freshly cut and faultlessly brushed, his suit had just been pressed, his shoes shined, his nails were immaculate—everything about him led you to believe that his friendship would be worth cultivating.

After presenting himself with grace and poise he introduced his mission as follows: "I heard you were a

Mason and so I came to you to ask you about some of their practices. Some things have been happening to me which I am sure resulted from the activities of the Masons. How do they go about recruiting members?"

"They do not recruit members," he was told. "If a man signifies his wish to belong to the lodge, he is voted upon by the organization, but no active recruiting is ever done."

"That's just it," he continued. "They do not openly try to get you in but they do under cover things to get you. I made up my mind I never would join them a number of years ago but they have been after me ever since."

"What do you mean, after you?"

"Well, it started this way. I noticed when I went on the street that some man would be following me, watching every move I made. At first it just amused me, but then it got to be annoying. I tried to shake them but they were always on my trail."

"Well, why would they shadow you?"

"They wanted to get something on me to make me join. They were afraid that if I did not join I would expose some of the things I know about them. You see I looked into their practices and they do a lot of things I don't like. That is why I made up my mind not to join them. Well, they know I know too much and they are either going to make me join them or they are going to get me."

"What do you mean, get you?"

"Just that. When they found I would not join they began to change their tactics and they are now trying to get me. At first they tried to hit me with their cars. I almost got involved in several accidents and I am sure they set the stage for those on purpose. You know how they do that. Well, about a year ago they started a new wrinkle. They are trying to poison me."

"No, no. You surely must be wrong. They would not run you down on the street, hit you with their cars, or poison you."

"Oh, you don't know the tenth of it, and you probably won't believe it when I tell you, but it is all true. I don't dare eat out at all any more. They will poison my coffee. The waitress will bring it, I will take a taste of it and it will be all right. Then they will pass behind my chair and drop the poison in it. I can never catch them actually dropping it in but when I taste it it is different and I know they have poisoned it. They will do the same with my vegetables and everything else I try to eat in a public place. Now I have to get all my own meals at home. Then they got to putting it in the fruits and vegetables I would buy and I could only buy canned goods so as to keep them from getting it in. I am not getting enough to eat because of all of this and it is undermining my health. It has gotten to the point where I just must do something about it."

"What do you think should be done?"

"I think steps should be taken to stop them from doing such things. What chance has one poor lone man against a powerful organization? They can do just what they want to do and when they start in on a man they will surely get him. They will probably get me but I would like to expose them so as to break them and save other poor fellows from the fate I will likely suffer. They are just like a gang, once they go out to get you, you might as well give up."

And so this man would talk on and on in the same strain as long as he had an audience. You might think that you

were especially selected to hear these most intimate dis-
closures of personal intrigue, but he would go on in the
same fashion to anyone who would listen to him.

This young man appeared to be on a search for the
truth, but was he? Let us see.

In the first place, probably all the objective facts he
reported were true. He probably did see people on the
street, walking in his direction. He probably did get into
near accidents and may have been nearly run down by
passing cars. He probably did have funny tastes when
he ate in public places. Who has not had all these things
happen to him? Is there only one possible answer to all
these things, and is that answer that he was being at
first sought as a member of a particular fraternal order,
and latterly persecuted because of his refusal to join?
We recognize the obvious distortion of emphasis here.
If one wants to get the truth he must consider all sorts of
possible explanations. This man had entertained only
one possible hypothesis, one which seems ridiculous to
us.

Suppose we point out to him this fallacious nature of
his reasoning, what will he do? Continue to give us more
evidence of the same sort. In a sense all that he says is
believable. Men have been poisoned. Gangs have spotted
certain individuals because they considered them dangerous to their operations. Why should we doubt this
man? Because of a very simple and apparent defect in
all his arguments. He shows that he is concerned more
with believing his interpretation than he is in testing its
truth. If you should be interested enough to live with him
for a time and to organize certain checks to determine
whether he is correct in his assumptions, you would find
him getting more emotionally insistent on his interpre-

tation the more negative evidence you discovered. You would learn that he was dominated by the wish to believe rather than the wish to discover the true state of affairs. The wish to believe is the soil in which delusions grow.

But why should anyone wish to believe that he is spotted for extinction by a powerfully distributed fraternal organization? If such a suggestion occurred to him it is more likely, you may argue, that he would wish just the opposite and fight against such a horrible interpretation of the events which he described.

How delusions of persecution develop. Rather than attempt to account for the growth of this particular delusional system, it may be better to describe the general principles of such delusional development. These general principles have been derived from studies of many cases.

Two essentials underlie the development of a delusion of persecution. The first is a conceited personality. The conceit may vary in degree and may be disguised as self-esteem, ambition, virtue, or some similar worthy trait; but conceited the person must be. Often the victim poses as a very modest person; he will tell you that he has very little regard for his own interests, he is concerned with the social good, and such high sounding interests. But a little observation of him will belie his words. His meticulous care of his person is just one bit of evidence of his high regard for himself.

The second requisite is a failure of the person to accomplish all the things he feels he should be able to accomplish. This failure may be a professional failure, it may be an economic failure, it may be a failure in achieving a satisfactory love adjustment. The two latter are most likely to cause trouble of this sort because they are the hardest types of failures to admit. Hence the development of the rational type of defense mechanism.

When a conceited person has failed, what shall he do? He cannot admit that he has really failed; he cannot admit that he is deficient; he begins to hunt for excuses to account for the discrepancy between his abilities and his actual accomplishment. He feels that others have underestimated him, that they are jealous of him, or that they have actually tried to interfere with his success because they are afraid of him. Placing the blame on others is much more satisfying than admitting his own deficiencies. He forthwith adopts the former hypothesis, and sets out to prove that he is right in his interpretation.

This scheme for saving our face is as old as the hills. We have an illustration of it when Adam blamed Eve after he was caught eating the forbidden fruit and Eve in turn blamed it on the serpent. We are led to believe that the serpent blamed it on the devil; the devil presumably was willing to take the blame. We see children getting out of scrapes by saying that some one told them to do the thing for which they are reprimanded. If a young man fails to get a position, it is not because he lacks training or is deficient in his ability to sell his services; some one else had a "pull." If a man embezzles funds, he blames it on some woman who demanded luxuries he could not otherwise afford. If a woman falls, it is because some vile man seduced her.

The tendency to blame others is fostered by parents and teachers who make an insistent search for the blameworthy person when any misconduct arises. The child soon learns that he can squirm out of a predicament if he will exaggerate the influence of other persons when he is caught.

Once having developed the habit of casting the blame on others, the tendency grows apace. At first it is enough to place the blame on one other person. Shortly it dawns on the victim of this habit that such an excuse is not so flattering. It is a tacit assumption that the other person is better than himself. If one person can keep me down that person must be better than I am. So the way is paved for the next step, that of believing that several persons are in league against me. I could handle one person, but when they organize a league against me I am powerless. This feeds my vanity still more. The persons in league against me are quite important persons; they are devoting all their energy and time to thwart me. The Masons, the Catholics, the government, no organization is too great or too powerful to be selected as the force to keep me from demonstrating to the world what great powers I have.

Hence we can see that the delusion of persecution illustrated by the young man who thought he was being poisoned had its beginning in a very simple and apparently harmless distortion of emphasis.

What can be done about it? When it is deeply rooted as in the illustration we have given it is almost impossible to uproot it. But the lesson from this picture is obvious. The tendency toward developing delusions of persecution is really an outgrowth of the tendency to blame others for our difficulties. If it is to be stopped it must be averted in its earliest phases. Any young person who finds himself blaming others when he fails should fight this impulse as he would fight some vicious disease. For it is a vicious disease once it gains lodging in a person. As we have said before, failure should be a stimulus to make us fight harder. Blaming others is a poor substitute for fighting.

Delusions of grandeur.   The process we have been describing may not stop with delusions of persecution. Having become convinced that others are plotting against him, the victim of the delusion may ask himself: "Who am I that all these great organizations should be so concerned with persecuting me?" He concludes that he must be some great person and casts about to see whom he might be. He has discovered some great secret that these people would like to steal from him; he is therefore a great inventor. He knows too much about the secret schemes of these people; he is therefore some great reformer, perhaps the Messiah himself. Perhaps he has royal blood in his veins and the actual rulers are usurpers of the power he should rightfully possess. Perhaps he has great military prowess and they are afraid that he might defeat them were he to come to his own; he is Napoleon or Alexander the Great.

In every hospital for mental diseases we can see persons who have delusions as to their own identity. Such persons amuse us and seem totally irrational in their thinking. When we see, however, the steps of perverted thinking which lead to these conclusions on the part of these persons, their delusions do not seem so strange.

Delusions of disease and unworthiness.   Not all persons justify their failures by blaming others; some go to the opposite extreme and become very critical of themselves. They are certain, in the beginning, that they have the ability to accomplish anything which they set out to perform; if failure comes it must be because they did not use their abilities properly, they must have made some mistake along the line. Usually such persons are strict self-disciplinarians. Self-mastery and self-negation are, they believe, the highest virtues; if practiced sufficiently these virtues must bring the reward of success. Failure means self-blame.

Some of these persons blame their poor success on ill-health. They are certain they had the right plan of life and would have succeeded had not poor health intervened. The more they fear failure the more they hide the real fear and stress the fear of disease. Seemingly they take great care of their health, but in reality they do very foolish things. They want to be ill, really do things to make themselves ill, or believe they are ill when they are not, but through it all put up a great pretense of taking excessive care of their health.

Of course, this emphasis enables them to pity themselves and to obtain pity from others. No one could blame a person for failing when he is ill; indeed, he deserves credit for putting up as good a struggle as he has, in view of his poor health.

Beneath the illness a motive is often to be found which changes the whole situation completely. This was the case in the illness of Mrs. X, an illness which lasted for years and which baffled the wisdom of many physicians. It began just before the time that her daughter's wedding was to take place. In spite of the terrible pain of which she complained, the physicians could not determine upon a diagnosis and advised her to rest and to await more specific developments. This suggestion drove her frantic and she complained so violently that they at last decided upon an exploratory operation. Nothing was discovered and she was so informed. This was all that was needed to provide fuel for a new series of complaints. She was sure that the surgeon had injured her by operating on her. Queer twisty feelings developed in her stomach, crept toward her heart and lungs and she was sure both were affected. Because of all the hubbub the wedding, of course, was postponed. When she seemed to get better another date was set, but again it had to be deferred because she had a fresh attack. Finally the young man became angry and issued an ultimatum that the marriage must take place or he would break off all relations with his sweetheart. Thereupon the mother had the most violent attack she had yet experienced; but the young man made good his threat, broke his engagement and, a year later, married another girl. Strangely enough, soon after hearing this news, the mother improved rapidly. The only recurrence she has had was when the daughter almost became engaged to another young man. This woman was actually fooling herself as well as her daughter. She praised her daughter for making so many sacrifices for her, not realizing that she was enslaving her daughter by her intense selfishness, and that the sickness was a ruse to maintain her control.

It is but a short step from this blaming of disease to a feeling of total unworthiness. The martyr not only glories in disease but in his mental and spiritual unworthiness. If he could only sacrifice himself for others who are more worthy than himself he would gain his greatest happiness—so he argues.

Martyrdom, again, is merely a device to save one's face. The martyr has failed, but the failure he parades is usually of a different sort from the failure he is trying to hide. He hides a real confession of failure by developing a species of holiness through his self-abnegation. The martyr, in short, parades his holiness to cover his defects. He is just as self-centered as the one who develops delusions of persecution; he is merely showing it in a different manner.

Where does this delusional trend have its beginning? In the sympathy of certain individuals for those who confess. One little boy who had learned this lesson well had the habit of quickly confessing to his mother his naughty deeds before she had a chance to find them out on her own account. She could not punish him when he showed the proper repentant attitude and confessed. Confession pays the debt, so why not confess and confess, and so pile up a credit balance in our moral account? That is what this boy did and that is what many adults do.

2 **Can false beliefs be avoided?** Certainly no one wants to believe that he is being persecuted when he is not; no one wants to believe that he is Napoleon, the Messiah, or a millionaire when he is not; no one wants to believe that he has a disease when he is sound; no one wants to believe that the earth is flat when it is round. Yet none of us would dare to make the statement that all our beliefs correspond exactly to the truth. Try as we may some of our beliefs will be radically false, some will be almost true, and some will have in them about as much truth as error.

The only solution to this dilemma is to put just as much confidence in a belief as rational demonstration of its validity justifies. We have never found an exception to the truth that $2+2=4$ and it is impossible to conceive a situation in which this would not hold true. Such a belief stands for itself, and it needs no defense from you or from anyone else. When a belief is of doubtful validity it does need defense. Consequently when you feel called upon to defend a belief you may be sure that the validity of that belief is questionable. The more it needs defense the less reliable it is.

Isn't it absurd, then, that we should ever defend any

belief? If it cannot stand on its own feet it should fall. Truth is nothing to fight about. If it is true there is no need for a fight and if it is doubtful, the procedure should be to investigate and not to fight.

Why cannot we say: "I would like a certain thing to be so, and because it gives me comfort, I intend to live as though it were so." Suppose, for example, I find it more comfortable to live if I act as though others could be trusted. Do I have to believe that all men are trustworthy in order to obtain such comfort? Do I have to force others to agree that all men are trustworthy, or do I have to fight with them if they tell me that they believe that some men are dishonest crooks? If we can just get this viewpoint we can develop a livable attitude toward life, an outlook on this world and its affairs, and can be reasonably happy living according to this outlook. If we live as though a certain thing were so, recognizing that in many cases it is not so, then we will not need to build up any rational defense of our code of living, nor fool ourselves that we know the ultimate truth about human beings.

Should we disbelieve everything? One other warning is necessary before leaving this subject. Some immature individuals, realizing the danger of rigidly adhering to a belief, go to the other extreme and hope to escape trouble by saying that nothing is certain, therefore they will believe nothing.

They think there is a virtue in denying very obvious truths, even those derived from pure reason. They have been told by the same persons certain mathematical and scientific principles and that there is a Santa Claus. Discovering that there is no Santa Claus, they ironically declare that there is nothing else, either.

Here again, we permit our emotions rather than our intellects to change our beliefs. A woman, who believed thoroughly in retributive punishment after death, had no hesitation in condemning to everlasting fire those who "died in sin." But when her only son died in a drunken brawl she changed her religious beliefs overnight, and believed heartily in a "second probation" after death. This simply illustrates what is happening all the time. Why not admit that your emotions determine your outlook on life without attempting to rationalize this outlook and defend it with a pretense of reasoning?

Rules for correct thinking. Some of the principles we have discussed in this chapter may be summarized as follows:

1. Learn to distinguish between the two kinds of belief: the beliefs that arise from personal preference and those which follow inexorably from rational thinking.

2. Arguments developed to support a belief which is personally desirable are likely to be fallacious. You are more likely to be concerned with winning your point than with clear thinking and will distort your thinking almost invariably.

3. Be sure to get in a realm where you have no emotional prejudice if you would train yourself to think clearly. Heated discussions may be fun, but they do not help clarify thinking.

4. Be willing to go anywhere and to accept any conclusion when clear thinking leads you.

5. Because you have reached a conclusion is no reason to favor that conclusion. Your thinking may have been in error. Be as critical of your own beliefs as you are of those of others. Yes, be more critical of your own.

6. Do not rest upon formulated beliefs. They are

merely resting places to permit you to get your breath before beginning a new journey in the land of thought.

7. Learn the technique of clear thinking until it becomes second nature to you. Learn to recognize a fallacy from afar.

8. The greatest danger of clear thinking is the wish to believe. Beware of any conclusion that gives you too much comfort. Remember, thinking is vigorous exercise, a sort of a game. Beliefs are resting periods between playing periods. You cannot mix the rest periods with the periods of activity.

QUESTIONS

1. Outline the arguments to prove that there is no direct causal relationship between belief and truth.
2. How would you define belief?
3. How would you define truth?
4. Where should we expect to discover the source of sound beliefs?
5. What is the emotional element in relation to beliefs that tempts us to entertain false beliefs?
6. What distortion in our reasoning do we adopt to support a belief?
7. State four principles that are involved in clear thinking.
8. Describe how emotions distort our thinking.
9. What rule can be applied to enable us to escape emotional bias?
10. Distinguish between an intellectual contradiction and emotional bias.
11. Show why loyalty has no place in the realm of reason.
12. What is the importance of being willing to change a belief?
13. What emotional satisfaction does a person derive from fixed beliefs?
14. What does the emotional fervor with which we hunt for supporting evidence tell us about our confidence in a belief?
15. How does doubt in ourselves lead to intolerance for others?
16. Show how a belief can be an escape from intellectual doubt.

17. What is meant when we say that belief can be a form of complacency?

18. What is rationalization?

19. What does zeal in argument often signify?

20. What is the wholesome thing to do when we find ourselves very anxious to believe a certain thing?

21. Memorize the five rules in the technique of clear thinking.

22. Think of some instances from daily life where it pays to maintain a questioning attitude.

23. Can all problems ultimately be reduced to questions so specific that they can be answered by "yes" or "no"?

24. What unwholesome uses may be made of questions?

25. What effect should a question have upon a person?

26. What should the thinker do with contradictions?

27. Show how an experiment should be designed to give a direct answer to a specific question.

28. What does the normal man do when he discovers that he has made a mistake in his reasoning?

29. Why is it useless to argue with a person who appears to be irrational?

30. Show how an error in reasoning can be used as a defense mechanism.

31. In what two ways may facts be distorted?

32. Give illustrations which indicate how facts are distorted in the way we perceive them.

33. How do scientists attempt to overcome perceptual errors?

34. Explain how selection of evidence may enable one to distort the truth.

35. How does science protect itself from the danger of generalization?

36. Under what circumstances does it pay to generalize?

37. In what way are analogies useful?

38. Wherein lies the danger in using analogies?

39. What is a delusion?

40. Distinguish a delusion from an error of reason.

41. What sort of person is most likely to develop a delusion?

42. What factors in the story told by a deluded person make it difficult to refute his arguments?

43. What happens when you argue with a deluded person?

44. What is the element which lies behind a delusion which must be dealt with if any improvement is to be made?

45. What two essential elements underlie the development of a delusion of persecution?

46. Show how a delusion is simply an adaptation of the necessity to "save one's face."

47. How does one learn to blame others for his difficulties?

48. Explain how the tendency to blame others develops into a delusion of persecution.

49. How can the tendency to blame others be corrected?

50. Show how a delusion of persecution can be transformed into a delusion of grandeur.

51. What type of person is likely to develop delusions of disease and unworthiness?

52. How can a person use a delusion of disease to avoid some unpleasant situation?

53. Explain the way martyrdom develops.

54. Explain how a person may entertain false beliefs and still never develop a delusion.

55. Show why disbelief of everything does not solve the problem of rational errors.

56. State the rules for correct thinking.

CHAPTER VIII

COUNTERACTING DEFECTS

"When William Pitt, the Earl of Chatham, was secretary of state of Great Britain, an admiral came to him with the complaint that he had been given an impossible task. In reply Pitt picked up his two gouty crutches, shook them at the admiral and shouted with scorn, 'Impossible? Sir, I walk on impossibilities.'

"If Pitt with his swollen, painful joints could hobble around on crutches and do his work, what right had a robust admiral to complain about a few difficulties? How often it is the strong man who hunts for an excuse while the handicapped man makes a heroic struggle and accomplishes the seemingly impossible.

"A handicap can be used as an excuse for laziness or cowardice or it can be used to make you buckle down to the hard work that is necessary to overcome it." [1]

What are handicaps? When we speak of a physical handicap we think of a man who is unusually short or tall, one who is maimed—having one leg or one arm, for example—one with deficient hearing or vision, and other such manifest physical differences. A difference which makes him unable to compete on equal terms with his fellows is a handicap. Any disadvantage which makes it difficult for him to compete with his opponents, whether the difference is natural or artificially imposed, is a handicap.

[1] Morgan, John J. B., and Webb, E. T., *Making the Most of Your Life*, Long and Smith, 1932, p. 23.

239

Now, a handicap is not necessarily an evil. In sports the superior player is given a handicap, that is, an additional barrier is erected to make his performance more difficult, thus placing him on more equal terms with the other players. The handicap should be an extra incentive to make him play the harder. If he had no handicap he could win easily and in all probability would not exert himself as much as when he has the handicap.

Obviously if two players are too far apart it is ridiculous for them to compete. You would not expect a man with a wooden leg to run the hundred-yard dash against a man with two legs. The handicap would be so great as to make such a contest ludicrous. The one-legged man admits that he cannot compete in a foot race with a two-legged man, and lets it go at that. He need not have his whole life disrupted because of such a situation. He would feel humiliated only if a great deal of emphasis were placed upon foot racing; he would be totally discouraged with life only if foot racing was the sole way to achieve anything of value.

The term handicap has no significance except in comparing the performance of different individuals. Furthermore, it has meaning only in reference to specific performances. A man with one leg may be handicapped in foot racing but this has no bearing in his attempts to compete in spelling, in chinning himself, and the like. Consequently, whether a man is to be pitied or not because of some handicap depends upon the value we place upon the acts which the handicap interferes with.

Should handicaps be overcome? Some educators have insisted that a person should devote his major energies to overcoming any handicap he might have, the idea being to make all persons as nearly alike as possible. This process can be carried to an absurdity, as is illustrated by the following fable.

"In antedeluvian times, while the animal kingdom was being differentiated into swimmers, climbers, runners, and fliers, there was a school for the development of the animals. The theory of the school was that the best animals should be able to do one thing as well as another.

"If an animal had short legs and good wings, attention should be devoted to running, so as to even up the qualities as far as possible. So the duck was kept waddling instead of swimming. The pelican was kept wagging his short wings in the attempt to fly. The eagle was made to run, and allowed to fly only for recreation; all this in the name of education. Nature was not trusted, for individuals should be symmetrically developed and similar, for their own welfare as well as for the welfare of the community.

"The animals that would not submit to such training but persisted in developing the best gifts they had, were dishonored and humiliated in many ways. They were stigmatized as being narrow-minded and specialists, and special difficulties were placed in their way when they attempted to ignore the theory of education recognized in the school.

"No one was allowed to graduate from the school unless he could climb, swim, run, and fly at certain prescribed rates; so it happened that the time wasted by the duck in the attempt to run had so hindered him from swimming that his swimming muscles had atrophied, and so he was hardly able to swim at all; and in addition he had been scolded, punished, and ill-treated in many ways so as to make his life a burden. He left school humiliated, and the ornithorhynchus (duckbill) could beat him both running and swimming. Indeed, the latter was awarded a prize in two departments.

"The eagle could make no headway in climbing to the top of a tree, and although he showed he could get there just the same, the performance was counted a demerit, since it had not been done in the prescribed way. An abnormal eel with large pectoral fins proved he could run, swim, climb trees, and fly a little. He was made valedictorian." [1]

Why should any person be made to feel that the main business of his life should be to excel in some characteristic in which he is obviously deficient? Why should he be made to feel that if he cannot make up this deficiency and excel his fellows in this particular that, somehow, his life is a total failure? To humiliate and shame a child because he cannot do some specified act is about as senseless as humiliating an eagle because he cannot climb a tree.

Development of inferiority feelings. Inferiority feelings are not an essential sequel to handicaps; they come only when the person so handicapped is made to feel, somehow, that he has been cheated. Instead of holding up before a handicapped child the goal of superiority in the thing in which he is lacking, he should be taught to evaluate himself fairly and frankly. He should be taught willingly to admit that there are some things he cannot do and should learn to have absolutely no desire to do those things. It is the desire to do what one cannot do which produces discouragement.

Your actual capabilities and limitations are not nearly as important as the attitude you take toward them. For

[1] Burnham, William H., "Success and Failure as Conditions of Mental Health," *Mental Hygiene*, 1919, *3*, pp. 391–392.

it is this attitude which determines what you will do about it. If your attitude is one of discouragement you will rest on your oars, make all sorts of excuses for not trying, and consequently you will accomplish little of anything. If, on the other hand, you hopefully try to make of yourself the most that there is in you, you will continue to fight, no matter what your handicaps may be.

A wholesome attitude is absolutely dependent upon an honest evaluation of your every capacity and every handicap. If you discover you are very deficient in any one capacity this discovery need not produce discouragement; it should lead to a frank abandonment of any hope in that direction. If you have a fair chance to compete, even though it may be with some disadvantage, you should enter such a struggle with a full understanding of what it will involve in the way of extra effort. If you are superior in some trait you may enter into its development with every assurance of success in that direction.

The stimulating effect of a handicap. Knowledge of a handicap may provide one of the most stimulating elements in life, and, if properly used, may be a tremendous asset to an individual. Improperly used, it may be a detriment and a means of distorting and ruining a person's entire life. The greatest possible advantage that can come from a handicap is the motivation it provides to overcome its effect. This process is known technically as compensation. It takes two forms: direct and indirect.

1. *Direct compensation.* The classic example of direct compensation is the story of Demosthenes, the great Greek statesman who lived three hundred years before Christ. He was weak-voiced, lisping, and short of breath; the letter R was especially troublesome to him and he enunciated very poorly.

"We are told that he overcame these physical dis-
advantages by practising with pebbles in his mouth . . .
trying to shout down the breakers on the shore at Pha-
lerum . . . reciting while running up hill, learning to
deliver many lines in one breath, and speaking before a
mirror to correct his gestures. More than once he failed
when he rose to address the people. At his first attempt
his periods fell into confusion, and he was met with shouts
of laughter. He built, we are told, an underground chamber
where he daily practised his voice and delivery, sometimes for two or three months at a time, shaving one side
of his head in order that he might resist the temptation
to go out into the streets." [1]

This story is often used to teach children with any sort
of handicap the value of persistent effort and the implication is that any handicap may be surmounted if the
sufferer persists in his endeavors. It is quite probable that
Demosthenes was a persistent and indefatigable speech
student, but it is also likely that the extent of his original
difficulties was exaggerated in the interests of making a
good story. If one has a minor defect it is well to encourage him to persist in direct effort to overcome it. Such
persistence is a wholesome thing and probably helps to
develop worthy character traits as well as to overcome the
specific defect.

If such a story is used to encourage one with a major
handicap to persist in its mastery, the effects of such
teaching may be pernicious. One young man with a hair
lip, and who stammered dreadfully, persisted in his ambition to be a criminal lawyer in spite of advice to the
contrary by his supervisors. He gave up only after years
of vain struggling to master his speech difficulties and,

[1] Packard, A. W., *Demosthenes*, G. P. Putnam's Sons, 1914, pp. 28–30.

while he made considerable progress in this direction, he had failed in his law studies because he spent all his time on his speech. Every time this young man was approached on the subject he replied, "Demosthenes overcame his speech defect and so can I."

If one has a defect of any kind, he should be encouraged to improve himself and to overcome that defect if it is at all possible. We do not mean to imply from the above incident that speech defects are not subject to improvement. Most of them are. Work to overcome any defect you may have, but do not stake your whole life and career upon superiority in your weakest characteristic. The danger lies, not in trying to overcome a defect, but in devoting all your energy to that pursuit, and losing your perspective in doing so.

2. *Indirect compensation.* If one had a handicap he should be stimulated by that handicap to fight, to make something of himself; but it may be the part of wisdom to attempt to excel in some characteristic different from the one in which he is handicapped. Putting forth an intense struggle to excel in some trait because one is lacking in another is called indirect compensation.

If indirect compensation is to be successful one must never permit himself to entertain the feeling that he has chosen a poor substitute. If he fights with the feeling that he can never be quite as good as though he had excelled in the trait in which he is handicapped he will never get the deserved thrill from his success. If one works to be an author *because* he cannot be a prize fighter, he will always feel a certain amount of chagrin even though he wins international fame as an author. Such chagrin is pointless and foolish. It is just as worthy to excel in one thing as in another. It is a much smarter thing to attempt to achieve excellence in a specific direction because you have capabilities in that direction than it is to attempt excellence in one direction in order to hide the fact that you are lacking in another. Can you imagine an eagle, after he has learned to soar high in the heavens, discounting his achievement because he has not the ability to learn to climb trees? Or can you imagine a squirrel mourning a wasted life because he is unable to compete with the eagle?

Unconscious compensations. We have been advocating the conscious and unbiased evaluation of all capabilities and handicaps as a prerequisite for wholesome adjustment. This procedure is relatively easy when one has a handicap which is so obvious that it cannot well be ignored. Where the handicap is not so violently thrust upon one's attention it is much harder to recognize one's limitations, especially where it concerns some character trait. Consequently, one is very likely to fail at a proper evaluation, and any compensatory behavior is likely to be carried out unwittingly. This has several unfortunate consequences.

In the first place, outsiders are much more likely to arrive at a true appraisal of your abilities and limitations and to see through your attempt to conceal them. For example, suppose your honesty is not as wholehearted as you might like it to be. If you fail to recognize this fact you are likely to go to the other extreme, to consider yourself meticulously honest, and to demonstrate this fact to yourself and others by an excessive display of honesty. When a theft has occurred in which you might have been implicated you protest your innocence in such an excessive manner that all your auditors are inclined to doubt you. This may happen whether you are implicated in the crime or whether you are absolutely innocent. The person who has no unconscious qualms about his own integrity is not likely to overdo his protestations of innocence.

In the second place, an unconscious compensation will seldom eliminate the emotional dissatisfaction which accompanies the unrecognized deficiency. One will experience a continued, inexplicable dissatisfaction which is apparently groundless. Accomplishment in some other direction, instead of bringing satisfaction, will merely add to this dissatisfaction. The poor victim will work hard, will make an apparent success, and will grow more restless and unhappy all the while. It is only when a straightforward evaluation of oneself is made and any deficiencies faced squarely, and a conscious adjustment made, that one gets the relief from emotional tension which is so necessary for a happy life. When you see a person who is apparently succeeding, piling one victory on top of another, and at the same time growing more and more dissatisfied with himself and with life in general, it is pretty certain that he has some unsatisfied longing. His outward success does not satisfy because it is an unconscious substitute for what he really wants.

It is better to recognize your wants, decide rationally whether it would pay to attempt to achieve them or to forego them, and act accordingly, than it is to deceive yourself as to what you really want and then go through life in a continual groping for you know not what.

Furthermore, an unconscious compensation is not likely to take the form that is rationally the best for the whole situation. For any one handicap there are a great number of possible compensatory activities. Some are more suitable than others and the sensible thing to do

is to make a valiant attempt to view the whole situation
with the purpose of selecting the very best form of compensation.   To jump into the very first thing that is
unconsciously suggested to you places the odds against
you at the very start.

Some specific forms of compensation. Almost any
form of conduct may be compensatory in its essential
purpose. We shall consider only some of the more common forms. Throughout the following survey we should
be continually reminded that each form has its value
when used consciously and rationally. When used without a keen awareness of its function any type of behavior
is likely to be distorted even to the point of being grotesque.

1. *Compensation by contrast.* The most common form
of compensation is effected by emphasizing the opposite
of the characteristic which it is desired to hide. The
bantam rooster is the one who makes the biggest display in the barnyard. The tiny man is very likely to
strut and display his importance. The person with the
least degree of authority is likely to impress you with
his sense of importance; the office boy is likely to be
much more pompous than is the president of the company. The boy who has most fear in his heart is likely
to do the greatest amount of bragging about his courage. The girl who is most impressed by young men is
likely to be the loudest in voicing her indifference to
them. Life is replete with illustrations of this sort, and
we are all familiar with them when we see them in the
other person, but strangely blind to them in ourselves.

When the exaggerated form of behavior is of a highly
moral nature the disguise is much more likely to be effective than in the simple illustrations just cited. For

example, a woman living with her daughter and son-in-law manifested in all her conduct the most extreme unselfishness. She would not accompany them on auto rides or to the theater, saying that she did not want to detract from their enjoyment of each other. She selected all the undesirable tasks around the home and insisted upon doing them. She would always take the inferior portions at dinner, making it plain that she wanted her children to have the best. The climax came when she prepared a large roast and insisted upon eating but a tiny portion of fat so that her daughter and son-in-law could have the rest. The young man protested that she would be doing them a favor by eating a healthy portion since he did not want to eat cold roast beef all the rest of the week.

It is a good rule to follow to look for a domination by the opposite trait when a person is thus extreme in his behavior. This rule applied here. It developed that this woman had been impressed with the danger of mother-in-law interference, had almost wrecked her son's home by such interference and selfishness. In her zeal to be unselfish in order to avoid a repetition of her error she went to the opposite extreme.

This stress upon a moral trait to counterbalance a questionable one may be valuable. Certainly it is better to be overhonest than to be a thief, it is better to be too generous than to be selfish, it is better to strut than to submit too readily to all those who may have larger bodies, or it may be better to deprive oneself of luxuries too rigorously than to be a glutton.

But why cannot a person secure a balance without overdoing the manifestation of the compensating activity? Normally, one should be able to strike such a balance. When he overdoes his activity it is usually a sign that he is afraid of the trait he is endeavoring to restrain. This fear makes him overestimate its force and so he has to put more weight on the other side of the scales. He not only balances the suppressed trait but has to add enough weight to make up for the fear factor.

In such cases it would be better to face squarely the undesirable trait and by direct dealing eliminate the fear in the manner described in Chapter III. The degree of excess which a person manifests is a measure of the amount of fear which is present. Compensation is not the best way to deal with a fear. It should be adjusted directly.

2. *Substitution of an unrelated trait.* A girl who could not carry a tune and whose ability on the piano was near the vanishing point was taught to console herself with the following ditty:

> "I cannot play, I cannot sing;
> But I can try like anything."

Such sentiments are little consolation, however, for obvious and enduring failure. This girl learned the value of emphasizing her other qualities and revised the ditty as follows:

> "I cannot play, I cannot sing,
> But failure now has lost its sting;
> For I can swim and I can run
> And I have made a hole in one.
> My math. I get with little strain;
> I think I have a fertile brain."

She had made a good adjustment because she had learned to stress the importance of the things she could do.

In seeking a substitute, care must be taken to select some activity in which one has more than an even chance of succeeding. The danger in this form of compensation arises from the tendency to select something as a substitute which is too difficult. If this is done and the person fails in the substitute as well as in the original activity, his sense of inferiority is only increased. The object of compensating is to build up a feeling of self-confidence; therefore the activity should be one in which the person has considerable promise of success.

For example, a boy who had a small physique and who was teased unmercifully by his comrades decided that he would excel in intellectual pursuits. He made this choice not because he had any great assurance that he would make a scholar but because it seemed like a noble pursuit and one which others would be forced to respect. It happened, unfortunately, that he had only mediocre mental ability and was never able to make the spectacular showing in his school work that he set out to do. As a consequence, he became more dejected than ever and considered himself a total failure. An examination revealed that this boy had striking musical talent which had never been exploited. He was encouraged to take up the violin and became extremely successful. All his inferiority feelings disappeared in view of this success in music, and he no longer was obsessed with the feeling that he was weak physically and only average in intellectual activities.

3. *Reforming others.* A rather inferior method of compensating is to set out to reform others. This may prove to be a satisfying process to the one who makes use of it for two reasons. It makes one feel nobler to be engaged in the business of uplifting others, for the simple reason that one cannot lift up another without proceeding on the assumption that he is better than the one he is help-

ing. In the second place if one can get occupied with the defects of others he becomes distracted from his own shortcomings.

One may make a good reformer if he has been tempted to commit the acts from which he is trying to rescue his fellows. But he makes a still better reformer if he has once succumbed to the temptations that he is afraid his inferiors cannot master. The best temperance reformer is the converted drunkard. A good reformer must at least be one who would be peculiarly susceptible to the vice or condition he is opposing. His reformation activities are, it can be seen, a compensation for his own weaknesses. An illustration will make this point clear.

"A young unmarried preacher—a High Church Episcopalian—several years ago gave promise of being a very successful man, but now, through a number of peculiar characteristics and contradictory forms of behavior, seems about to ruin his career. When he first accepted the position in which he is serving, his impression upon his congregation was striking—most of his people thought that he was remarkably able. That impression has been entirely changed within one short year because of his abnormal attitude in relation to women. His sermons show that he is personally and vitally concerned in the message that he is delivering. He gets very much in earnest, pounds the pulpit, shouts, goes almost into a frenzy in the storms against sin, which to him is a synonym for any form of sex conduct. Practically all his sermons are of this type. He is calm and almost uninteresting when he deals temporarily with any purely theological theme; but is intense when raging against dancing, short skirts, flapperism, bobbed hair, rouge, and vice, which to him all belong in the same class. So violent is he in his antagonism to any form of courtship that he forbids the young boys and girls of his parish to walk home from church together. If any young girl disobeys this injunction she is barred from being confirmed. It must be a choice with her whether she will give up all social relations with men or give up confirmation. In order further to protect innocent girls from male wiles, he himself often escorts them home from service, giving them each a kiss upon parting. In spite of the fact that he raves against immodest dress, his room is decorated with pictures—some of which are advertising posters—showing girls clad in scanty apparel.

"He seemingly has a Herculean task to ward off the advances of all the spinsters in the parish. He will come home, for instance, and almost in a frenzy begin to denounce a certain woman who has had the temerity to invite him to some function. He will throw up his arms and almost scream in his denunciation of her wiles in thus trying to seduce him. Finally, he will become calm and accept the invitation. However, despite his acceptance, he will act in a boorish and churlish manner to the imagined seducer. His hostess, on these occasions, naturally thinks him rude and resents his needless rebuffs. He thus makes himself hateful in order to repel advances he merely imagines. He seems to take delight in defaming the characters of innocent girls in his congregation. He selects some especially attractive girl and talks about her in the most degrading manner to others of his 'fold' without grounds for so doing. In one such instance, this scandal-mongering came to the ears of the girl's relatives and he was confronted with it by the girl herself. He had absolutely nothing to reply, but since that time has seemed afraid of this girl and avoids her as if in terror. He carries a pistol to protect himself from imagined pursuers. There is probably mental justification for this, for he actually has injured many persons. As a matter of fact, however, no one has made any threat to do him bodily harm. When he meets those whom he has defamed he becomes unctuous, flattering, and fawning in a sickening fashion. Although he seems to think all his parishioners are vile he takes little apparent interest in their spiritual uplift or salvation, in spite of his eloquence against vice; and when called at night to visit the bedside of a dying parishioner, he has been known to refuse to go, and to show no concern upon learning of the neglected individual's death.

"All this is obviously a defense mechanism. The minister is trying to live a celibate life. When some female appeals to him as a possible mate, he is horrified by the thought; but, instead of blaming himself for the thought, he condemns the manners, dress, or character of the innocent woman." [1]

This case is probably a little extreme, but it illustrates a type of compensation which may be present in a milder degree in many reformatory activities. Certainly, if one is to be of real service to his fellows he cannot be dominated by the personal conflicts and emotional biases which this young man showed so clearly. Such behavior is of no value to the man who uses it nor to those whom he is presuming to help.

Let it be remembered that the specific forms that compensation may take are exceedingly numerous and complex. These are selected merely because they illustrate important aspects of the whole process.

Hidden dangers of inferiority feelings. The descriptions thus far given show clearly some of the dangers that

[1] Morgan, John J. B., *The Psychology of the Unadjusted School Child*, Macmillan, 1924, pp. 155–157.

result from compensatory activity. The latter form of reforming others contains elements both of obvious danger and some more subtle threats. We shall now consider some still more insidious dangers which develop from an unwise emphasis upon inferiority feelings.

1. *Admission of defect to win praise.* The inferiority complex has become so popularized that almost everybody is willing to admit that he has one. Such an admission comes easily because it does not imply anything so very dangerous and, besides, such an admission has all the ear-marks of modesty. A person may feel quite virtuous in his confession that he has an inferiority complex. Since it is not taken any more seriously by most persons than a "poor memory," a headache, or a cold, it furnishes an excellent device for getting out of things.

It takes little observation to ascertain that it is easier, in the long run, to be too modest than it is to be too boast-ful. If a person makes pretenses beyond his capacities he faces the necessity of living up to his boasts or suffering humiliation. Once our friends discover that we have over-stated our abilities they take great delight in exploiting us, watching us writhe when we get in over our depths, and finally laughing us out of court.

If, on the other hand, we begin by understating our ability, even to the point of confessing a definite inferior-ity, what an opportunity to bring the expression of sur-prise to our comrades when they see a marvelous per-formance instead of the failure they anticipated!

Even a child learns this trick, as was shown in a little girl who always prefaced what she did with some such statement as "I cannot do that," "That is too hard," and then, with a smirk, did a creditable performance.

The danger in this type of defense is that others may

take your statements seriously, believe that your ability is limited, and thus make you lose confidence in yourself. You begin by belittling yourself in order to increase the self-esteem that you can create by surprising people, and may end by convincing both that you amount to but little. Modesty is a valuable trait but if overworked may slap back.

2. *Inferiority to exploit others.* Another trick that is often learned very early in life is that if we parade our deficiencies we can make the other fellow do all the work. After the armistice was signed, it became the general policy of the army to discharge officers who were the least important in the service of demobilization. A particularly efficient man often found that he had difficulty in getting his discharge when he desired it. When this condition of affairs was rumored abroad every man who wanted to get his release immediately became as inefficient as possible—each tried to outdo the other in incompetence.

A child, who was not as adroit as the army officers, on discovering that she could not escape washing the dishes for her mother, screamed, "I'll break them if you make me do them."

Now, if this ruse to exploit others could be permanently successful there might be little reason to decry it. Why should a person not exaggerate his incompetence in a task he does not wish to perform? The reason is that, although this device is begun in trivial situations, it will grow on one and, eventually, it will spread to such an extent that it will undermine your own self-esteem.

3. *Denying the existence of an inferiority.* The most serious danger in connection with a handicap of any sort is the tendency to deny its existence. Such a course is merely storing trouble which inevitably will tumble down upon you at some future time.

If you blind yourself to your limitations, your friends, feeling sorry for you, will avoid doing or saying the things which would make you conscious of them. Since all persons are not friendly, the opportunity of humiliating you will provide too strong a temptation for them, and they will feel called upon to inform you of your unknown limitations. A person who is honest with himself is never shocked at any criticism by his friends or by his enemies.

How to deal with handicaps. If you evaluate yourself properly you are then in a position to work toward improvement. If you decide that your handicap is something that has the possibility of being overcome, how can you accomplish this?

By the following procedure: Recognize your faults and then act as though you did not have them.

For example, Theodore Roosevelt overcame in this manner the ill-effects of a weak body, unprepossessing appearance, and a fearful disposition. "He noticed that strong boys played active games, swam, rode horses, and did hard physical work. He became active, rode, played, and worked with a vengeance and became a model of physical endurance. He observed that other boys met fearful situations with grit to overcome the cause of the fear. He found that he became bold when he faced terrifying cattle in the roundup in the spirit of true adventure. When he mixed with people he found he liked them and did not want to slink away from them. He found that when he greeted people with his exclamation of 'dee-lighted' it was impossible to be afraid of them. . . .

"He captured health by acting as though he were healthy. He overcame his fear by acting as though he were not afraid. He outshone his physical appearance by acting as though he were just as attractive as anyone else.

"No one knew better than Roosevelt himself that he had handicaps. He never duped himself into believing that he was courageous, strong, or handsome. His success in acting as though he did not have handicaps depended upon clearly recognizing his defects; but he never nursed them. . . .

"Recognizing your faults and then acting as though you did not have them is a sure way to build up self-confidence. If you try to act as though you did not have them, without yourself admitting them, you only succeed in making yourself ridiculous." [1]

If you want to be a coward, refuse to face yourself as you are. If you want to be a fighter, face every limitation you have as a challenge and decide the best thing to do about it. If there is no chance to gain anything by attempting to overcome it, accept that fact as a good sport. If you have a fighting chance to win there is no greater challenge that you can possibly receive than that of making good on this fighting chance.

Imagined inferiorities. We have been discussing possible ways of adjusting to real handicaps as well as the dangers that may result from the various ways in which a person attempts to overcome his handicaps. A genuine handicap is not essential, however, for the development of a feeling of inferiority. Quite the contrary, it often happens that an inferiority based on an imaginary handicap becomes a much more vital problem than would be the case were the handicap a real one. If we know the cause of a feeling we can deal directly with that cause

[1] Morgan, John J. B., and Webb, E. T., *Making the Most of Your Life*, Long and Smith, 1932, pp. 20–21.

and effect an improvement. When the cause is unknown the problem becomes much more baffling and requires much more insight.

1. *Sources of imaginary inferiorities.* The source of any feeling of inferiority is in personal comparisons. When the handicap is a real one the comparison is so obvious that no one need voice it for the owner to appreciate his handicap. Where the handicap is not a real one, or is a very minor one, any emphasis upon it must be the result of some expressed appreciation of one's competitors or some indicated disparagement of oneself. A great many conditions may bring about such comparisons.

Parents may be partial to one child and openly or unconsciously may show this favoritism. The child in disfavor, instead of assigning this favoritism to personal bias by his parents, assumes that there is something wrong with himself. Not knowing just what it is, he watches himself, compares himself with his brothers and sisters and draws his own inferences as to his inferiorities. He is very likely to misjudge abilities, but the accuracy of his judgment has very little to do with his feelings in the matter.

If the parents are not responsible, often outsiders start these feelings. They continually make personal remarks before tiny children, comparing their looks, their dispositions, their resemblance to one or the other parent, and openly show their approval or disapproval. The effect of these speeches is much greater than their makers appreciate. It will be a boon to civilization when a ban is placed upon all personal remarks made about children in their presence. It should be regarded just as boorish, just as much an indication of poor social training, to say, "Isn't Mary a pretty girl?" meaning she is prettier than

Susie, who is listening to the comment, as it would be to say, "Mrs. Smith, I think your dress is much prettier than Mrs. Jones' dress," in the hearing of Mrs. Jones. Children have been known to retire from the presence of such poorly cultured, but socially prominent persons, with blushes of shame expressing their wish that people would not talk about them.

Another element in modern life which gives birth to and nourishes feelings of inferiority is the competitive system in school, business, and industry. The school is by far the most prolific breeder of these feelings through the competitive system, because it gets the children in their formative years, and when they are ripe for the formation of different attitudes.

If competition is conducted only between persons of fairly equalized ability, and if it results in a shifting of victors continually, so that no one excels for any long period and no one continually loses, it may be of value. Where it is unbalanced it is always a bad thing for the loser. He becomes more and more hopeless, and either gives up and accepts his inferior rôle, or retaliates upon his more fortunate comrades in some subtle fashion. In many schools the duller children form an organization to tease and persecute the good students. They call them names, shun them, or even actually injure them, attempting to turn the tables and make themselves feel superior to the "sissy teachers' pets" even if it is in nothing better than a rowdy fight.

2. *Imagined inferiority leads to social difficulties.* If one has a real inferiority he tries to change his status by self-improvement of one sort or another. The person with an imagined inferiority may attempt to do the same thing, but he realizes that his inferiority is not so much

the result of his lack of ability; it results from the ill will of other persons. You may do excellent work, but if you have the ill will of the one whose task it is to judge your work you may be certain that it will be depreciated; you never will be able to please him.

This fact is soon made apparent to the person with an imagined inferiority. He tries to improve, hoping that the attitude of his parents, teachers, or supervisors will change as his work improves. As he discovers his error he is very likely to change his tactics and attempt to get square with the person who disapproves of him. He has done all he can to win their approval; having failed in this, his attitude turns to one of hatred and malevolence.

In other words, the person with an imagined inferiority does not fight his own inferiority, he fights the social situation which produced it. He realizes that a change in his status comes from changing others and not from improving himself. He must spend much more time in handling other persons than he does in effecting his own self-improvement. If we fail in overcoming a real inferiority we may turn to some other activity as a compensation; if we fail in overcoming the disapproval of others, we easily are led to hate them for making us feel so uncomfortable.

An illustration may make this point clear. A little girl was humiliated by her teacher because she did not show the right spirit of coöperation in a class project. This project was to consume a whole week and involved placing on the blackboard a great amount of material. Each child was supposed to do a part of this work. On the first day Mary got into a tiny scuffle with the girl standing next to her. In order to punish her the teacher refused to permit her to enter into the project throughout the remainder of the week. Furthermore, she made continual references to her naughtiness and used the entire week to humiliate her. The teacher thought she was motivating her to be more social so that, on future occasions, she would be more coöperative. Instead, this girl was made to resent the whole proceeding. She hated her teacher for making her feel so inferior, and hated the work that the other children did. The outlet of these feelings was attained by a rather natural act, but one which brought a storm down on the head of the girl. She climbed in at a basement window of the school on Saturday night and erased all the work from the blackboard.

The teacher, after discovering who had erased the material, wanted to punish her for her vindictive conduct. She thought that this behavior showed an anti-social attitude. Quite to the contrary, it showed a social attitude which had been frustrated in its objective. Many hateful and vindictive acts are thus initiated.

Strutting is often a reaction to an inferiority feeling which has resulted from the slights or insinuations of others. If the recipient of this treatment is not adroit in his knowledge of other persons he is likely to attempt to influence them favorably by showing off before them. He has the erroneous notion that people like us for our superior talents. As a matter of fact, the reverse is more likely to hold. We do not gain friends by strutting. So, when the humiliated individual tries to gain the favor of the one who insulted him by displaying his talents, he merely incites the other person to renew his efforts and is virtually inviting more insults.

Note the vast difference that is likely to exist between the fight which is stimulated by a real handicap and one which is produced by an imagined handicap. The former may be a very wholesome type of fighting, and may end in a remarkable victory, or at least in some degree of self-improvement. The latter is directed against the one who brings the inferiority to light, is motivated by a feeling of hatred for this individual, and can end in nothing but a bitter fight which seems so far removed from any inferiority feeling that its significance is not likely to be apparent to either contestant or the outside observers.

Hate is one of the most harmful attitudes that it is possible to cultivate. Mental health cannot be complete when hate is a large element in an individual's life. But hate cannot be avoided by attempting to feign the opposite attitude. If, however, the cause for the hate is recognized, it may be readily supplanted. This mechanism which we have just described is one of the most frequent causes of hate. Indeed, it is such an important cause that it would be well to consider it whenever hate appears. We tend to try to injure the person we hate. If we hate him because we were unable to obtain his love, and if this failure is so poignant because it makes us feel inferior or incompetent, the situation is merely aggravated. If you cannot win a person's love you do not increase your self-esteem by hating him. Either renew your efforts to gain his affection, or give up frankly and turn your attentions to others with whom you may have more success. It is a very unwholesome thing to blind yourself to the real problem by hate.

Our reason for saying this about hate is that a great many mental disorders have hate as a large factor in their development. Of course, in these mental diseases the hate is greatly exaggerated and we do not mean to imply that anyone who hates will become pathological. But it would pay an individual to avoid hate in the realm of his emotions as vigorously as he would avoid contamination by an infectious organism. Avoid hate as you would avoid putrid food.

General principles. Some general principles about inferiority feelings and their treatment may be summarized as follows:

1. Frankly face any handicap you have or may think you have. You gain nothing by attempting to deceive yourself as to your capabilities.

2. If the handicap is a real one, and is so pronounced as to make competition with others extremely difficult, do not try to compete in any endeavor in which it plays a part. Do not give up such activities with any spirit of resignation. There should be no remorse or chagrin connected with such a course.

3. You can achieve indifference to a real handicap by devoting your energies to something you have ability to do. Such an activity should not be regarded as a substitute for the handicap, but it should be viewed as an activity having merit of its own without reference to the handicap.

4. If the handicap is not pronounced it might be overcome by increased work and effort. Such a program should be undertaken with a full sense of the risks involved and that the odds are against you. The spirit behind it should be that of entering a game; it is fun whether you win or lose. You know that you are likely to lose, but in that case you can feel proud that you put up a good fight. If you win, the feeling of achievement will, of course, be magnified because of the original handicap.

5. Many handicaps are unreal. They are the product of unfortunate contrasts and comparisons by other per-

sons. Learn to evaluate yourself fairly and do not be led to exaggerate your deficiencies because of unkind remarks by others.

6. If persons under-rate you, you can gain their approval more by gaining their friendship than by demonstrating your ability to them. Do not show off. They will hate you in turn for that.

7. When people persist in making you feel inferior, you are likely to hate them. Avoid this tendency as you would a plague. It does not increase your self-esteem to hate one who has humiliated you; it lowers it. It does not increase his regard to have you hate him; he feels justified in his disparaging view. Hate for others is the poorest possible method of adjusting to any difficulty whether it is a real injury, a real or imagined inferiority, or an accidental slight.

QUESTIONS

1. Name two effects that can result from a handicap.

2. Define handicap.

3. What function do handicaps serve in sports?

4. Show the bearing that gross inequality of ability has upon competition.

5. If the ideal of education were to make persons alike, what would be the necessary procedure in relation to handicaps?

6. Show how the attempt to make all persons alike can be reduced to an absurdity.

7. Without competition there is no handicap. How could you arrange competitions so that no one would feel that he was handicapped?

8. Under what circumstances do handicaps lead to feelings of inferiority?

9. Why is the attitude a person takes toward a defect more significant than the defect itself?

10. Upon what does a wholesome attitude toward your limitations depend?

11. What is meant by compensation?

12. What beneficial effect may come from knowledge of a handicap?

13. What is meant by direct compensation?

14. What precautions should be exercised in urging persons to use direct compensation?

15. What effects may follow attempts to compensate directly for a major defect?

16. What is meant by indirect compensation?

17. Under what circumstances is it a good plan to use indirect compensation?

18. What unfortunate possibility should be avoided in using indirect compensation?

19. Why are unconscious compensations dependent upon failure to evaluate one's abilities properly?

20. Name three unfortunate consequences of unconscious compensation.

21. Show how scrupulous honesty might indicate an unconscious compensation.

22. Explain why unconscious compensation defeats its own purpose.

23. From daily life select a number of forms of conduct which you think illustrate compensation by contrast.

24. What is the characteristic of compensatory behavior that makes the observer suspect its true nature?

25. Show how it is fear which makes a person go to extremes in his compensatory reactions.

26. Why is compensation inadequate to dispel fear?

27. In selecting a substitute activity what precaution should be taken?

28. Why does reforming others increase self-esteem?

29. Why is the service of the reformer who is compensating likely to be of little value to those he is presuming to help?

30. How can you account for the popularity of the "inferiority complex"?

31. Why is it unwise to overstate your abilities?

32. What is the advantage of being modest?

33. What disadvantage may result from being too modest?

34. How can an inferiority be used to exploit others?

35. What is the most serious danger in connection with a handicap?

36. State the rule for dealing with handicaps.

37. What is the source of imaginary inferiorities?

38. Describe three ways in which this factor operates to produce imaginary inferiorities.

39. Show how hatred may develop from a feeling of inferiority.

40. Describe the way in which a person is led to maltreat the person whose love he craves.

41. What may strutting indicate?

42. Why is it the fighting of the person with an imagined inferiority is so likely to be unsuccessful?

43. Show why hate is seldom recognized as a result of inferiority feelings.

44. Memorize the general principles for dealing with inferiorities.

CHAPTER IX

EXAGGERATING DEFECTS

As a young man L. had all the promise of making a great success of his life. He was very intelligent, had a good education, was very robust, and had a very pleasing personality. Now, at the age of 56, he is holding down a very ordinary clerical position in a large corporation, and has not been promoted for the past twenty years. His failure is the outgrowth of some very unfortunate traits which he permitted to develop without realizing their significance. He learned to enjoy ill-health.

In his early twenties he was offered a position which involved considerable responsibility. The prospect of the strain which would be involved, according to his way of thinking, worried him considerably, and he postponed deciding for several days. During the interval he became more and more disturbed emotionally until he actually suffered a digestive upset. This illness he interpreted as evidence that he was physically incapable of the strain that the new position would involve, and he refused to accept it.

He did not admit to himself or to anyone else that he had refused because of his fear of responsibility, but gave poor health as an excuse. Shortly after this he married a very sympathetic woman who took great delight in caring for his health. He then began a round of physicians, taking every conceivable examination in his search for symptoms. He read all sorts of medical books, and was certain that he had every disease which the books described. Physicians told him repeatedly that he was in the best of health, but he refused to believe them and was continually taking all sorts of drugs and patent nostrums.

His main topics of conversation were his stomach, diets, and exercise. That this was all nonsense was illustrated by the fact that he would eat a hearty meal and then on top of the feast consume a special diet which his physician had prescribed. Now, a middle-aged man, he will tell you what prospects he had of success, but how he was prevented from reaching the top of the ladder because of his ill-health, which had hounded him all his life. His friends dropped him one by one, until now he has no one to listen to his woes but his wife. He is very sorry for himself.

The offices of physicians are literally filled with men and women of this sort, who have nothing wrong with them but who insist that they have. If one physician tells them they are normal they will drop him, go to another, and another, until they find one who will give them bread pills and listen to their tales of woe. They are called neurasthenics.

How the enjoyment of ill-health is learned. Like most defense mechanisms, neurasthenia does not spring forth fully developed; it begins very early in life and is not recognized as a disease until it is deeply rooted in the poor victim.

These beginning stages can be seen on all sides. A child is neglected, punished for his mistakes, made to do unwelcome tasks, and held to a strict routine as long as he is well. When he becomes sick he discovers that the attitude of all those around him is changed. They no longer make any demands upon him, they shower him with affection and satisfy his every whim. He enjoys all this tremendously in spite of the pain from the illness. The observing child cannot fail to notice the change in this whole picture when he recovers his health. He has to be "broken in" all over again. His mother will tell him that he has been spoiled, that he cannot expect all the attention he received when he was sick, now that he is well. In other words, being ill is a very advantageous condition, while health brings all sorts of discomforts which are really more painful than the physical pain of his illness.

How ill-health may be an advantage. Not only is the child who has been ill affected by this treatment. His brothers and sisters notice that he is getting all the attention, while they, who are well, are being slighted. If they complain about this situation they are told that their brother is ill, and hence deserves the utmost consideration. They wish they might be sick and share some of the benefits. Many a child has begged to be taken to the hospital in order to have his tonsils removed because his brother had such a good time having his out. Experience teaches all of us that if we want attention we should get ill; if we stay well we get little of it.

Furthermore, illness enables us to get out of all sorts of unpleasant tasks. The plea of illness never fails to be effective. If we could just regulate our illnesses we could float through life on a bed of roses.

A class was notified ahead of time that they would be given a quiz. At the appointed time about twenty-five per cent of them were absent, presenting excuses of illnesses in great variety. The next time the instructor announced a quiz he added that if any student absented himself from the quiz for any reason at all, sickness included, he would receive zero. All were present. Did this announcement actually improve the health of the class to that extent?

Illness as an unconscious defense mechanism. How much are these people aware of what they are doing? In some instances, especially in the early stages, it is quite likely that there is a conscious exaggeration, if not an actual pretense, when there is no illness at all. While this may be so, there is little value in determining just how much of an illness is real and how much it is exaggerated. We all know that a headache, which is a real headache, may be very annoying if we have a hard task to perform. The ache becomes almost unbearable under such circumstances. The same headache pains us much less if we have a very desirable occupation ahead of us. Actual pain is different depending upon other circumstances. The slightest indisposition is sufficient when we want to escape, but it takes very great suffering to stop us when we are intent on some game.

Even though, in the beginning, an ailment is exaggerated because it is effective in getting us out of a task, there may be an actual increase in the symptoms after we have so used it. In other words, we may use illness as an excuse to fool others, and later find that we are fooling ourselves. An instance in point is the following: A girl developed the habit of telling her friends that she had a headache in order to excuse herself from invitations which would interfere with her work. Having given such a deliberate excuse early in the evening, she would later discover that she actually had a headache. This girl was essentially honest. After excusing herself she would tell herself, in order to appear honest to herself, that she did not feel so well and, in a short time, she actually felt justified in having offered the excuse she did. She had actually developed a headache in order to prove to herself that she was truthful.

Once this habit of escaping the responsibilities of life by complaining of pains and aches gets root in us it grows very prolifically. Should we give any less plausible reason for shirking we should gain disapproval and we would, through shame, be forced to take our place and work. No one will blame us for being ill, so we escape and win sympathy at the same time. Should we get the feeling that our friends entertained a fleeting suspicion that our aches were not real, all we have to do is to exaggerate a bit more and they are again deceived. So we increase the severity of the symptoms until they become all-consuming.

Forms of neurasthenia. Some neurasthenics specialize in a specific ailment, learn all that they can about it and play up those symptoms alone. Others are more versatile and change around from one disease to another according to the fads of the day or according to their own caprice.

1. *Escape from vague fear.* It can be seen that the disorder will never be cured by attention to the disease which is presented. The more the patient is examined the more he likes it. The greater detail he can recount as to his symptoms the more likely he is to divert the mind of his examiners and auditors from the real cause of his disorder—which is an attempt to escape responsibility.

He seems to be worrying about his health, but he is not. He is afraid of life, but transfers this fear to a fear of illness. It really is a marvelous defense reaction.

The method of treatment used to be rest. This suited the patient exactly. He adopted his symptoms to escape struggle and then some good physician prescribes rest. It is just perfect.

Lately the prescription is more likely to be work of some sort. This is much better than rest, but it still fails in that it does not direct its influence to getting rid of the main issue, which is a fear of life's responsibility in general, or some specific difficulty. Neurasthenia can only be understood as a means adopted to distract attention of both the patient and outsiders from the real conflict.

Most of the so-called "nervous breakdowns" of college students are of this type. Students complain that they are overworked and are forced to drop out of college to take a much needed rest. Here it may be no more than a fear of failure in school which becomes so insistent that work and study are impossible. The "nervous breakdown" enables the student to escape possible failure and to "save his face" at the same time. Of course there are students who do have to drop out of college because of genuine illness. These neurasthenics are merely taking advantage of this fact, and sneaking out with those who merit a temporary release from college.

2. *Escape from specific conflict.* Sometimes the thing from which the neurasthenic is trying to escape is more specific, yet something which he dare not openly admit to himself or to others. The following case illustrates this.

A young man who had a very fine position with prospects of advancement had to give up his work and go to a sanitarium for a prolonged rest. It seemed a particularly unfortunate situation, for he had planned to be married in a few weeks. He complained bitterly at his ill-fortune. He would lose his position because of the illness, he could not support a wife with no position, and the marriage had to be postponed indefinitely.

He was after a time discharged from the hospital, returned to work, and was again able to look ahead with great hopes for a successful business career. Since he was in such fine circumstances, another date was set for the wedding. A short time before the wedding was to take place he had another "breakdown," and had to give up his position and go to the hospital for another prolonged period. He again expressed great sorrow that the wedding had to be abandoned and all his friends as well as the friends of his prospective bride were very sympathetic. However, a physician who understood such things took him in hand, and it was discovered that he had a hidden antipathy for marriage, which he did not recognize clearly, but which dominated him. He could not express this fear outwardly and refuse to marry the girl whom he had be-trothed, so he took flight in his illness. Certainly what this man needed was not rest or medical care so much as to have his attitude toward marriage straightened out.

A person who has developed the habit of escaping by the route of illness is likely to use the same device in all sorts of various situations. He will remain well as long as things run smoothly, but whenever some difficulty arises, no matter what its nature, he will immediately turn to his health instead of facing the issue squarely.

Treatment of neurasthenics. How should people of this sort be treated? Should we all get "hard-boiled" and treat sick people with less consideration? This would hardly be wise as a general policy for, in so doing, we might be cruel to a person who was genuinely ill. Most physicians have in their memory at least one case where they became very stern with a convalescent patient and forced him to become active in his business before he was physically able to do so. One experience in which the results of such drastic treatment were unfortunate is enough to put us on our guard against general insensitiveness to illness in others. It is, of course, just this fact that the neurasthenics play upon.

It is not so much a question of whether we shall be sympathetic or rough in our treatment of others. We should try to discriminate, and help the person adjust to the thing which is driving him into illness. It is strange how blind we may become in cases of this sort. For example, a mother brought her boy to a hospital with the story that he had a queer illness. Every morning he was too sick to go to school and had to remain in bed until about the middle of the morning. He then seemed to be better for the rest of the day, could get up and play, only to have another spell the following morning. In the hospital he was put to bed, but was soon able to be up and around. When he was given a task in the hospital one morning he complained that he was ill. He was immediately put to bed. After another patient had done the work assigned to him he informed his nurse that he was better and wanted to get up. He was gently told that since he had been ill he must stay in bed all day. Sick in the morning, in bed all day, was the rule. It took but a few days of this sort of treatment to cure him.

The treatment that is needed is a real change of character. These persons need to be reëducated in their fundamental attitudes toward life. They are cowards, hiding behind human sympathy to escape the battles of life. Teach them that the thrills of life come from the conflicts one has to face and they will no more want to escape by becoming ill than a ball player will want to go to bed each time an important game is to be played. The neurasthenic needs to be taught to be a fighter. Instead he is usually babied and petted until he himself becomes certain that he cannot face the tiniest difficulty in life.

Let us repeat, in order to understand the significance of exaggerated complaints of illness, we must remember that the victim of this defense is using the illness as a distraction device to draw the attention of others from the real difficulty. As long as they can be interested in his illness they are not likely to look further, and therefore they miss the real significance of the complaints.

Hysteria. The flight from a conflict into complaints of illness may fool other persons but it does not deceive the patient himself very successfully. Consequently, the conscientious person, becoming aware of the deceit, actually develops symptoms of organic disease, feels the aches that accompany illness, and becomes convinced himself that he is ill. When this point is reached we have a disorder which is called hysteria by medical men. Hysteria takes a great many forms, but the central factor in all cases is the adoption of the symptoms of an actual disease in order to disguise a genuine mental conflict. Let us consider some of these.

1. *Forgetting.* Even under ordinary circumstances our memories play queer tricks upon us. If we have two conflicting appointments we are very likely to keep the one we prefer and totally forget the other. We forget to pay bills, our obligations to do unpleasant tasks, past events whose recollection annoys us, and even the names of persons we do not like.

Other persons are very tolerant of a poor memory and, for this reason, we can readily get them to accept the excuse that "We forgot." Not only do others accept such excuses but we blithely exonerate ourselves from blame on the same grounds. A man with a good "forgettery" has a relatively easy time covering his mistakes. We escape punishment from others and, at the same time, keep our own consciences quiet.

Most persons object to the theory that we forget because of the escape it furnishes us. They hate this explanation because it robs them of a very excellent means of escape from difficulties. They argue that memory is a physiological function, wholly dependent upon the operation of the nervous system. Granted that the nervous system is necessary to effect memory, it is possible to set up a habit of forgetting just the same.

For example, suppose a little boy fails to do as he was told. If he says, in excuse, that he did not want to do it, he is likely to be punished. If he says it was too hard, he is likely to be scolded. If he refuses point-blank to do it, he is likely to be forced to do it under supervision. If, on the other hand, he says he forgot, he is likely to be excused. He may begin by offering the excuse of forgetting when he remembered, but he is likely to end by really forgetting. He learns to forget because he learns that it pays to forget and those who accept this excuse are teaching him to do so. If you do not believe that forgetting is a good excuse try on your instructor the various excuses just suggested and compare the results with the excuse that you forgot.

In spite of our willingness to accept forgetting as an excuse we all recognize that it is a poor one. If, for example, a young man fails to keep his appointment with a girl and then offers the excuse that he forgot all about it, the girl is very likely to retaliate by saying that he was not interested in the appointment or he would not have forgotten. And the girl is right. If he continues in his apology and explains that he was studying, at a party, or interrupted by friends, the girl may rightly contend that he was more interested in the other activity than in the appointment. She thus has a measure of the degree of interest he has in her. If he will choose to permit his studies to interfere with his appointment he thinks more of his studies than he does of her. You can hardly conceive of a boy forgetting his own birthday, but when a man forgets his wedding anniversary it means that he is not particularly interested in that day.

When a person forgets in this manner it does not follow that he has hysteria. Such forgetting is normal. But the same principles, in greatly exaggerated form, furnish the explanation of the gross memory losses which in hysteria assume a pathological aspect.

Pathological forgetting may take two forms. In one the individual forgets everything connected with a particular subject while he remembers other things which occupy the same range of time as the forgotten subject matter. In the other type everything occupying a certain period of time may be forgotten. In either case the forgetting may be suspected to depend upon some conflict if it comes in in a queer fashion and especially if his memories come back miraculously.

The degree of forgetting varies greatly. In some extreme cases the individual forgets how to read, write, and speak. He seems to be a little child again. In other instances, while he cannot tell you anything about a certain subject or a definite period he does retain much of what he learned. If these cases are studied it is usually found that the forgetting has served him some definite purpose in precisely the same way that the milder forms of forgetting benefit the normal man.

We may conclude that memory is a function which

varies according to the needs of the individual involved. He may begin the habit of forgetting for some relatively trivial reason and suffer no serious consequences. But once the habit is started, it may grow until it is used in an abnormal manner and large sections of the person's experience may be apparently lost. We say apparently, for the reason that with suitable methods the memories may be restored. The habit of forgetting is a poor habit to cultivate.

2. *Sleepwalking.* In Lady Macbeth, Shakespeare offers a classical example of sleepwalking:

Gentlewoman. Lo you, here she comes! This is her very guise; and, upon my life, fast asleep! Observe her; stand close.

Doctor. How came she by that light?

Gentlewoman. Why, it stood by her; she has light by her continually; 'tis her command.

Doctor. You see, her eyes are open.

Gentlewoman. Ay, but their sense is shut.

Doctor. What is it she does now? Look, how she rubs her hands.

Gentlewoman. It is an accustomed action with her, to seem thus washing her hands; I have known her continue in this a quarter of an hour.

Lady Macbeth. Yet here's a spot.

Doctor. Hark! she speaks; I will set down what comes from her, to satisfy my remembrance the more strongly.

Lady Macbeth. Out, damned spot! out, I say!—One, two; why, then 'tis time to do't.—Hell is murky!—Fie, my lord, fie! a soldier, and afeard? What need we fear who know it, when none can call our power to account?—Yet who would have thought the old man to have had so much blood in him?

Doctor. Do you mark that?

Lady Macbeth. The Thane of Fife had a wife; where is she now?—What, will these hands ne'er be clean?—No more o' that, my lord, no more o' that; you mar all with this starting.

Doctor. Go to, go to; you have known what you should not.

Gentlewoman. She has spoke what she should not, I am sure of that; heaven knows what she has known.

Lady Macbeth. Here's the smell of blood still; all the per-
fumes of Arabia will not sweeten this little hand. Oh, oh, oh!

Doctor. What a sigh is there! The heart is sorely charged.

Gentlewoman. I would not have such a heart in my bosom
for the dignity of the whole body.

Doctor. Well, well, well,—

Gentlewoman. Pray God it be, sir.

Doctor. This disease is beyond my practice; yet I have known
those which have walked in their sleep who have died holily in
their beds.

Lady Macbeth. Wash your hands, put on your nightgown;
look not so pale.—I tell you yet again, Banquo's buried; he
cannot come out on's grave.

Doctor. Even so?

Lady Macbeth. To bed, to bed! there's knocking at the gate;
come, come, come, come, give me your hand. What's done
cannot be undone. To bed, to bed, to bed!

Doctor. Will she go now to bed?

Gentlewoman. Directly.

"In this picture one can see in Lady Macbeth a ter-
rific attempt to submerge the memory of her horrible crime
to keep it from coming to the foreground. The event
is too powerful an influence, however, and she is forced
in sleep to give reign to it and reënact the horrible murder
scene." [1]

In sleep the ordinary person is able to lay aside the
activities of the day. His dreams usually represent a
carryover of some insistent thoughts, emotions, or activities which do not easily retire into the background.
When there exists some profound disturbance, as in the
case of Lady Macbeth, the sleep may be so disturbed
that activity may take place. This activity often gives
a clear indication of the nature of the disturbing influence.

Milder sleepwalking episodes merely indicate that

[1] Morgan, John J. B., *The Psychology of the Unadjusted School Child*, Macmillan, 1924, pp. 108–109.

the person has not been able to relax from some exciting situation. For example, a boy who was very much interested in baseball, and who had witnessed an exciting game, rose in his bed the night after the game and yelled, "Go it second! Go it second!" A woman who had been much disturbed by the loss of a ring got out of bed, took a lamp, and began searching for the lost ring. A boy whose dog had died cried in his sleep and called for his dog by name.

All these simple cases indicate that the sleeper had not been able to recover from some sort of emotional strain. With such recovery the sleepwalking episodes will naturally disappear.

When one is torn by a severe mental conflict, when guilt obsesses one's every thought in spite of all attempts to repress it, as in the case of Lady Macbeth, the sleepwalking episode becomes more significant. It tells us that the subject has made a mighty attempt to forget but, in spite of seemingly normal behavior when awake, the memory still persists to torment him.

Whether or not sleepwalking should be taken seriously depends, therefore, upon the nature of the underlying emotional tension. The only cure is to relieve this tension. In simple cases this is easy; when it involves a moral struggle it is more difficult.

3. *Fainting spells.* Some fainting episodes are, of course, the result of purely physical disturbances. Others are essentially an escape from an emotional situation which is too much for the subject of it. A person who faints away at the sight of blood is obviously unable consciously to face the blood with the associations he has built up around it. He runs away from the emotional strain by going to sleep.

Some persons never faint; some have fainted only once or twice in a lifetime and then when confronted with an exceedingly gruesome spectacle; others develop the habit of fainting on the slightest provocation. In any case it is a form of running away from reality and in extreme cases may be pathological.

The habit of fainting may be cultivated by the solicitous interest of onlookers and through the fact that the fainter gains some end by this device. One girl had so enslaved her mother by her fainting that she could get anything she wanted. She expressed a desire for a car on one occasion and, although the mother could ill afford one, she remarked to a neighbor, "We must get a car or Mary will have a fainting spell."

A teacher had a boy in her class room who was supposed to have epilepsy. Care had to be taken to prevent any undue excitement so that he would have no fainting spells in the presence of the other children. One day he was asked by the teacher to perform some simple task but, not wanting to do it, he replied, "If you make me do it I shall faint." The teacher, perceiving that the boy was using the fainting device to gain his own ends, told him, "All right, you have your spell, and then you can do the assignment." Seeing that his ruse was discovered, he gave a sheepish grin, performed the task, and did not faint.

Here again, if an individual has tried to suppress a particularly painful experience, it may bob up in spite of his efforts, and cause him to go into a sleeping or fainting spell at any inopportune time. In such a sleeping spell he may dream or enact the horrible episode much the same as might occur in an ordinary sleepwalking episode. The following case illustrates this:

"A young woman, twenty-nine years old, intelligent, sensitive, hears one day abruptly some disastrous news. Her niece, who lives next door, has just died in dreadful circumstances. She had thrown herself out of the window in a fit of delirium. The young woman rushes out, and comes, unhappily, in time to see the body of the young girl lying in the street. Although very much moved, she remains to all appearances calm, helping to make everything ready for the funeral. She goes to the funeral in a very natural way. But from that time she grows more and more gloomy, her health fails, and we may notice the beginning of the singular symptoms we are going to speak of. Nearly every day, at night and during the day, she enters into a strange state; she looks as if she were in a dream, she speaks softly with an absent person, she calls Pauline (the name of her lately deceased niece), and tells her that she admires her fate, her courage, that her death has been a beautiful one. She rises, goes to the windows and opens them, then shuts them again, tries them one after another, climbs on the window, and if her friends did not stop her, she would, without any doubt, throw herself out of the window. She must be stopped, looked after incessantly, till she shakes herself, rubs her eyes, and resumes her ordinary business as if nothing had happened." [1]

Sleep is a desirable means of getting respite from the cares of the day; fainting spells may be useful on rare occasions to escape when a particularly loathsome experience confronts one; but each person needs to cultivate the ability to meet most situations, whether pleasant or not, without running away into a fainting spell. The best treatment for chronic fainters is to train

[1] Janet, Pierre, *Major Symptoms of Hysteria*, Macmillan, 1913, p. 27.

them gradually to face situations involving emotional strain.

4. *Double personalities*. Every person who is at all honest with himself will recognize that he is the victim of conflicting tendencies. We all have good and bad impulses existing side by side. What do we do about it? We attempt to formulate some code of behavior and to adhere to it in spite of impulses to the contrary. Sometimes we wonder how some of the temptations which come to us could originate within ourselves. It would be a comfort if we could believe that they came from elsewhere. Hence we evolve explanations to save ourselves the undesirable admission that these thoughts and impulses are our own.

A simple method is to blame companions, but often it is hard to prove that they gave us any untoward suggestions and we dare not openly accuse them even if we do try to make ourselves think they are to blame.

We may blame evil spirits, original sinful impulses, or develop other excuses even more absurd. One is the development of a secondary personality.

Tendencies in this direction can easily be observed in simple situations which confront many children. Suppose a child does something "naughty." The mother may say, "Who has gotten into my little girl? Surely that is not my girl acting that way, it must be some outside naughty little girl has gotten into you." What a wonderful device for the child to use to get out of blame. All she needs to do in the future is to blame her bad behavior on the naughty little outside girl. Other expressions for this same thing are: "Jack must have gotten on your back." "Satan must have talked to you." "A naughty spirit must be in you."

This tendency to dissociate the personality and to assume two separate individuals, one doing good acts and one doing bad deeds, usually does not get very far because it is too strange to deceive others and we cannot take it very seriously ourselves. Some few individuals, nevertheless, are able to carry this process to great extremes with the aid of a memory gap between the two. With the tendency to blame a hypothetical individual and a convenient memory, such persons can easily retire to a different "personality" when circumstances get out of hand.

A recent illustration of this was the case of Mr. Robins. He left home with the intention of keeping an appointment with President Hoover which promised to be quite unpleasant for him. He did not appear at the White House when he was scheduled, and it was thought for a time that he had met with foul play. Some weeks later he was found in a tiny country community. He had assumed another personality, had taken a different name, and had totally forgotten his former existence. When his wife first appeared to him he did not even remember her. However, his memory soon came back and he resumed his former existence. He had conveniently become another person to avoid a possible unpleasant situation.

If one can successfully make his memory do such tricks it provides a very successful escape from difficulties. Popular stories such as Stevenson's *Dr. Jekyl and Mr. Hyde* serve to increase the credulity of the public, and they think that this change depends upon some mysterious accident in the individual. It is not any strange power that effects such changes; it is the habit of the subject of wishing he could escape into another person; a vivid imagination of the type of person one would select if he could escape; and, finally, an emotional shock great enough to motivate one to effect the final forgetting act.

Another illustration of this mechanism is found in the case of a preacher who secretly wished he were a business man instead of a preacher. One part of him wanted to preach and would not let him make the change; another part of him wanted to make the change; so he had a lapse of memory and effected the transition. The story is as follows:

"On January 17th, 1887, the Reverend Ansel Bourne, an itinerant preacher, drew a considerable sum of money from a bank in Providence, and then entered a tram car. This was the last incident which he remembered. 'He did not return home that day, and nothing was heard of him for two months. . . . On the morning of March 14th, however, at Norristown, Pennsylvania, a man calling himself A. J. Brown, who had rented a small shop six weeks previously, stocked it with stationery, confectionery, fruit, and small articles, and carried on his quiet trade without seeming to anyone unnatural or eccentric, woke up in a fright and called in the people of the house to tell him where he was. He said that his name was Ansel Bourne, that he knew nothing of shopkeeping, and that the last thing he remembered—it seemed only yesterday— was drawing the money from the bank in Providence.'" [1]

In double personality we have still another form of running from reality. Instead of facing life frankly we run into another personality which we have artificially created. It may seem a long distance from "chasing Jack from your back" as a child and changing from a preacher to a shopkeeper, but the mechanism is the same.

5. *Sensory defects*. "Didn't you hear me call you?" yells the irate mother.

[1] Hart, Bernard, *The Psychology of Insanity*, Cambridge University Press, 1931, pp. 65–66.

"No, mother, I did not hear you at all," replies the panic-stricken boy, certain that he is going to feel the effects of the anger his mother is displaying.

To his amazement his mother subsides and no punishment is forthcoming. He got out of being spanked merely by saying he did not hear. Grand! He forthwith develops a hearing defect; when it is convenient he does not hear things.

"Why do you make so many mistakes in reading? Can't you see?" asks the teacher.

"No, my eyes hurt and I cannot see," replies the boy and so gets out of a scolding for his poor reading.

So, we are teaching these children to turn off their sensory apparatus when it is convenient for them to do so much as they would turn off a radio receiving set. By displaying defective eyes or ears they are escaping punishment or scoldings and are getting out of unpleasant tasks.

This serves as an excellent defense. If I say I did not hear a command no one can prove that I did. Even if tests prove my hearing to be normal, I may still have failed to hear because of absent-mindedness. If we succeed in using such a defense it is possible to build up a habit of poor vision or poor hearing when the sense organs themselves are perfectly normal.

Some of these cases go undetected for a long time until some accidental circumstance proves to the victim and to others that the defect is not physiological. In other cases the subject is too eager to make the defect sound plausible and thus builds a trap for himself.

This latter condition came out very clearly in the case of a college student. She had complained of poor vision all her life and some one had read to her all through her school career. She really could not read. She described her

visual disorder as a very unusual thing. Ordinary things
she could see as well as anyone else. When she looked at
printed matter, she contended, she could see only the
upper half of the line of type. It was as though some one
were holding a sheet of paper over the lower half of the
print. To be sure, if this explanation were correct, she
would have great difficulty in reading. Anyone can prove
that to his satisfaction in a few moments. However, such
a visual defect is impossible. The structure of the eye
would not permit such a condition, and a few tests proved
conclusively that this explanation was in error. The girl
had depended upon others for so long that she could not
read, but the deficiency was due to lack of training in
reading and not to poor vision. She had succeeded with
this story for years until she began to fail in her work in
college and was forced to submit to a thorough examination.

"All of us value our senses so highly that it is hard to
realize that a person could give up the use of his eyes or
his ears without being forced to do so by a direct physical
injury to the sense organ. That a mental conflict, a
central disturbance of a complex sort, can result in the
loss of the use of a sense organ that is organically intact
is shown by the following case.

"A colored boy, apparently about twelve years of age,
was found by the police wandering near one of the south
side parks in Chicago. He said that his name was Frank
Coleman, but was unable to tell where he lived or how
he came to the place where he was found. He was taken
to the detention home, where unsuccessful efforts were
made to locate his home.

"One morning, shortly after the beginning of his residence at the detention home, he appeared unable to

speak or hear. He made signs indicating that someone had grabbed him by the throat, and that as a result he was unable to use his voice. He could not hear what was said to him, but managed to understand a little through signs that were made and through watching the lips of the speaker. His writing was so poor that this means offered little help. He understood simple things that were written, but his replies were mostly unintelligible.

"For four weeks he remained mute (unable to talk), except for two instances when he was heard to utter sounds. One was when he was made to scrub a floor and the other was when he wanted a cigarette. That his deafness was not absolute was shown by the fact that he winked whenever a loud sound was made behind him. He also showed signs of sorrow when his mother was mentioned by a person whom he could not see.

"At first an attempt was made to force him to speak by frightening him with an electric current that was harmless but decidedly unpleasant. All such attempts only served to make him more and more resistive, a condition in which all suggestions or requests met with immediate opposition. Finally, he was made to understand that he would be put to sleep and thus be made to talk. He was placed upon an operating table and ether administered. As he became unconscious he yelled, 'I'll talk if you let me go.' . . . This experiment proved that he could talk . . . and in about twenty-four hours he was hearing and responding normally." [1]

While drastic means are sometimes resorted to in cases of this sort because they are so extreme, in milder cases the better plan is to discover what motive lies behind the

[1] Morgan, John J. B., *The Psychology of Abnormal People*, Longmans Green, 1928, pp. 33–34.

sensory defect. If a person exaggerates a sensory defect it may be assumed that it is to his interest to do so. Change the circumstances so that it will be markedly to his advantage to hear and see and he will overcome the defect with miraculous speed.

6. *Motor disorders.* When a person is afraid, worried, excited, or expectant, he is very likely to make little jerky movements, finger his garments, pull at buttons, tremble when he attempts to make a movement, drop articles, spill his food, and the like. In some extreme emotions his muscles may be so affected that he cannot move but becomes rigid and paralyzed. We all recognize these motor reactions as indicators of emotional excitement whether they occur in ourselves or in others. But we have no means of telling the nature of the emotion behind these movements except by indirect inference. If the subject of them has no hesitancy in revealing his mental attitudes he will tell you whether his trembling is the result of intense joy or of fear. He will let you know whether he is paralyzed because of anger or fear and will let you know the reason why he has either emotion.

On the other hand, he can very easily dissimulate if he finds it to his interests to do so. He may do this by misrepresenting the emotion behind the actions or he may accomplish it by directing attention to the motor behavior, exaggerating it, and insisting that there is no emotion to account for it. Such a defense is particularly effective because the activity is quite apparent and the observer is quite intrigued by bizarre actions of any sort. So, all the patient has to do is to tremble a little more violently, pull his buttons with greater insistence, twist his body a little more vigorously when he attempts to do anything, or let his helplessness become more pitiable, and he has his friends on his side, sympathizing with him and looking no deeper than the apparent organic defect for the cause of his trouble.

The significance of these motor disorders was demonstrated during the recent war. Men with injuries were taken to hospitals for treatment. As their limbs recovered the prospect of going back to the trenches became too much for some of them and, unconsciously, their symptoms were prolonged. The actual wound may have been healed but the individual found himself unable to move the injured member. The fact that these paralyses were not organic was demonstrated when the armistice was signed. With the prospect of a return to the trenches removed, a great proportion of these persons recovered the function of their members immediately.

Disorders of this sort furnish the bulk of evidence for miraculous cures of one sort or another. When a person has to drag himself about with the help of crutches at one moment and the next throws his crutches in the air and walks normally, the remarkable "cure" has been due to the removal of the emotional situation which was behind the paralysis. Instead of assuming, as the result of such a "miracle" that an organic disease was cured, the conclusion should be that the disease was functional and not organic; that is, it was a defense mechanism established because it enabled its owner to escape some mental conflict.

There have been cases where a seeming organic paralysis appeared and disappeared in ways which showed that the motor organism was intact in spite of an apparent organic disease. Janet cites one instance where a man was paralyzed when awake but was able to get up and walk about during his sleep.

"A man of thirty-two usually remains in bed, for both his legs are paralyzed. . . . In the middle of the night he rises slowly, jumps lightly out of bed,—for the paralysis we have just spoken of has quite vanished, takes his pillow and hugs it. We know by his countenance and by his words that he mistakes this pillow for his child, and that he believes he is saving his child from the hands of his mother-in-law. Then, bearing that weight, he tries to slip out of the room, opens the door, and runs out through the court-yard; climbing along the gutter, he gets to the housetop, carrying his pillow and running all about the buildings of the hospital with marvelous agility. One must take great care to catch him, and use all sorts of cautions to get him down, for he wakes with a stupefied air, and as soon as he is awake, both his legs are paralyzed again, and he must be carried to his bed. He does not understand what you are speaking about, and cannot comprehend how it happens that people were obliged to go to the top of the house in order to look for a poor man who has been paralyzed in his bed for months." [1]

If your legs carry you where you do not want to go it is possible to refrain from such journeys by becoming paralyzed. But what an inefficient method of adjusting to such a situation! After all, one could be carried there, so the barrier is not insurmountable. And how much easier it would be to face the real issue—the fact that part of you wants to go and part of you does not want to go—and adjust to it in a rational manner instead of refusing to go anywhere in order to refrain from making one undesirable type of journey!

If you wish to see this mechanism in embryonic form

[1] Janet, Pierre, *Major Symptoms of Hysteria*, Macmillan, 1913, pp. 28–29.

watch a little boy going on an errand he does not want to perform. He drags one foot after another in the most painful manner; he can hardly make them move; they are nearly paralyzed. Then watch the same boy using the same legs a moment later to run to the store to buy himself an ice cream cone. It is obvious that the difference is not in his legs; it is in the motive behind the walking. Why not use as much intelligence in attempting to understand extreme paralysis in hysterical individuals when they serve such obvious purposes?

7. *Nausea.* It is easy for nausea to become associated with mental conflicts because emotional upsets usually involve the digestive apparatus, and the nausea can come, in the first instance, as a direct emotional reaction. If the nausea, in and of itself, serves to change the issue to the advantage of the sick person, it will likely be repeated and may easily grow into a habit.

A woman thirty-five years of age practiced almost day and night for months to train herself to participate in a piano recital. She reached a high degree of perfection and looked forward eagerly to the night when she would appear in public. Unfortunately, just as she was about to make her stage appearance she became exceedingly ill, and of course could not appear. The next day she could talk of nothing but her misfortune at getting ill just as she was about to make her appearance on the stage. She was "so angry and so humiliated that she did not know what to do," so she talked about it incessantly. Why should she get sick just at the wrong moment? It seemed most unfortunate until the history of this woman was unearthed.

When a little girl in the primary grades she was called upon to recite a lesson in which she was not prepared.

She became terror-stricken, and as a result of the intense emotion became actually nauseated. The attention of the teacher and pupils was directed to the illness; she was nursed most carefully, and did not have to recite. She was a smart little girl, and the next time she saw a similar danger—that of being forced to recite what she did not know—she actually induced nausea by poking her fingers down her throat. She helped the emotion along with her fingers and became nauseated again. This became so easy for her and was repeated so often that she was excused from recitations.

When she became older she realized the folly of this escape and broke the habit. She had not used it consciously or unconsciously since her school days. But in the stress of excitement and some fear as to the outcome of her appearance in recital, the old habit pattern came back and she became ill in spite of herself.

8. *Operative diseases.* The climax of adopting a physical disease in order to escape from a mental conflict comes when a person is able to deceive his physicians to the point where they will operate upon him and when he will fool himself to such an extent that he is willing, and even anxious, to undergo such operations. It is a clever physician who has never been deceived by hysterical individuals. They will develop tender areas, swellings, temperatures, and will show a fairly consistent picture of tumors, inflamed appendices, stomach ulcers, and the like.

On the other hand, a physician who has been deceived by patients of this sort has been known to become over-cautious and to treat as hysterical a genuine organic difficulty. After a physician has treated as an hysterical patient a woman whose autopsy showed that she died of an abdominal tumor, he is likely to be rather loath to diagnose any more individuals as hysterical, and so becomes an easy prey for persons who have no organic difficulties but are genuine hysterical patients. He argues that if he operates unnecessarily the patient will probably recover from the operation, and no great harm is done; but if he fails to operate when he should have done so, and the patient dies as a result of his neglect, he feels that he has been guilty of a grave error. Hence it is better to err in the direction of too much treatment than in the direction of too little. But it is too much treatment that produces hystericals, and so we continue to have them.

Prevention of hysteria. Hysteria will not be eliminated by evolving more discriminating tests to prove whether or not a disease symptom has an organic basis. Such a contest between the physician and the patient is always won by the patient, for there is no limit to the degree that even a tiny symptom may be exaggerated.

The solution will come by training persons to develop the type of personality and character that will make the use of disease symptoms to escape a mental conflict impossible.

In the last analysis, the hysterical individual is a grown person using babyish tricks to solve his problems. He plays upon the sympathies of other persons; he is playing mean tricks upon himself, and all in a very childish fashion.

The use of these various symptoms may not be as dangerous as other mechanisms which we have described. The victim of hysteria will not become so mentally deranged as to be considered insane by legal authorities; he will not find himself committed to an institution for the care of the mentally diseased. No, he stays outside of public institutions to annoy his friends, neighbors, and physicians with his troubles. If he has means he may go to private sanitaria; he fills the coffers of less scrupulous physicians, and provides a continual annoyance to physicians who do their utmost to maintain a high standard in their practice.

All these tricks that they use are childish ways of running from reality. They indicate that the child has not been taught to face life and its problems. Suppose it is a moral issue; why run to a disease to escape admitting that one has been tempted to do an undesirable act? Teach a child to face his temptations squarely and fight them directly, and he will not resort to illness.

But of course the main trouble rests with the adults who have these children in their care. They themselves do not want to admit that the child is motivated by improper drives, and they accept the ruse that the child offers even more readily than he does himself. It is this gullibility on the part of teachers and parents, as well as physicians, that provides the soil in which hysteria and neurasthenia grow.

QUESTIONS

1. Can you think of anyone whom you know who is using health as an excuse for not facing the realities of life?

2. Describe in your own words the behavior of a neurasthenic.

3. Describe how neurasthenia develops.

4. What treatment could you accord a neurasthenic of your acquaintance which might help him to get rid of his symptoms?

5. How do you suppose he would respond to your treatment?

6. If a mother is kind to her child when he is ill, she tends to teach him to use illness as a defense mechanism; if she ignores him she is regarded as hard. What should she do?

7. Show how we may deceive ourselves with a device originally adopted to deceive others.

8. Show how a real illness may turn into a feigned illness merely because of faulty emphasis.

9. Why is escaping responsibility through physical complaints so effective?

10. In brief, what is it that underlies a fear of illness in the neurasthenic?

11. Why is the rest cure ineffective?

12. Why is it that the neurasthenic response can in no sense be looked upon as a heroic reaction?

13. Why is it that some physicians are deceived by those who feign ill-health?

14. Show why it is more important to discern the reason for the feigned illness than to determine on a specific method of handling the person.

15. What is meant when we say that these persons need a real change of character?

16. What is the fundamental distinction between neurasthenia and hysteria?

17. How can wishes play tricks upon our memories?

18. Why are most persons willing to accept poor memory excuses?

19. How does hysterical forgetting differ from normal forgetting?

20. Describe the two forms that hysterical forgetting may take.

21. In what sense can forgetting be called a habit?

22. What is meant by sleepwalking?

23. What do minor sleepwalking episodes indicate?

24. What determines the seriousness of sleepwalking?

25. Of what value to the individual is fainting?

26. In what way may fainting be developed into a habit?

27. Compare sleeping and fainting.

28. How should chronic fainters be treated?

29. In what different ways can we get rid of the blame when we have an unworthy impulse?

30. How can mothers inadvertently teach children the beginnings of the "double personality" defense?

31. Explain how extreme cases of double personality may grow from simple beginnings.

32. Show how double personality can be considered as a habit.

33. Show how it is possible to teach a child to develop a functional hearing defect.

34. What is the difference between failing to hear because of absent-mindedness and because one did not want to hear?

35. Can an intense desire to see or hear actually increase visual and auditory acuity?

36. Can you explain the extreme illustrations given in the text as exaggerations of the same tendency in normal persons?

37. How would you handle a person with a visual or auditory defect of a functional sort?

38. What does motor incoördination usually indicate?

39. What lies behind most "miraculous" cures?

40. Show how fear can produce a functional paralysis.

41. Explain why fear may readily cause nausea.

42. Describe the manner in which nausea may become habitual.

43. How could one overcome the habitual tendency to become nauseated in minor fear situations?

44. Why is it that a person with a functional disease can induce a physician to operate upon him?

45. Why is the attempt to prove that the hysterical patient is using trickery likely to prove fruitless?

46. What form should the prevention of hysteria take?

47. In general, what is the purpose of the hysterical person?

48. Why must the prevention of hysteria begin with adults who have children with hysterical tendencies in their care?

CHAPTER X

CRIME

Some persons seem fated for ill-fortune. Helped out of one difficulty they fall into another and another, in what appears to be a fatal interplay of forces beyond their control. Analysis of such cases usually displays a strange inability to profit from experience, and to learn some simple lessons of living that any child should be able to grasp. They seem unable to manifest the ordinary common sense which is so necessary an adjunct to a successful life. The following case is typical:

A woman was arrested for stealing two loaves of bread and was taken to the county jail. Here she told such an incoherent story that she was transferred to the psychopathic hospital for further study.

When a young girl, she had fallen in love with a man who tried to get away from her by taking a job as woodsman in a Western state. She followed him and lived with him for a number of years, although he refused to marry her. She gave birth to three children and as he refused to support her adequately she came back to the Middle West, placed the children in a home, and got a job.

Soon she found another man with whom she lived and to whom she bore three more children, although again she did not marry. This second consort abused her almost as much as the first one had done, and it was in desperation that she went out to steal some bread to feed the children.

This pathetic story touched the heart of the social worker and an unusual effort was made to help her get a fresh start in life. A position was secured for her in a fine home as cook. This position she gave up after two weeks, saying that she would not work with that "old hen." Her employer was, in reality, a very fine and considerate woman. A second job was secured with similar results.

She was then given a job in the kitchen of the hospital and here displayed a number of peculiar traits. She had quarrels, in turn, with practically every employee of the hospital, each time the responsibility for the difficulty resting on the other person. Periodically she would fail to appear for work, and give as her reason that some one had hurt her feelings. Each time the squabble was patched up and she returned to work.

She had borrowed money from the social worker, and one would suppose that when she received her monthly pay check from the hospital she would repay part of her debt. Instead, she spent her first month's pay having enormous portraits made of herself. One of these she sent to the first man with whom she had consorted, another to the second man, one to each of the institutions where her children were maintained, one she hung in the kitchen where she worked, and one she hung in her bedroom.

The second month's pay she used as a down payment on a fur coat. Since these expenditures exhausted her resources she had to borrow from the social worker in order to live for the remainder of the month.

One morning when she failed to appear for work the social worker went to the rooming house where she lived, found her room locked and gas fumes coming from the

cracks in the door. An entrance was made. The gas had
been turned off and she was found lying on her bed with
her picture propped up in front of her while she read the
Bible.

In her spare time she played solitaire, stacking the
cards invariably so that she would win.

In spite of all this, she had a fairly pleasing personality.
She greeted everybody with gay cordiality and was always laughing and making "wise-cracks." She had normal intelligence as far as the standard tests were concerned, but she did not know how to meet the ordinary
situations of life.

After several months she disappeared, leaving a most
scathing note denouncing the social worker who had
helped her so much and everyone in the hospital who had
any position of authority.

Shortly after her disappearance a most elaborately
engraved announcement was received telling of her marriage. About the same time the social worker received
a letter saying that at last she had found the man of
her dreams.

Where do we get common sense? A medical man
would diagnose this woman as a "psychopathic personality." Personality is the consolidation of past experiences into a unified whole which is able to move according
to principles which have resulted from those experiences.
A wholesome personality has some consistency of action and thought, and makes continual readjustments
in accordance with the lessons which each new experience brings. The sick personality fails to effect this
unification; each new experience finds him just as un-
prepared as a child, and he makes just as foolish blunders
as would an inexperienced baby. Common sense, the

ability to meet the ordinary situations of life with intelligence, comes from experience. When we discover a
person who has it to a marked degree we know he has
had a rich experience and has been able to profit from
it. When we find one who lacks it we know that he is
lacking in experience or that, having had the requisite
experience, he has been unable to coördinate it. This
woman's history shows that she had had sufficient experience to enable her to learn, but that she failed to
profit by it.

Why does one person profit from his experience and
another fail to do so? If those who fail were lacking in
intelligence we might attribute it to that factor, but
these psychopathic personalities are normal or superior
in intelligence. Perhaps their training has been different.
We believe that there is a specific difference in the training of these persons which in a large part accounts for
their peculiar reactions to life.

These persons uniformly show a history which indicates that they have been shielded by other persons,
or by circumstances, so that they did not have to stand
the brunt of their own mistakes. This happens when
comrades, parents, and teachers are unusually lenient
or of a fine disposition; or it happens when the individual
as a tiny child has such a charming personality that almost anybody does anything to help him. Perhaps, in
some cases, the two combine. These conditions often
continue into later life, and merely accentuate the pernicious habits started earlier. The illustration of the
woman just recited is a case in point. She did more silly
things while in the hospital and deserved less consideration than most of the other patients, and yet she had
more done for her than anyone else in residence. These

persons learn to get what they want by playing on the sympathies of those around them, and each time they succeed in this game they become more incapable of developing ordinary common sense. They do not have to look after their own interests, everybody does it for them. The man who takes life seriously marvels that they can be so flippant about serious predicaments. But why should they not be flippant? Some one will get them out of every "scrape" they ever have.

Are they immoral? If morality involves consideration for the rights of others, then they are immoral, for they have no consideration for anyone but themselves. They will take all the favors offered to them but feel no obligation to be of service to anyone else. They are loving persons, but their love is the love of a leech; once they get a hold upon another person they will drain the last drop of blood from him and then forsake him as of no further value, probably berating him for not having given more.

They have a silly sort of chronic optimism. No matter what happens they take for granted that it will come out all right, but assume no responsibility for making things turn out fortunately. The responsibility is wholly upon those around them. If outsiders do not shoulder the obligations, they take on an aggrieved air and cannot understand their lack of consideration.

One does not need to go to a psychopathic hospital to find individuals who have personalities of this sort. Girls of this sort who are successful are commonly known as "gold-diggers"; if they are unsuccessful they are given the title of "leech," "vamp," or something worse. Men of this variety are known as "gigolos" or "lounge lizards." These names are applied to psychopathic personalities in their beginning stages, if they acquire a suitable host. Those who cannot attach themselves suitably end up in the poor farm or some worse institution. If they get a mate who will submit to all their vagaries they loudly proclaim they have found the "ideal of their dreams."

The cure for this condition is to teach them the need for reciprocity in social life, the advantages of give and take. It does no good to chide them, or to make them suffer some arbitrary punishment. This will merely drive them to greater lengths to win sympathy, and does not get to the core of the trouble, which is faulty education in social relations.

In their mildest forms, psychopathic personalities do no particular damage to society. They are pests, make considerable unhappiness, but make themselves more unhappy than they do others. When the type of attitude which underlies their behavior becomes extended it may do specific damage, especially when it leads to outright criminal behavior.

Criminality. To apply the term criminal to a person tells you very little about that person. The act which the condemned man may have committed may vary all the way from some very trivial act to the most atrocious outrage against human rights. To apply the name to those who have repeatedly violated the legal code does not help much. Recently Michigan attempted to define crime in this manner and imposed life sentences on those convicted four times. As a result a man was given a life sentence for carrying a pint of whisky. The sentence was later commuted. Nor does the appellation criminal furnish any information as to the motive that may have actuated the act. A man might steal from a variety of motives: He might be attempting to wreak vengeance upon an enemy. He might be doing it to get food for a starving family. He might have some mental disease. He might do it because he hated society in general, and because he thought the world owed him a living. He might do it because he was proud of his prowess as a pickpocket. It might have been the result of a wager. The possible causes could be multiplied indefinitely.

In other words, crime is a legal term to denote the fact that a law has been broken. To apply the term to a person tells you nothing about the personality of the individual to whom it is applied. And yet we continue to commit this error. We brand as a criminal a man who has gone afoul of the law. We then proceed to make other unwarranted assumptions. We say that if he has committed one crime he will commit others. We assume that there must be some taint in his blood. We do all this with little or no consideration of the circumstances of his crime or the motives behind it. If he is a criminal he becomes somehow different from the rest of us, and we ostracize him from our society.

This attitude is a carry-over from a very primitive conception of crime. In the early days of society a crime was considered only from the standpoint of those who had been injured by it, and the only motive behind treatment of the criminal was retaliation. The principle to which ancient society adhered was: "An eye for an eye and a tooth for a tooth." It made little difference what manner of man did the crime or why he did it; he had injured his fellow man and he was made to pay the penalty. We hated the criminal because he had injured us.

William A. White has given another very ingenious explanation as to why we hate the criminal man. He

says that in early times man hated what he conceived
to be sin and tried to get rid of it by transferring it to
some animal or person.   If this animal or person was
then gotten rid of the sin went along and the man was
freed from his guilt.

"The obvious principle embodied in the concept of the
scapegoat was the principle that evil could be gotten rid
of by transferring it to some object, animal, or even man
and then by getting rid of them the evil, of course, went
along. . . . Because man can shift a burden of wood or
stones from his back to that of another the savage imagines that he can as easily shift his burden of pain and
sorrow to another who will bear it in his stead. . . . On
the day of Atonement the Jewish high-priest laid his
hands on the head of a goat, confessed all the iniquities of
the Children of Israel, and having thus transferred their
sins to the animal, drove it into the wilderness. . . .
The principle which runs through these customs is clear
and seems to be a universal characteristic of man. Man
is always trying to get rid of what makes him unhappy
and if this is sin, . . . he tries to escape responsibility for
it. In punishing the criminal, therefore, he is not trying,
primarily, to get rid of sin in the abstract, that is a rationalization of his conduct, he is trying to get rid of that sin
which he feels resident within himself. The criminal
then becomes a handy object upon which he can transfer
his sin and thus by punishing the criminal he deludes himself into a feeling of righteous indignation." [1]

Whether punishment of the criminal is for the purpose of
retaliation or whether it is to make him the scapegoat for
our own sins, it is obvious that the treatment of the crime

[1] White, William A., *Principles of Mental Hygiene*, Macmillan, 1917, pp. 132–
135.

itself without consideration for the motives behind the crime does not get to the psychology of the criminal and does little or nothing to make the criminal into a more socialized being. On the contrary, our treatment is more likely to make the unfortunate individual more unsocial. After a period of imprisonment he is likely to be more embittered and feel more justification in repeating his nonsocial performances.

What few attempts have been made to consider the man who commits the crime have been rather absurd. If we can prove that the man was mentally unbalanced we excuse him from the customary penalty. Consequently our criminal courts become a burlesque of psychological knowledge wherein clever lawyers try their wits in proving that the criminal was "insane" in order to enable him to escape the penalties of the law. The objective in proving a man irresponsible for his acts should not be to enable him to escape the law; it should be to determine what treatment he should receive. If no treatment is available and if he has an attitude toward society which makes him dangerous, he should be incarcerated regardless of the enormity of his crime. If he can be cured steps should be taken to do so just as we would attempt to cure a man with a bacterial infection. He should not be returned to society until specialists regard him as cured.

From the psychological viewpoint a criminal is usually a man in mental ill-health, and to understand him we must know how and why he got into that condition. We should be concerned not so much with whether we should sympathize with him or hate him—such questions are irrelevant—but whether we can understand something about him. If we go into the subject we shall find that many of the attitudes and habits which underlie criminal conduct are the outgrowth of very early training, and that what appears to be a sudden outburst of a totally new criminal tendency is nothing but the bursting forth of what was in the individual for years.

We are all too anxious to ignore such tendencies in their incipient forms, merely trusting that things will, through some kind providence, turn out all right. We cannot do anything, we think, until some lawless act has actually been committed, and then, in high indignation, we set out to wreak vengeance upon the culprit. With a proper understanding of mental life, many criminal acts could be prevented. Prevention instead of treatment should be the paramount issue.

Nor should the student imagine that these problems of unethical conduct are totally removed from his immediate life and interests. We have tried in previous chapters to show that pathological individuals differ only in degree from normal individuals; we shall find that the same principle holds with those whose mental illness takes them in the direction of crime. If we concern ourselves less with the desirability or undesirability of the external behavior and more with the significance of that behavior as to the attitudes which they signify, we shall take a long step toward human understanding and toward the eradication of much undesirable conduct.

Criminal acts may indicate mental conflict. Whenever a crime is committed our inclination is to give first consideration to the crime itself. We try to find the offender only in order to make him pay the penalty for the crime and not because we have any interest in him or in the motives he may have had in committing the crime. This is merely another form of treating the symptom rather than getting at the causal factors behind the symptom. Let us see how differently some acts appear when we know something of the background.

1. *Fear.* An auto driver was arrested for speeding and crashing into a car at a crossing where he should have stopped. On the surface this looks like gross negligence and disrespect for the law. This is what actually happened. This driver was driving very slowly behind a delivery truck. The delivery truck driver put out his arm to signal for what our victim thought was a left turn and so he started to pass to his right. Just as he came up alongside of the truck, the truck started to make a right turn. Our driver slipped by but bumped the fender of the truck as he did so. He thought the damage was of no consequence and continued down the street. As he did so the thought came into his head that he was a "hit and run" driver. The daily papers had been waging a campaign against such creatures and as he thought of this he became frightened. Looking through his rear view mirror he saw the truck driver coming and thought he was trying to catch him. Thereupon he lost his wits and could think of nothing but getting away, so he speeded up, with the result that he did not look as intently ahead as he should have, and the accident occurred.

As is usually the case when we try to frighten people into obedience, the persons who need it least are the most affected while the hardened individual, toward whom it is directed, gives it little heed. This man was really a very careful and law abiding driver, who immediately magnified the trivial thing he had done, and lost his head as a result.

Many crimes are committed because the persons who committed them were afraid that some minor act which they had done would be discovered. Blackmailers play upon this fear and may drive their victims to desperation. While most of us recognize this situation, the less tolerant members of society are likely to contend that the victim should have lived such an exemplary life that he could not have been blackmailed. However this may be, certainly the correct interpretation of such a case demands that all the facts be known.

2. *Reaction against deprivation.* If we are denied one thing we are prone to feel that we should be permitted to humor ourselves in something else. If the doctor forbids us to eat candy, why should we not be permitted to take in more movie shows to make up for the deprivation? We are irritated by every deprivation and have a feeling that we must have something, and if we cannot have what we want we take the nearest thing at hand as a substitute. The thing we substitute may be some trivial and harmless affair so that it makes little difference to us or to society. Sometimes it takes the form of a criminal act. Here the results are bad but a student of human nature should understand why the act is committed. Such understanding does not imply that we condone the act. It is not a question of approving, but one of understanding.

Some illustrations will make clear how this process may lead to criminal acts. A boy of fourteen who had never been previously involved in any misdemeanor was caught stealing a car. It seems that the engine of this car was running as the boy walked past and he could not resist the temptation to get in and drive away. Of course he was quickly apprehended and scolded severely by his parents. Upon their intervention the police dismissed him. In a few months, to the surprise of his parents, he was involved in another automobile theft. This time he and several of his comrades worked together, took a car, changed the license plates and other identifying information, kept it hidden in a deserted garage, and took turns driving it.

This boy had what his parents described as a mania for driving cars. They had absolutely forbidden him to drive until he was sixteen and they could not understand why he had this craze to drive. A little investigation disclosed that this boy's urge to drive a car was largely the result of the categorical refusal of his parents when he asked to drive. Their flat denial made driving seem a very real pleasure to him; he spent hours in imagining he was driving, got road maps and planned long trips he would take, hung around garages and watched the mechanics work with cars, all of which whetted his appetite. It seemed to him an eternity to wait until he was old enough. Driving became a sort of compulsion which he could not resist. Here it seems fairly obvious that this boy's intense longing was at least partly the product of the restraining methods used by the parents.

The same principle applies in the case of another boy who had an uncontrollable desire to build fires. This urge dated from the violent reaction of his mother to his first attempt. He would build them in all sorts of places and at all times, day or night. Each time he was caught and punished seemed to increase the fascination that fires had for him. It seemed, from studying the boy, to be pretty obvious that his interest was largely stimulated by the negative form of treatment.

3. *Gratification of secret longings.* Many of us have secret longings to do little things which may be things we have been denied when we were little or which are symbols of those things. One young man had a strange desire to take a hobo trip, a thing which horrified his parents;

but the desire persisted until, at the age of twenty-five, he finally went on such a trip. After that he had no further desire.

One man, otherwise honest, will steal rubber bands and lead pencils. Another will pilfer every book he can lay his hands on. A girl stole money to take taxi rides. Her father had several cars and chauffeurs and she could go anywhere she wanted, but she had a continual longing to ride in taxis. We might go on with this list indefinitely. In truth, nearly every person has some little hidden desire which is totally silly to almost everyone else, but which represents a repressed urge which hangs over him like a shadow and which gets an outlet in strange ways.

A thing is silly or strange only so long as we do not understand it. It seems silly only because we do not know all the facts. For example, one boy of about ten stole other boys' spectacles, field or opera glasses, and lenses of all sorts. Why did he select such things to accumulate? Here is part of the story which explains it. He had been reprimanded by his teachers for doing poor work, especially reading. They had suspected eye difficulty and had his eyes examined, but found no difficulty sufficient to account for his trouble. About the time that most of the visual examinations and excitement about his eyes were in progress, he was very friendly with a boy who was doing excellent work in school but who wore very heavy glasses. These glasses seemed to our patient to stand for success in school, and his stealing of glasses and the accumulation of a collection of lenses of all sorts was a more or less unconscious way of adjustment to his poor school work. Instead of demonstrating a criminal disposition they indicated a very wholesome desire, the wish to overcome what he considered the cause of his trouble—poor vision. By dealing with the fundamental impulse the boy lost all desire to steal and the problem was solved.

4. *Desire for freedom.* Persons who have been unduly repressed in a great many different aspects of life confess that they are continually hemmed in with a feeling of oppression, they feel hampered even when there is no direct inhibiting force which they can point to. If asked to do something the first impulse of these persons is to say, "No, I won't do it." If told to refrain from doing another thing they immediately feel like saying, "I will, too." Especially when left to their own devices they have an urge to do something, they know not what, merely something they know they should not do. They say, "I just must do something or I will burst." Repression is synonymous too often with morality, and freedom with immorality. Hence, such repressed persons feel that they must obtain their freedom through some sort of immorality. They may break loose in some trivial behavior, and this is likely to be the case, but they may also perform some act which has serious consequences. The cause depends upon the same principle whether it is serious or trivial from the social viewpoint. Hence, while safeguarding society, which certainly must be done, the remedy lies in discovering the nature of the underlying repression, the way in which the attitude developed, and from these findings a reëducation program may be instituted.

In the following case it happened that the conduct of the patient had some serious consequences. A young man student in a large university did very good work during the entire fall term, the first year of his attendance at the college in question. For various reasons it was not practicable for him to visit his home during the Christmas vacation, and he was left practically alone in one of the dormitories. One day he built a fire in his room and started down to the shopping area of the town. Fortunately the fire was discovered before it had done much damage; but the possibilities of such an escapade were quite terrifying to the university authorities and the young man was arrested.

In his boyhood this young man had gotten into several escapades, and in each case was so severely reprimanded by his father that he had never repeated any of the breaches of morals in which he was caught. His urge toward morality was the restraint imposed by his father. After his father died he got into a situation which was more immoral than any he had engaged in during his father's life. This time he so keenly felt the need of some strong person upon whom to lean that he hunted up some man in an authoritative position and asked him to see to it that he did not repeat the act. This man acted much as his father had done, threatened him with dire punishment and watched him carefully.

When alone in the dormitory this boy felt an urge to do something; he wished his father or the substitute for his father were there to hold him in check, but since they were not there he felt that he must do something. This feeling grew and grew until it became an uncontrollable compulsion and he lighted the fire. He begged to be placed in the custody of some one who would guard him and force him to do as he should do. Having always been dependent upon other and stronger individuals he felt totally incapable of living a moral life without some one watching his every act. He was paroled to an uncle who agreed to take this responsibility.

In a sense this boy was not much different from those who live a moral life because they are afraid to do otherwise, for the reason that they believe an all-seeing eye is watching their every move, and that they will surely have to pay the penalty for what they do. If they were ever made to believe that they would not be seen or discovered they would most certainly lead very lax lives. Some students have been heard to confess that if they were not certain that they would be punished either in this life or the life to come, they would most certainly lead highly vicious and immoral lives. It may be better for a person to live a moral life under such duress than to lead an immoral one, but this is a poor type of virtue, because it is wholly negative. Certainly the positive principle with which the reader is already familiar is better than the negative avoidance of what will bring punishment. The principle we refer to is: Make it a rule to do those things which will be of positive benefit to yourself and to your fellows.

5. *Direct breaking out of repressed impulse.* If a person fears he has a tendency to do some particular act and at the same time tries to convince himself that he has no such tendency, it is quite likely that the feared behavior will break forth in spite of the attempted repression by the individual. He then builds up a safeguard to support his determination, which may be effective but often is not, because the person has not faced squarely the problem which is involved. The following instance illustrates a situation of this type.

A young man who was preparing for the ministry in a Presbyterian seminary was caught stealing, and caught under very unfortunate circumstances. The stealing in the dormitories had been going on for several months and, in spite of some very clever detective work, the thief had escaped detection. Finally, in desperation, the authorities had the locks changed on all the doors. This young man was selected as the one to make the changes and to take complete charge of the distribution of the new keys. In spite of these precautions, the stealing continued. Finally, it was traced to this young man, and much of the stolen material was found in his possession. When thus caught, he confessed, and was very contrite.

Was this simply a case of a confirmed thief, who entered the seminary to cover his tracks, and to carry on his profession under this added protection? His friends turned against him, and were all too anxious to call him a hypocrite, but their accusations did not solve the problem.

This boy confessed that as a young child he had learned to steal. The wrongs of stealing were so impressed upon him that he determined he would never steal again. With every temptation he endeavored to emphasize his moral qualities as a compensatory balance. His open avowal of religious creeds was an important step in this direction. He could not very well steal when he openly confessed that he was a Christian. In order to add further reënforcement he decided to enter the ministry. His taking up the ministry, instead of being an indication of hypocrisy, was evidence of a profound attempt to escape his temptation. In addition, he married a very fine girl, thus giving himself still more protection. He was so meticulously honest that he was the most trusted man in the dormitory. He did not try to achieve a position of trust in order to steal, but in order to build up his defense against stealing. The implicit trust placed in him, however, merely increased the temptations into which he was thrown, and proved to be his downfall.

6. *Disguise for a worse offense.* In other instances a criminal or lawless act may serve as a smoke screen to hide from the delinquent individual himself as well as from others the possibility of a more heinous offense. We all recognize this as a conscious defense device. A crooked politician often gets the public all stirred up about some minor breach of faith in order to distract their attention from some major graft. If a little boy can get his mother sufficiently excited about his soiled clothes she forgets about the damage his escapade did to the neighbor's car.

In somewhat the same fashion an individual can distract his own attention from some major temptation. He stresses what appears to him to be a minor offense and fails to see that it may be a scheme to hide some more serious temptation. Most crimes of this sort are extremely silly in appearance. A person will steal things which are of absolutely no value to him, will commit the theft in a silly and unintelligent fashion, will confess readily, and usually can give no motive for the crime.

For example, an intelligent boy of fourteen, who had no record of having stolen before, took some articles from the janitor's room in school. They were things for which he had no use—an old rusty razor, some milk checks which the small children used, a pair of pliers, and a couple of towels—he took them home and put them in a closet, took no steps to cover his tracks, and confessed when caught. He could give no reason for taking them, he had no use for them, he could merely say that he felt an impulse to walk off with them and he obeyed this strange feeling.

The motives for this stealing could not be ascertained by direct questioning, for the boy himself did not know. By indirect investigation a conflict of an entirely different sort was discovered which explained his stealing escapades. His mother (he was an only child) was very much afraid that her son would not have the proper respect for girls, and had taken great pains to warn him against the dangers which she imagined were in his pathway. She made her warnings very vivid and actually frightened him thoroughly. In giving him this instruction she used continually an analogy to drive her point home. She compared improper sexual behavior with stealing. The first clue we obtained as to this connection came in a very striking fashion. We were asking him about various things, his comrades, the games he enjoyed, and the like. He was casually asked if he had any girl friends. He grew suddenly tense, drew himself up and almost yelled: "No, I stay away from them. You will never get me stealing a girl." The fact that he used stealing in this connection together with the intense emotion which a very casual question brought forth gave us the clue which proved to be correct. He would not "steal a girl" but he could disguise from himself any such possibility by stealing useless articles in a peculiarly unintelligent fashion.

Stealing happens to be one offense that is often used to cover up more serious temptations. While stealing is condemned, it is condoned more easily than are other offenses, a fact which probably accounts for its use as a smoke screen. For example, married women who may be tempted to indiscretion will live highly respectable lives, but will commit petty thefts from department stores.

Criminal acts may indicate a pernicious attitude. In the acts which we have been considering, where the background is some sort of mental conflict, the outcome is more or less incidental to the main issue, and is often likely to be of an unexpected sort. We shall now consider a type of activity which is more directly the expected outcome of the underlying attitude of the individual. These cases are important because we can see the beginnings of the attitudes which account for them, long before they reach the stage of breaking forth in lawless behavior. It is a mistake to await the final outbreak when the attitude could be changed before that stage is reached.

1. *Hatred.* Hate is an emotion which the human race could well afford to lose. Try to dress it up and disguise it as we will, it nevertheless does much damage. Even such a term as "righteous indignation" will, upon analysis, prove to be but a disguise for an attitude which is anything but righteous.

If the person who entertains this attitude is a young child or if he is lacking in intelligence it is very likely to manifest itself directly and usually in a crude fashion so that any observer can see the hatred behind his behavior. Such cases can be dealt with directly. If a child slaps his mother, punches his brother, throws a book at his teacher, what should be done? Obviously, it is futile to attempt to teach the child the undesirability of the acts he performs. He knows that already, but is in such a rage that he does the first thing which suggests itself. His attitude toward his mother, brother, or teacher needs to be changed. This accomplished, his overt acts will take care of themselves.

The intelligent and mature man does not vent his

hate in such obvious forms. He is very likely to work
out elaborate schemes for getting his revenge on his
enemy, schemes which it may take years to carry out
successfully. Isn't the fundamental attitude of hate just
as important in such elaborate plans as in the explosive
actions of the little boy? Instead of viewing the situation in such an analytical fashion we are likely to be so
interested in the devices which are used that we neglect
the fundamental factors.

The earliest signs of this attitude are the daydreams
in which the little boy pictures his revenge upon the
teacher or the playmates who have wronged him. Sometimes these take concrete form in deadfalls, pits, or traps
which he constructs with great care and watches with
delight for his enemy to fall victim to. The so-called
practical joke is very often based on hate, although it
is disguised behind a form of specious humor. The girl
who, when asked to narrate the funniest thing that she
had experienced during the preceding year, told how
she had seen a man fall off a hayrack and get run over
by a car which was following the hayrack, certainly
evidenced a pernicious attitude toward life. Whenever
we glory in the downfall or the discomfiture of another
we are manifesting that we have a streak of hate in our
make-up. It is but a short step from enjoying the misfortunes of another when we had nothing to do with his
affairs to the place where we actively engage ourselves
in seeing to it that misfortune does come his way. Even
such a trivial thing as laughing at slapstick comedy evidences a small degree of hatred in the person who laughs.

Carried to more extreme lengths we find persons who
will devote the major portion of their lives retaliating
for a real or fancied wrong. They justify their conduct

by imagining that they are doing the Deity a favor in helping him punish those who justly deserve it. A recent news account narrated how a woman had been killed by her stepdaughter, who confessed that she had followed her stepmother for twenty years, waiting for an opportunity to punish her for whipping her when she was a little girl. One man studied for years in order to learn to play poker with sufficient skill to beat an enemy who was an expert poker player. Having learned to beat him he placed him in a position where it was easy to borrow some of his employer's money to pay his debts. Having started this little game he kept it up until the man had stolen a considerable sum and then set a trap so that he would be caught.

According to our courts such conduct is not criminal. According to the mental hygiene viewpoint it is the most heinous sort of crime that could well be imagined. Deliberately to set about to ruin a man in such a despicable fashion is certainly worse than absconding with funds; yet the law will condone with the former and punish the latter.

This type of hatred becomes still more significant and dangerous when the one who harbors it is ignorant of its true nature. He will disguise even from himself the hate he feels for the other person, and will even deceive himself into thinking that he really loves his victim, and that his cruel acts are really acts of kindness.

How subtly a person can hurt another is illustrated in the following incident. With tears in her eyes Esther, a girl of twenty, told how she had tried in vain to save her sister Maud, aged twenty-five, from a terrible sorrow. Maud had been receiving attentions from a man for several years whom Esther was sure was an evil influence. She had tried to warn Maud over and over again, but to no avail; the more she told her of the man's evil ways the more Maud seemed to increase her devotion for him. The climax had been reached when the man had made some improper suggestions to Esther. She pondered for a long time what she would do, and finally determined to tell her sister. To her amazement, when she did, Maud flew into a violent rage, told Esther that she was a vile, evil-minded person, and that she was trying her best to ruin her chance for happiness. She even accused Esther of tempting the man and then blaming him for what was her own fault. Esther was apparently much hurt by this ingratitude. After going through all she had in her attempt to help her darling sister, that is the thanks she got!

The truth of the situation was that Maud had an inkling of Esther's real motive, and for that reason was incensed with her bungling attempts to save her from the wiles of the supposedly bad man. Early in her life Esther had felt that Maud was the favored child, that she was always regarded as a good girl, while she, Esther, was considered bad and relatively worthless. She developed a hatred for her sister which she thought she had conquered, and her present attitude was one of extreme devotion. The hate persisted, in spite of the apparent love, and she was doing all these supposed acts of kindness with the underlying motive of spoiling her sister's chance for happiness. After seeing through this situation, Esther admitted that the supposed "advances" of the man were largely her imagination, and that what he had done was at her instigation.

The most dangerous form of conduct is the act which is apparently an act of kindness but which is motivated by an unconscious hatred. Beware of any kind act which brings suffering to the one upon whom it is bestowed. It is probably a disguised act of hate.

2. *Suspicion.* The attitude of suspicion is second only to hate as an incentive to do injury to others. We have already seen how suspicion may lead to the development of delusions of persecution. In such cases the object of these delusions is feared to such an extent that the deluded person may be tempted to retaliate or even to murder him. Where the suspicion has some ground in reality the attitude may be somewhat the same. The tormenting idea that another person is involved in schemes to encompass one's downfall can lead to but two reactions. Either one must retreat and protect oneself from the threatening danger, or he can take active steps to defend himself.

Such aggressive behavior is likely to be performed under a high degree of emotional excitement, it is likely to seem justified as a measure of self-defense, and it will have a moral flavor because the acts of the other person will be regarded as evil.

The first type of non-social behavior which grows from suspicion is spying. In some forms spying is not subject to punishment. The ordinary "stool pigeon" is usually within the law. On the other hand, an international spy is subject to the death sentence. Whether he comes within the law or not, no one has any respect for anyone who gains information in underhand ways and uses it to gain a personal advantage or to wreak vengeance on an enemy. The best way to make enemies and to lose friends is to become a spy and a talebearer.

Spying is, it should be understood, the smallest of the ills that may result from suspicion. The spying is merely a device to obtain evidence to justify the suspicions. Evidence gathered in this fashion must be biased and unsound. A scientist knows that he cannot be too anxious to verify an hypothesis or he will be prejudiced in his search for evidence. He will tend to notice every item which corroborates his hypothesis and will, in spite of himself, fail to see that which contradicts his hypothesis. If this is true with a scientist, who actually tries to overcome his bias, how much more so will it be with a person who is overanxious, because of his suspicion, to find evidence that the suspected person is guilty.

Having found what he conceives to be valid evidence that the suspected person is guilty, the fear in the mind of the suspicious person grows; he magnifies the possibilities of harm that may come to him until he arrives at a veritable panic of fear. He feels that he must do something, yet he must keep his plans to himself lest his enemy learn of his objective and outwit him.

He hides his suspicions more carefully the surer he becomes that they are founded in fact, lays his plans carefully and springs some trap upon his victim. Some of the most well-planned murders are committed by persons dominated by the attitude of suspicion. A man who is open in his attitude, who fights directly, will give some indication of his attitude before he gets to the point of committing violence. The suspicious person in the very nature of affairs gives no clue as to his attitude, unless he should go to the other extreme in his attempts to cover his tracks, and, for this reason, is often the very last person to be suspected when the crime is discovered.

In view of the carefulness with which the suspicious person conceals his attitude, is it possible to discover such attitudes in time to change them? Must we wait until a crime is actually committed before discovering this dangerous viewpoint?

A good way to determine whether a person tends to be suspicious is to get him to express his attitude about others. When a man accuses other persons of being sneaky, of suspecting his fellows, of devising plots to exploit others, or of being too secretive, it is fairly good evidence that he is disclosing the manner in which he himself feels. If, when such a person is found, provided he is discovered early enough, he is placed in positions which will reënforce his confidence in other persons, his suspicions may be laid. It would do little or no good to attempt to argue with such a person in an attempt to change his attitude. The attitude is built upon distrust and can only be overcome by building up, through experience, a feeling of trust.

3. *Egocentricity.* To be sure, there is a large element of self-centeredness in both hate and suspicion, and it may be that this selfish aspect is what makes those people so dangerous. In some cases we can have attitudes in which the selfish aspect is the most significant element. How far can selfishness, in and of itself, lead to non-social behavior? Presumably one can be self-centered and still do no particular harm to his fellows, but when the selfishness goes to such an extreme that the rights of others mean practically nothing as compared with the wants of the selfish person, all sorts of misdemeanors may result.

For example, a young man who had been idolized by athletic fans because of his achievements in this field, who had been pampered by his parents who told him that he was a genius, and who had been practically subsidized by business men, developed an extremely pernicious viewpoint on life. If he saw a tie which he liked he would proceed to take it, no matter who owned it, and would be apparently hurt if the owner objected. Such things are, as is well known, rather common among young students. With this boy, that was just the beginning. He walked off with a chair belonging to another student; he took books, pens, blankets, suits of clothes, and even a raccoon coat. This seemed to be going a little too far even for an athletic genius, and they began to protest. The genius did not deny having taken the things, but he could not see why any of them should object to his appropriating them. He did not even deem it necessary to present the customary excuse that he merely had borrowed them. He admitted that he had taken them, that he had no intention of returning them, and could not see why they objected. Was he not a great man? They should be honored to have their clothes worn and their belongings appropriated by so great a man. Did not business men outdo each other in getting royal visitors to this country to ride in their cars, to wear their clothes, to eat at their cafés, to occupy rooms at their hotels, and to accept the keys to their cities? He really felt injured that they did not appreciate him.

This may sound humorous were it not for the fact that the young man was serious in his contention. He would consume as much as an hour's time telling anyone who would listen how remarkable he was. Such discourses usually ended only when the patience of his listener was exhausted.

Not being content to express his egocentric attitude in such congenial quarters as the college dormitory, he carried it to the outside world and got into trouble. If he needed a tire he took it from the nearest car, much as he would take a tie from his roommate's wardrobe.

Intrigued by the whistle on an electric locomotive he proceeded to take one, and needing a storage battery to run the horn he appropriated one from a battery station. When arrested he took on an aggrieved air and could not understand why he should be so mistreated.

This attitude, of course, one recognizes as the philosophy of the person who believes that the world owes him a living and he sets out to collect. It pervades many phases of life and does a great deal of damage both openly and under cover of very sublime rationalizations.

QUESTIONS

1. Take each of the acts of the woman described at the beginning of the chapter and see if it cannot be duplicated by persons who are considered normal.
2. If it is not a single act which makes this woman seem peculiar, what is it?
3. Which word would you say best characterized her behavior? Immoral, capricious, unintelligent, selfish, uncontrolled.
4. What distinguishes a wholesome personality from a psychopathic personality?
5. What is common sense?
6. What is meant by a unified or integrated personality?
7. What two situations may account for lack of common sense?
8. On what grounds can we infer that the psychopathic personality lacks proper training?
9. What type of faulty training is usually found in psychopathic personalities?
10. What other results could come from the same type of defective training—some that have been previously studied?
11. Describe the attitude of psychopathic personalities toward other persons.
12. Why is it a poor attitude to expect others to take the brunt of your mistakes?
13. How can such an attitude be cured?

14. Why does not a psychopathic personality often find himself committed to a hospital for the insane?

15. Why cannot criminality be defined according to the kind of act committed?

16. Why is repetition of offense not a good criterion of crime?

17. Show how the same act might spring from diverse motives.

18. How should the use of the term criminal be limited?

19. Summarize the arguments to show that the term criminal should not be applied to persons.

20. What is meant by retaliation theory of crime?

21. Put in your own words White's theory that the criminal is a scapegoat.

22. What damage results from treating the crime instead of the criminal?

23. Why should not the insanity plea be used to exonerate a man?

24. Can you say that a man who injures his fellows is in ill-health mentally?

25. Where should the treatment of crime begin?

26. In what way do persons who violate the rights of others differ from normal individuals?

27. Describe how fear may make an innocent man break the law.

28. What conclusions can you draw about the limitations of fear to enforce lawfulness?

29. Show how deprivation may lead to breaking a law.

30. Give some illustrations of stealing to gratify some secret longing.

31. Show how a longing for something worthy may lead to a criminal act.

32. What wrong associations are often connected with repression and freedom?

33. How may such associations lead to criminal acts?

34. Show the ill-effects of morality which is based solely on the fear of breaking a law.

35. Show how battling a temptation may merely increase the strength of that temptation.

36. How can one crime be used as a screen for worse crimes?

37. Describe how such a screen may be used unconsciously.

38. What offense is most often used to cover worse impulses?

39. What differences in treatment should be used when an offense is based on an attitude rather than some accidental situation?

40. Why is it important to get the attitude behind an act?

41. What differences exist between a child and a grown man in the manifestations of hate?

42. How does hate begin?

43. What are some customary reactions of the child to hate?

44. Show how hate may lead to conduct which is not criminal, but which is pernicious, nevertheless.

45. Show how hate may work unconsciously.

46. Describe how an act which is apparently a kindly act may be a malicious one.

47. What characteristic of suspicion makes it so pernicious?

48. Why is it that spying does not allay suspicion?

49. What is likely to be the outcome of nurtured suspicions?

50. What is a good method to use to determine whether a person is suspicious?

51. Does egocentricity necessarily lead to criminality? Why or why not?

52. What kinds of unsocial acts does the egocentric person tend to commit?

CHAPTER XI

OVERCOMING EMOTIONAL DEPRESSIONS

A little four-year-old boy who had been playing in his yard, after considerable difficulty, wriggled through a hole in the fence, ran to the stream which ran along the far side of the pasture, and then settled down to play along its edge. He soon became so engrossed in his mud pies that he became careless of his footing, stepped upon a mossy stone, slipped, and fell full-length into the water. As he fell he scratched his arm on a bush beside the water's edge.

Without uttering a sound he scrambled out, looked himself over, and gravely started toward the house. He reached the hole in the fence, squirmed through, and as he ran toward the house, began screaming with great vigor. His pain, grief, fear, or whatever it was he felt, seemed to begin the moment he reëntered the yard and, consequently, within hearing distance of his mother.

His mother ran to the rescue of her darling boy, petting and comforting him with great enthusiasm. The more she soothed him the more violent became his convulsive sobs. Finally, from sheer exhaustion he subsided, the spasms became less frequent, and he settled down to change his clothes and to wash the few blood stains from his arm.

After you have finished laughing at this little boy, and after you have decided that he was simply crying to get his mother's petting, or that he was doing it to divert her attention so that she would not punish him for leaving the yard, look at yourself and you will probably recall instances where, even as an adult, you have been guilty of similar conduct.

If you recall an incident where you really had occasion to be grieved, and if your emotion was true grief, it may still cause the tears to start to think about it. On the other hand, if you used some minor misfortune as an excuse for self-pity you should take your supposed sorrow no more seriously than you take the weeping of the little boy.

Value of grief. When is one justified in being grieved? Grief has an important function in life and if that function is clearly understood we are not likely to let it be supplanted by self-pity—which may do us harm.

When you lose your money, when your job disappears in thin air, when your best friend dies, when you discover that your plans cannot materialize, when your confidence in other persons is shaken by the perfidy of some one you trusted; when any of these things happen you must change your course to make allowance for the unexpected misfortunes. You would prefer to go on the way you have been doing, but you cannot. Things are different—you must stop, you must change your plans, evolve a new philosophy of life, get a new ambition, or adjust to the loneliness which the loss of your loved one requires. Just how you will do this you cannot be sure; the blow is so sudden that you cannot adjust in a moment. You need time to think, to get your bearings. Grief is merely the name for the emotion you feel so long as you are in this state of dazed indecision. Grief, then, is a characteristic of the enforced inactivity which has resulted from some sudden, unwelcome, and unexpected change in your affairs. Its intensity is usually in proportion to the violence of the shock, and to the extent to which you must change your outlook on life.

True grief has an important function in life. It incites us to efforts to escape the discomfort which goes with it. This discomfort is a valuable spur to us to do something. We wish to escape our unhappiness and, consequently, look about us for some new adjustment. If it were not for the urge which arises from the unpleasantness of grief many of us would never readjust our lives when misfortune does come our way. We might succumb to inactivity and permit life to swallow us up instead of fighting back.

Distinction between grief and self-pity. If grief fails to perform its essential function, if it is unable to drive us on to a readjustment, we may find ourselves developing a chronic grief. Such grief may seem so much less painful than the prospect of facing life that we put all our attention upon the way we feel. We nurse our feelings instead of effecting a readjustment. If we were honest we would be forced to admit that this is a weak and childish way to respond to the unexpected misfortune, so we adopt a clever way of being weak and childish and still maintaining our self-esteem. We magnify the trouble which has befallen us. We picture to ourselves the extreme happiness of which we have been deprived. We contrast with this the terrible plight in which we find ourselves, and do all we can to increase the contrast. We tell ourselves and our friends that we need pity. If they agree that we need it, we use this as a justification of our contention that we deserve pity.

In short, self-pity is merely an excuse, a device to enable us to escape from the fight of life. The search for sympathy from others is often an attempt to gain support for our weakness and to justify our self-pity.

Cycles of elation and depression. Life never runs on an even keel for long periods. For a time our work may be crowned with success but there will be periods of relatively poor accomplishment if not actual failure to progress at all. In some individuals the periods of success may predominate while in others the periods of failure may be the longer, but that there will be changes one may rest assured.

The moods of a person, of course, tend to follow the trend of achievement. Periods of great achievement will be accompanied by emotional elation, great activity, and productive and active thinking. Periods of great depression will give rise to emotional depression, inactivity, and slow and confused thinking. It is quite natural for a man to be happy when he is making money and quite natural for him to be depressed when he is losing it. A wedding spreads joy, while a funeral engenders sorrow.

So long as these movements of elation and depression are consistent with the actual success and failure of the individual they are normal and wholesome. The mood merely indicates that the person is meeting the objective situations in the most fitting manner. When things are going smoothly one must be active and alert to keep up with the tide. When things have gone badly one needs to stop for breath and to get his bearings before making a fresh attack on the problems which confront him. The cause for the changes in mood lies in the external objective events of life and when this is the case the moods are wholesome even though they may be quite variable.

A danger arises when you turn your attention from the objective conditions, toward which you should be directing your efforts, to your own feelings and moods.

To be sure, in any case, you are aware of your moods, but they should be secondary and should not be cultivated for their own sake. If, during a period of success, you turn your attention to your happiness, you will work up an artificial elation, will fan it to feverish heat, attempting at the same time to keep your objective activities up to the level of your happiness, and thus lose your grip on the essential problems which confront you. Having lost your judgment because of your interest in your own happiness, you begin to make mistakes and precipitate a worse failure than would have been the case had you kept your head.

Having paved the way for failure because of your devotion to your own happiness, you lose your grip on objective problems and things go to smash—your feelings of happiness with the rest. Since you have taught yourself, during the period of success, to bask in your own feelings, you again place too much interest in your feelings when you are failing. You overdo your feelings of depression and, instead of placing the emphasis upon clear thinking, you use all your energy in being emotionally depressed.

Furthermore, you exaggerate your manifestation of grief in order to "save your face," just as the little boy who fell into the stream "saved his face" by yelling to gain his mother's sympathy. He was to blame for wandering from the yard, but he escaped censure by claiming the pity of his mother. You probably were indiscreet in your excessive zeal in periods of success, but you escape the feelings of remorse and the condemnation of your friends by pitying yourself and claiming their sympathy.

What is the solution? First, it is well to recognize that life is ever changing. If you are successful you will in-

evitably encounter periods of less success. If you are failing you will reach a time when you will be more successful. Failure to recognize and to act upon this principle
of life is as foolish as for a sailor to assume that the skies
will continue to be clear forever merely because they are
clear today, or to fear that there will be storms eternally
because he is now in the midst of one. Success and failure
follow upon each other as inevitably as night and day,
although they do not come with the same regularity.

In the second place, if you have recognized this changing nature of life, keep your eye upon objective events so
that you can adjust to them instead of attempting to
adjust to the way you feel about things. Enjoy the
weather—yes; but do not forget how to trim your sails
when the storms come.

If you take the fighting attitude toward the struggles of
life you will never be beaten. "The trouble with Bill is,"
remarked a business man, "that he never knows when he
is licked. He gets an awful drubbing, but bounces back
like a rubber ball, with a whole bundle of new tricks and
with unbounded energy to try them out. He acts as
though he were enjoying life just as much when he is
getting the worst of it as when he is on top of the world."

A man is never whipped so long as he keeps fighting,
and he will continue to fight, and enjoy it, so long as he
keeps his attention fixed on the objective factors in the
struggle instead of his own happiness or unhappiness.

Feelings of failure. Whining when things do not go
right is the defense mechanism of the weakling. The
fighter does not expect to stay on the peak of success continually; he learns to enjoy a ride on the toboggan as
well as the climbing up the mountain. It makes little
difference whether one is on the top or the bottom, whether

he is climbing up or sliding down so long as he is alive to
the situation and maintains his control and poise through
it all.

If one succumbs to the temptation to be subjective
instead of objective he is sure to develop feelings of
futility and failure no matter what his objective situation
may be. If he is having success he looks ahead with foreboding and if he is failing he becomes excessively despondent. He develops an outlook on life which is sure to kill
all his initiative. He wishes to escape reality because he
has not learned the fun of facing it.

In other words, the causes for the feeling of failure are
to be found in the attitude of the individual rather than
in the objective circumstances upon which he and his
friends may try to fix the blame. Two men lose their
earthly possessions; one fights on, and the other whines.
Two women lose their husbands; one makes a readjustment, while the other devotes the remainder of her life
wishing that she might join him. The same conflict may
lead to an heroic attempt to adjust in one person; it may
lead to a mental disease in another; it may result in a complete surrender or a silly wish to leave this life in still
another. If we examine the different forms that the feeling of futility takes in different persons we will discover
the same fundamental principle in all of them.

As everyone knows, the great danger in the feeling of
futility and in emotional depressions is that the victim,
in a fit of despondency, may go so far as to attempt to
end his life. If the reasons for such despondencies can
be understood this danger may be avoided in many instances, and, even in mild cases where such an outcome
would never occur, an understanding may lead to a more
wholesome outlook upon life.

Forms of emotional depression. First let us examine some of the forms that emotional depressions may take and then we can study the specific reasons for their development.

1. *The unidentified craving.* Anxiety is a very painful feeling. It may be backed by some indefinite fear or some wish which is hostile to the ideals of the individual. This latter condition leads to a fear that one may violate his moral codes. He does not know just what he wants, what moral code he may violate; he can tell you nothing specific about it, but he knows he is unhappy, afraid, and beset with worries. These vague worries are not as likely to lead to a violent emotional depression as the complaints of the worrier might lead one to believe, but sometimes they do, as is evidenced by the vagueness of the reasons given by some individuals for their extreme depression.

One person writes: "I am consumed with a great urge to fulfil my destiny. I have some mission to fulfil but am unable to measure up to this call when hampered by fleshly limitations. I seem to be hemmed in by clouds so that I have lost my vision of the future and all life seems so futile to me now. Life once promised me so much. Yes, I have work, a home, loved ones; but these are so unsatisfying." All these are extremely tenuous reasons for becoming extremely depressed, but this person could give no more specific ones.

There is evidence that these seemingly vague impulses are based on specific experiences which have been repressed and forgotten by the victim of them. They have submerged the specific events but have retained the emotional tone which went with them. They know not what they fear, but the fear is real to them nevertheless. It is the fact that the reason for the anxiety is repressed that makes such cases so difficult to deal with.

2. *Feelings of futility.* A very severe failure, or a series
of minor failures following upon the heels of each other,
may induce a feeling of failure which is so striking that
the victim of these events may drift into a very despondent
mood.

One girl of about thirty, after working for five years in
a very fine position where her work was praised very
highly, was forced to resign because the president's daughter needed the job. She secured a second position but
lost it in a few weeks. With little difficulty she secured
a third but lost that one in a week. Despondency gripped
her. What was the use, she complained; she could not
get along with anyone, her parents had taught her to
shun people, her efficient work had not seemingly been
of much value, she was too old to learn to make friends;
what was the use? However, after nursing her dejection
for a time, she became more lively, got another job in
which she made good, and she recovered her grip on herself.

Sometimes a failure which appears to be trivial leads
to the deepest dejection. For example, if a girl has failed
in love and has taken up teaching as a substitute, she is
likely to place far too much emphasis upon her success
in teaching. Should the principal criticise her in the slightest particular she feels that she is a total failure and wants
to quit. If it were simply a failure to please this principal
she could easily adjust to it. Instead, she argues to herself: "I have failed in love; I gave up all hope of ever being happy but hoped to forget in my teaching. Now, I
have failed in my teaching. I must be a total failure."
Thus, because of a seemingly trivial reprimand, she develops a case of the "blues."

It is well to find something with which to console ourselves when we are disappointed, but it is well to recognize the fact that such consolations are always greatly overvalued.

3. *Self-pity*. In a great many instances the victim of a depression is a self-centered man who takes himself much too seriously. Thinking that the universe revolves around him, his failure looms to tremendous proportions, and he begins to feel sorry for himself and for the universe as well. The objective man takes his defeats as well as his victories as part of a game and views them as passing incidents. His joy or his grief may be real, but they do not stop with himself. They lead to further activity of a wholesome sort. The egocentric person, on the other hand, is glad for himself when he succeeds, or pities himself when he fails.

Since he regards himself as an important part of the universe in general, he believes others must pity him also. As he looks around he discovers, sadly enough, that they do not pity him. They appear to be about as much absorbed in their own interests as he is in his. They do not appreciate him. How can he make them see his importance? He tries to appear unfortunate in their eyes and, if unable actually to impress them, he may spend much time imagining how sorry they would be were he to be the victim of some accident. They would then regret their lack of consideration for him; they would mourn his loss and appreciate his importance. He visualizes his mother, his father, his relatives, his friends, and even his enemies gathered around his casket weeping bitter tears over his loss. He delights in imagining their awakening to the fact that he was an abused and neglected individual.

All such imaginings and the self-pity which is the foundation of them are very infantile. They indicate that one has not developed very far in his social emotions. A better social adjustment is the only permanent cure for self-pity.

4. *Thwartings.* Some adults have never outgrown the childish refrain: "If I cannot win I won't play at all." If they see themselves playing a losing game they become depressed. In a child this attitude appears foolish, in some grown individuals it is also ridiculous, in others it is disguised as a lofty moral standard. Whether an extreme depression appears to be noble or idiotic, it is usually a variation of the same inability to lose with a good grace. To be sure, one does not want to lose all the time, but neither should he expect to win all the time.

Thwarting is never sufficient justification for a severe depression. The person who becomes depressed because of thwarting alone is like the little boy who, when he found that a door would not open on the first trial, screamed at the top of his lungs and threw himself on the floor in a veritable tantrum.

These persons who go to pieces because of some simple thwarting often manifest the false notion that if they cannot have what they want they have somehow been cheated. They loudly proclaim that they have been "disillusioned," and take on an air of sophistication. This unfortunate reaction on their part is due to the fact that they had their eyes fixed on a certain goal and, because they failed to attain that specific thing, can see no value in anything else. Those who act in this fashion are like little children who get their minds set on obtaining a certain piece of candy and will move heaven and earth to get it.

Attitudes of outsiders toward the depressed person. When the reason attributed for the depression seems trivial to us we scoff at the foolishness of the person who indulges in it.   When the reason involves something which we evaluate highly we are more inclined to credit the reason. For example, when a girl becomes despondent because she has an incurable skin infection on her face, when she has acquired a loathsome disease, when she has been indiscreet and is being made to suffer social ostracism because of the intolerance of her neighbors— in any of these cases we are likely to feel that the load is too much for her to bear. We feel that the depression is not overdone and that she needs our sympathy and any help that we may be able to give her.

In some cases the depression which the individual is experiencing seems to be the result of his own ill-considered acts; and then outsiders tend to gloat over him, saying that his suffering is a just retribution for his sins. Especially if we were injured by his activity are we likely to be pleased to see him suffer.

Whether we are inclined to laugh at the depressed person, whether we are likely to pity him, or whether we are pleased that he is being paid for his injuries to us, these are not the important elements in the situation. The essential need is for him to become more objective and less involved in his own emotions. If we are the outsiders we can do the most good when we keep our feelings to ourselves, and do the things to make the depressed person more objective. If we are the person with the "blues" we can help ourselves by avoiding those persons who have any feeling about our situation, one way or the other, and cultivate those who stimulate us to objective activity.

Causes of feelings of failure. It should be apparent that excessive emotional depressions are centered largely

around the feelings of failure which grip certain individuals. We are justified in branding these excessive depressions as menaces to human welfare. We should be anxious
to discover what gives rise to them, and to use this knowledge to eliminate them. However, we shall learn that we
can make little progress by attempting to deal with the
depression directly. We must get behind the depression
to the situation which caused it, and we shall find feelings
of failure to be the central core of the difficulty.

Feelings of failure should not be confused with the
popular inferiority feelings. The latter are often real
incentives to achievement. Feelings of failure are the
hopeless depressions which govern the individual when
he is absolutely certain that there is no further use in
trying. He does not feel inferior—he is sure he is beaten.
Let us examine some of the causes for the feeling of
failure.

1. *Excessive zeal.* A frequent forerunner of an emotional depression is a burst of unwarranted zeal. As the
school year was nearing a close, Earl F. was overtaken by
an extreme emotional depression. He sat inertly, staring
into space, oblivious to his surroundings, and apparently
very much dejected. Only eight months before he had
entered college with an enthusiasm and a display of
unbounded energy which had been the envy of his classmates for months. He worked hard at his studies, entered
all extra-curricular activities into which he could worm
his way, and seemed to have not a care in the world.
Why this change? About a month before the complete
break he had shown the beginnings of a different attitude.
He became listless, indifferent to his school work, talked
despondently, and proclaimed loudly that the year had
been a failure. As a matter of fact, it had been anything

but a failure as far as objective measures of his success were concerned.

The reason for this situation was not difficult to find. He had come from a home of limited means; his father had opposed his entering college on the grounds that it was a waste of time, a place for wealthy boys to play, filled with lazy individuals who would ruin his son. This opposition merely whetted Earl's appetite to go to college, and he had contrived with great difficulty to get enough money to enter.

Some of the money he had borrowed and he felt that he owed it to those who had backed him to make the best use of his time. This desire to make good, to "show" his father, to merit the help he had received, all conspired to drive him on with a feverish zeal, and he overexerted himself. Toward the end of the year he became physically fatigued, could not sleep at nights, worried about the coming examinations, speculated as to what people would say should he fail, and through all this worked himself to a morbid pitch of excitement which ended in the feeling of futility and depression.

The person who works with a feverish zeal which taxes his powers beyond their capacity, especially if he worries along with his work, is headed for an emotional depression. We are so imbued with the urge for efficiency and accomplishment that such persons are encouraged and praised, with seldom any recognition that the zeal might be an indication of some unnatural drive. It may be a bad sign when a person manifests feverish zeal.

2. *Fixed ideas.* "Don't be a quitter." It makes no difference what you start, we are told by certain moral advisers, never give up until you have accomplished what you set out to do. Some of us may need such encourage-

ment so that we will not give up when a small amount of opposition faces us. There are some persistent individuals, on the other hand, who persist for reasons which should be understood, and who get into difficulty, and encourage failure for themselves because of this unreasonable persistence.

We see the beginnings of this in the tiny child when he screams for an interminable period for some toy or a piece of candy upon which he has set his heart. Offer him great rewards as a substitute, and he still persists in his silly demands for the piece of candy. He has so overvalued it, at least temporarily, that he loses all sense of values and sees no worth in anything else.

Such behavior seems idiotic to the sophisticated adult who looks on, but it is not so different from various things which the adult may take very seriously. He sets his heart on a certain girl, and because he cannot get her becomes morbidly depressed, and thinks life is a total failure. There are millions of other boys who do not have her affection, and they do not desire to give up all hope for that reason. Why is she so valuable to him and not to the others? Merely because he has the fixed idea that he wants her.

If you should walk through the wards of a hospital for mental diseases and make a list of the various reasons that persons give to explain why they are depressed you would find a rather ludicrous assemblage of paltry desires which have been frustrated. They have trifling value to the observer but are of extreme worth to the one who cherishes them. It is this overestimation that makes them important.

When you set your heart too fixedly on the attainment of any one thing you are headed for a possible emotional depression. The way to avoid danger of such a depression is to be sure to achieve the objective you set for yourself or to refrain from being too set on that particular goal. Goals stimulate a person to activity, but if the goal is too rigidly defined it offers a threat of depression should one be unable to get it. It is good emotional insurance to refrain from being too fixed in your ambitions.

3. *Feeling of moral guilt.* Probably nothing builds up a feeling of despair quite so effectively as the feeling that one has made some irretrievable error. Sometimes there are intangible acts such as "sinning against the Holy Ghost" or "profaning a hidden law."

In other cases it is some concrete act which has been overvalued by uninformed moral teachers or by charlatans who reap a harvest by playing upon the fears of credulous boys and girls.

A very intelligent and successful business man consulted his physician to discover whether he was losing his mental balance. After the examination was completed and he was assured that his mental processes were perfectly normal, that he had no diseases of any sort, and that his nervous system functioned perfectly, he still appeared somewhat hesitant to leave and finally said: "Are you sure? In spite of your reassurance I am still mortally afraid of insanity. If I am all right why do I have this awful dread of it? Cannot you help me get rid of the fear? I might as well be insane as to suffer all this tormenting fear of it."

After an extensive study it was found that this man's apparent fear of insanity was a symbol of a feeling of guilt which he had carried with him from his boyhood. He had been told that if he manipulated certain parts of his body he would lose his mind. Having done this, he was filled with a dread of the consequences. He was assured by his physician that such acts never caused insanity, that these stories were circulated by ignorant enthusiasts or patent-medicine quacks, and that he need have no fears on that score. When he was able to believe implicitly the statements of his physician his depression and suicidal impulses vanished.

It is a mistake to teach a young person that any act has fixed and unchangeable consequences. Any act is but one part of a vast complex set of events which in turn fit in with a never-ending succession of intricate patterns. It makes no difference what an act is, it may be modified in its effectiveness by subsequent acts.

Combating depressions. Two little children were playing on the beach one day when a big wave knocked them both down. One sat where he had been deposited by the wave, and cried and cried. The other little child no sooner hit the ground than he was up, running away from the wave, yelling in great glee. Having been knocked down he did not wait for fate to pick him up. He picked himself up.

These two children grew up and both met adversity. They were about to enter college when their father died and left them penniless. The first boy bemoaned his fate, gave up the thought of a college training, took an inferior position, and throughout the remainder of his life complained about being cheated by the death of his father just at the time when he needed him most. The other boy was merely incited to greater zeal by the penniless condition in which he found himself. He worked his way through college and has become a successful business man. The first boy had learned the habit of failure; the second boy had learned the habit of fighting.

Now, the moralist may point to the latter person as an example of the way we should all act; but what if one finds that he is in the class with the depression tendency? Suppose one likes to pity himself, to seek sympathy from others, and to take every misfortune as an excuse for laziness, failure, or even suicide. How can one get over such a tendency?

1. *Build up a good physique.* There is nothing that will kill an emotional depression quite so effectively as bubbling physical energy. A robust man is stimulated to fight when he encounters a difficulty, while the weakling is inclined to yield to the slightest opposition. Having once started on the road to discouragement various things conspire to make a fight more difficult. The discouraged man will sit in an inert posture, his digestive processes will be retarded due to the emotional tension, the processes of elimination will be disturbed, and as a result poisons will be sent through the body instead of being cast off. All these things tend to make him physically weak and even ill. Having suffered some disappointment, and then having added to it physical flabbiness or pain, it is no wonder that the depression grows to enormous proportions. He exaggerates his misfortune to fit his feelings of physical weakness, and so the process goes on in a vicious cycle; the physical weakness accentuating his feelings of depression, and the depression increasing his physical ill-health.

In mental hospitals and sanitaria where these persons have been given careful study it has been discovered that the first essential is to build up their physique. They are given treatments to eliminate the poisons in their systems; they are given good food, sunshine and, as soon as they are physically capable of it, are given work and exercises to stimulate the bodily processes. It is surprising how often recovery from the emotional depression comes with the restoration of physical stamina.

If this works in hospitals with severe cases how much more effective it is when practiced by individuals with minor spells of the blues!

A very definite explanation of this relation of the blues with physical vigor is found in the nature of the emotional depression. Such an emotion causes a slowing of the action of the stomach and intestines. This tends to make poor digestion so that less value is obtained from one's food. The intestines do not function properly, the victim tends to become constipated, and poisons which should have been eliminated are spread through the body. Practically every case of emotional depression is accompanied by constipation.

Now, it is easier to give a person a hot bath, a cathartic, a good meal, a game of golf or tennis, and plenty of sunshine than it is to attempt to talk him out of his trouble or to cajole him into thinking that his trouble is "not as bad as it might have been."

The slightest spell of the blues is a signal to do something to improve your physical health, even though the cause of the blues may be something quite definite. In fact, it would be a very good plan if you used any misfortune, any bad news, as a signal to take extra precautions concerning your body. If you did you would find that you do not have the blues. The trouble is that most of us do not have the "sand" to act in such a manner. It is so much easier to slump and to "enjoy our depression," to pity ourselves. Consequently, each one of us should have a friend whose business it is to see that we do use extra precautions at the first sign of discouragement. He would be a much more valuable friend than the one who sits you down and says, "Tell me all about it," and joins you in a melancholy duet to the accompaniment of tears. When you begin to get blue you do not need anyone to weep with you. You need some one to make you build up enough physical reserve so that you can "take it." Depression and physical weakness go together, as do hope and physical vigor.

2. *Learn the true value of events.* In only a small proportion of instances have those who become depressed failed in any real sense. They have centered their attention upon some minor phase of life, have decided that failure in this small sphere will be a true measure of their limitations, and thus come to overvalue its significance. Recovery from a depression involves, consequently, the restoration of a balanced perspective.

For example, a girl of twenty-four became very much depressed because, as she expressed it, she was a quitter. Viewed by an impartial observer she would not have been judged to be a quitter, but from her narrowed perspective she condemned herself as an individual with no persistence or stamina. She had been an honor student all through college. She had been president of her class, had been editor of the school paper for two years, and was chief of the editorial staff for the senior year-book. All these offices she held with honor to herself and to the satisfaction of all those concerned. After graduating she returned to her home in a small town and spent nearly a year in idleness because she could find no occupation to her liking. During this period of idleness her mother continually urged her to find something to do, impressing upon her the evils of idleness, until finally in desperation she accepted a clerical position with an irritable, slave

driving spinster of fifty years of age. Nothing could be
farther removed from the type of work she had pictured
for herself. No one could be more different from the sort
of person she would have enjoyed working with. Furthermore, there was no opportunity to advance from the undesirable position to anything else. She had visions of
herself spending years in the company of this unhappy
woman, and eventually growing into the same sort of
misanthrope. She told her mother she did not like the
job, but her mother renewed her warnings against the
terrible sin of "quitting," told her that none of their
family had ever been quitters, and made the girl feel that
she must either stick to this job or admit that she was a
total failure. In spite of this the girl did become unusually exasperated on one occasion and did give up the job.
Then began a series of innuendoes and taunts by her
mother which finally culminated in an attempt at suicide.

This last act increased the poor girl's feeling of worth-
lessness, since it proved beyond doubt that she was a
real quitter. She had not only quit her job but had attempted to quit life as well. Now the family began an
even worse type of badgering. They watched her day
and night, and plainly told her that they did not trust
her. They took on aggrieved attitudes, as much as to
say that the girl had totally disgraced them, and their
sole interest in preventing another attempt was to save
their own reputations and not to keep the girl alive. Consequently, her depression became even more profound
because of their whole-hearted denunciation.

It can be seen that this whole situation was built upon
a thorough distortion of proper perspective. The girl
could see only one issue: "Am I a quitter or am I not?
I am a quitter. Since quitting is an unpardonable sin I

am in a hopeless condition. What is the use of any attempt on my part to do anything? I wish I could die."

This girl's conclusion was false because she began with a faulty premise. She accepted the statement of her mother that quitting was invariably a mortal sin. Anyone knows that it may be a virtue to quit under some circumstances. If this girl could believe that leaving the undesirable job was a sign of stamina—that she would have been a weakling had she stayed—she could be able to get a different emotional attitude toward the whole situation.

This end was achieved in a very simple fashion. She was given a position which involved the type of work she liked, with persons who were pleasant to deal with, and in a short time her self-confidence was restored.

Let us repeat a previous statement—despondency and a feeling of failure often come from overestimating factors which in themselves do not warrant the importance we attach to them. Money assumes a gigantic importance for the man who has recently lost his savings. All the girls in the world have no value when compared with the one who has just jilted the lovelorn swain. He can see nothing but his tremendous loss. Years later he may change his viewpoint, may even believe that the separation was a fortunate event; but now he can see nothing but desolation.

We can all develop so as to gain a greater breadth of vision, a greater perspective on life, and in so doing we are insuring ourselves against depression.

3. *Be active.* Did you ever see a person who was emotionally depressed and who was, at the same time, actively engaged in a stimulating occupation? More than likely, the depressed person is physically inactive as well

as mentally slow. Physical inactivity, as we have seen, encourages depression through affecting the bodily functions; but it also takes zest from life because life loses all its purpose.

In order to convince yourself of the vicious effect that inactivity can have in making you feel depressed, try this little experiment. Some day arrange things so that you have absolutely nothing to do. Do not read, work, play; but just sit. Let your mind wander particularly on your position in life, what you have accomplished, and what you have failed to perform. If you continue such idleness and ruminations for a day, you will almost surely not be very bright and cheerful at the end of the day. Then, as a contrast, arrange a day in which you do not have a minute to pause, where one activity is followed by another in rapid succession. At the close of such a full day you will very likely be tired, but it will be a happy fatigue, and what a delicious sensation when you relax! Multiply the former idle days and you will have a chronic depression; multiply the busy days and you will develop a happy outlook on life.

Such wholesome activity should not be confused with the excessive zeal which, as we have pointed out, often foreshadows failure. Wholesome activity is not feverish activity; it is not motivated by worry or by fear, it is the response of a healthy organism to the stimulation of tasks which need to be performed. Wholesome activity is pleasurable.

Unconscious causes of depressions. A good physique, a true perspective on life, and wholesome activity are effective means of combating emotional depressions when these are based on causes which are relatively apparent. In some cases, however, the depression may be a device to conceal from view some situation which is much more vital to the person than the depression itself. In these instances, the patient wants to be depressed because it is much more gratifying to his pride or to his moral sense than the admission of the true state of affairs would be. In other words, a depression may be a defense mechanism. It may be used by a person to distract attention from something which is really of much more importance than is the depression itself. There may be a great many unconscious reasons why a depression may be adopted in this fashion. We shall discuss only a few of the most important.

1. *To gain affection.* A depression may be used either consciously or unconsciously to gain sympathy and attention. We are all familiar with the swain who tells his faithless sweetheart that life is not worth living without her, that he must end it all, in order to bring her to terms. She feels that he must love her or he would not be so disturbed by the fact that she has rejected him.

Training for such behavior begins very early in life. If a child is cheerful his mother is very likely to assume that he needs nothing from her and to neglect him. If he is tearful and unhappy she will immediately devote a great measure of attention to him. She will inquire into the cause of his ill-humor, will wait upon him assiduously, and attempt in every way to cheer him up. When he wants love what more natural than for him to repeat the procedure which brought him love before?

In adult life we are not so likely to admit that we are using a depression as a device to make others love us. If the trick were too apparent to others it would not bring the desired results, and if it were used consciously we would feel chagrined to admit that we had to use such a childish means to win the love which we so much desire. Few of us want the feeling that we are loved merely because others feel sorry for us. We may use this device, but we must do it without being aware of it ourselves.

The following incident illustrates how the real cause of a depression may be concealed behind another preferred cause. A man of about forty years of age failed in business. As a result of this failure he developed a profound depression, sitting for hours in the same position, his frame racked with convulsive movements which were apparently repressed sobs, repeating the statement that life had no more interest for him. His friends became so sorry for him that they got together and reorganized his business so that he could make a fair start toward recovery, but he became worse and said that he could not make a go of it because of his mental condition. He could not be induced to take hold again.

By means which we need not describe here, it was discovered that he was depressed for a reason quite other than his economic difficulty. Years before he had developed the notion that his family did not love him as an individual, but only as a means of providing them with material comforts. This made him work frantically to give them everything they could wish, but at the same time increased his hunger for what he considered real affection. He often wondered if they would love him were he penniless. Why should he be a slave all his life if he never got the love he wanted? Poverty would punish them, if his notion were correct, and at the same time would provide a test of their love. This unconscious urge to get love through other means than his money really made him use poor judgment until he did fail. While he had subconsciously hoped that poverty would increase their love for him, he found that it did not. A son and two grown daughters both openly upbraided him for his mistakes and made covert remarks whose malicious significance he could not readily mistake. This revelation was so disturbing that he went into a real emotional depression, whereupon they became sorry for him and treated him with some consideration. The slightest sign of recovery brought forth urgings to return to his business so that they could again have the luxuries they had previously enjoyed. The poor man faced the alternative of remaining depressed and getting a little sympathy, or returning to business and getting no consideration except as a provider. He did not want to get over his depression, for it meant the accentuation of his hunger for love.

Of course, he never voiced this, the real reason, for his depression. He continually complained that he was a failure in business, that he was too old to begin again, that his mind was affected by the shock to such an extent that he could not be successful again. All this served to distract his attention from the real reason and certainly hid his real motive from his family and friends.

In such a case, the only successful remedy was to arrange matters so that his family loved him without reference to his earning ability. Being provided with love, he would have no further reason to be depressed.

2. *Self-punishment.* The wrongdoing of the ordinary man is usually more or less of an accident. He becomes so intent upon some objective that he loses his perspective and is led to do things the harmfulness of which he does not quite appreciate until it is all over. He is carried away by his enthusiasm to do things he would probably not do in his calmer moments. Having done the undesirable act he is more surprised than others at his

conduct. He excuses himself, convinces himself that there were mitigating circumstances, and proceeds to forget it. The emotional chagrin and the sense of shame persist, however, and hang over him like a shadow. They attach themselves to any unfortunate event that is less shameful than the one he is trying to forget, and he is outwardly depressed over this trivial external situation. All his friends feel that he is exaggerating the significance of the apparent cause of his depression, but there seems to be little that they can do about it. He actually nurses his sorrow, and seems to resent it when others attempt to alleviate it.

The way in which such a set of circumstances can conspire to make a person depressed is shown in the life of a young woman accountant. She began her business career with a feeling of inferiority. She thought that a woman in the business world was a sheep among wolves; that she must protect herself by constant vigilance if she wanted to advance in rank and salary. Soon after she began work she discovered that a trusted employee was falsifying accounts. She got all the evidence together, sprang a trap on him and he was discharged. As a reward she was promoted. This sort of trapping was repeated on several later occasions and each time she was praised for her cleverness and given concrete rewards. Then she became suspicious of one of the high executives in the corporation for which she was working. She began cornering him in the same way; but just as she was ready to spring the trap on him, he killed himself.

She told herself that she was not responsible for his death; she talked it over with her friends and they reassured her, telling her that she was in nowise to blame. She remained outwardly very calm, soon forgot the episode, and for a number of years seemed to have forgotten it. A new situation arose in which she was at enmity with another high official, and was in great fear of losing her position as a result of this dissention. To her surprise she found evidences of dishonesty on his part. She began to search for more evidence, and was on the point of getting it when an accident occurred which made her take a vacation. Her sister was killed in an automobile accident. She had never been very close to this sister and they had not lived in the same house for years; but she was very much upset by the death, and could not work because of her grief. This all looked like a logical depression until her vacation was prolonged and it was noticed that the depression became worse every time returning to work was suggested. She thought she was depressed over the loss of her sister. Under the surface, on the other hand, there was quite a different situation which was somewhat as follows:

She did not want to go back to work for, if she did, she would continue the investigation of the official. On the other hand, her success depended upon catching him, and what was the use of working if she was afraid to do the thing which was obviously her duty? When she did perform her duty it led to the suicide on the part of her victim. She was really responsible for one suicide. What if this other executive should kill himself! Then she would have the blood of two men on her hands. She ought to go back. She was afraid to go back because she did not want the blood of this other man on her hands. If she went back and did not trap him, they might trap her. Were they not all a pack of wolves? What to do? Fate helped her out and gave her the opportunity to grieve over the loss of her sister. One cannot work when an emotional depression is taking all one's energy. Consequently, she emphasized her grief to such an extent that she was able to deceive both herself and all her friends.

Obviously, such a depression could not be cured by consoling her for the loss of her sister. She did not want consolation for that, it was an opportune event for her. She needed to face the issue which lay behind her depression. Should she become more tolerant of her employers who were not honest? Should she be straightforward in her knowledge and give the executive a chance to make good? Or, should she continue her policy of climbing to glory on the bodies of her suicidal victims? Having faced the issue, she made an adjustment, and the depression over the death of her sister vanished in thin air.

The fighting habit. To sum up, the only sure cure for emotional depression is to develop in each person the habit of fighting. Depressions are an escape from reality, while facing reality necessitates continual fighting. But fighting is not enough; it must be happy fighting. Life is not a bitter struggle as some disgruntled persons would have you believe, it is a *happy* struggle such as you witness in an intense game. Consequently, the attitude of the fighter is much more important than the fact that he continues to fight.

What is a wholesome fighting attitude? It is the feeling that, in and of itself, the game of life is worth playing. The playing is the valuable part, whether one wins or loses in any objective sense. When one plays his part valiantly and happily he has succeeded, regardless of the number of counts he has piled up on any artificial scale.

It is the artificial values which some have set up which tend to destroy the wholesome fighting attitude and to breed discouragement and depression.

Man does not take life as he finds it. He builds artificial ideals and standards, sets them up as goals to be attained, tells himself that if he does not gain these objectives he has failed as a man, and so comes to overvalue his ideals. If he can keep his perspective and see these ideals as man-made devices to spur him on to achievement, he will be normal. When he gives them such importance that failure to attain them in a specified time, and in a particular manner, brings such disappointment that he wants to give up—then he has taken his first step toward an abnormal emotional depression.

QUESTIONS

1. Give some instance from your own experience where a person seeks to escape blame by soliciting sympathy.
2. What is the function of grief?
3. Explain the relationship between indecision and grief.
4. What behavior would you expect from one who is incapable of grief?
5. What factors lead to self-pity?
6. What common factor is to be found in self-pity and the search for sympathy?
7. What essential factor of life accounts for changes in mood?
8. How can one judge whether moods are normal?
9. Why should moods follow objective events?
10. What happens when a person devotes his attention to his moods instead of to the circumstances which influence his moods?
11. Explain how elation and depression become excessive.
12. What two precautions may be adopted to avoid cycles of exaggerated elation and depression?
13. Can you defend the statement: "A man is never whipped until he believes he is"?
14. Explain the advantage of being objective.
15. If we analyzed vague impulses and worries what would we be likely to find?

16. How may trivial things be invested with unwarranted value?

17. What could one be led to infer when a deep depression grows from an apparently trivial cause?

18. Show how egocentricity may grow into self-pity.

19. Describe some possible imaginings of the person who pities himself.

20. What is the reason for learning how to lose?

21. Why is thwarting not sufficient justification for a depression?

22. Describe the danger of a fixed, unchangeable goal.

23. What three attitudes may outsiders take toward the person who is emotionally depressed?

24. What should be the nature of the influence by outsiders upon the depressed individual?

25. Explain the relationship between feelings of failure and emotional depressions.

26. Distinguish between feelings of failure and inferiority feelings.

27. Explain how zeal may be a forerunner of depression.

28. Why do we so often fail to see the significance of excessive zeal?

29. What are some good and some bad ways of handling a person who works with feverish zeal?

30. Show how fixed ideas may lead to depressions.

31. Show why the intrinsic value of an objective may be totally unrelated to our estimate of its value.

32. Why are feelings of moral guilt not always indicative of actual guilt?

33. In what sense can specific acts be said to have different values?

34. Explain the significance of the following statement: The way a person acts when he is buffeted is more important than the kind or degree of buffeting.

35. State three rules for overcoming emotional depressions.

36. Explain the relationship between digestive processes and emotional behavior.

37. What rules can be applied to aid one in overcoming mild spells of the blues?

38. What harm may "sympathy" do in the case of a depression?

39. Describe what a friend should do when one becomes despondent.

40. Explain just what is meant by gaining perspective.

41. What effect does perspective have upon our evaluation of the different aspects of life?

42. How does activity effect changes in mood?

43. Name two unconscious causes of depression.

44. Show how we may learn to be depressed in order to gain affection.

45. Show the way in which depression to gain love may become unconscious.

46. Explain how self-punishment may be hidden and disguised.

47. State in your own words what is meant by the fighting habit.

CHAPTER XII

HOW TO GET THINGS DONE

"I wish I were back in high school," complained a college freshman. "There we knew what we were expected to do; the teacher gave us definite lesson assignments, we had small classes and knew we would have to recite every day, so we had to get our lessons. We did what we were told to do, and then we knew we were through. Here it is all so different. No one tells you just what you should do or when you should do it. You never know when you will be called on to recite. The professor expects you to take notes on his lectures, but never tells you what is important and what is not. I used to get good grades in high school, but it looks as though I would flunk here."

This is the actual record of one freshman's complaint, but it voices the feeling which may be found in varying degrees in many a college student. It also expresses the way a lot of people feel about life. Some students never discover what college is all about until they are nearly through, and many a man gets over halfway through his life before he feels at home at living. It is all a confused maze. Why?

It is largely because these people continue to depend upon others to take the initiative in planning work, they do only what they are told to do, and when a job is finished can only await further orders before beginning any new task. In high school our complaining freshman had learned to be a good soldier, he could take orders and execute them; but when he was not given orders he knew of nothing to do but to loaf, and consequently was accomplishing nothing. Then he blamed his teachers for not giving him specific instructions as to what to study and when to do it.

College offers many young persons their first opportunity to exercise executive ability. They have the opportunity for planning their own work and for issuing orders to themselves as to exactly how it should be carried out. They are for the first time their own boss. To some college students being their own boss merely spells freedom to do as they please—which is nothing. To others it offers an opportunity to become self-directed individuals. They are given an opportunity to demonstrate what they are able to accomplish. If you would study successfully, you must handle your studying as an executive would handle his business or industrial organization.

How to study effectively. Having arrived at the conclusion that the only person who is really going to make you study is yourself, that industry or laziness depends upon yourself, you are in a position to analyze the problem of efficient study in detail.

1. *Discover the purpose of each course of study.* Your purpose is to get a grade that will enable you to pass or to attain honors. Yes, but that is merely incidental as a record that you have discovered and fulfilled the deeper purpose of the course. Keep asking yourself what it is all about, what you are expected to know, what of it after you do know it. Is the primary purpose to accumulate a great many facts? Then get the facts and master them. Is it to teach you to reason? Then use your reason. Is it to teach you how to do certain things? Then do

them. You cannot study a foreign language, a science, geometry, literature, or philosophy in the same way. Try to state specifically the objective of each course at the beginning and then revise your statement repeatedly as you learn more about the subject matter.

2. *Pretend you are preparing to teach the lesson.* Many a person who has taken a course and has later been required to teach that course has awakened to the fact that he did not begin to learn the content of the course until he began to teach it. The implications from this are apparent. The student is too likely to be concerned only with getting the material clearly enough to "get by" an examination. Let him pretend that he must explain the content of each lesson to some imaginary comrade—not too bright a one—and he will be astonished at the different feeling he has about the lesson.

3. *Make up examination questions to give to yourself to test your knowledge.* As you prepare these pretend you are making the examination to test the knowledge of your imaginary pupil. Ask yourself what he should know about the lesson and then try to devise a question that will ascertain whether he has the knowledge he should have.

4. *Develop an interest in each subject.* The use of the three foregoing rules will help to make a subject interesting. In addition, you may develop interest by maintaining a questioning attitude toward every phase of it. Keep asking yourself: "What of it? Now that I know that, what bearing has it on the scheme of things? Doesn't that contradict this other bit of information I just learned in another course? Is it a real contradiction? If so, which is right and which is wrong?"

Keep up such a barrage of questions to yourself and you will find the driest subject teeming with interest.

It is only ignorance that breeds indifference. The more you question a subject the more interesting it will become. Be not so much concerned about what to believe or what to disbelieve. Instead, look upon doubt and intellectual uncertainty as a challenge and you will have no trouble with maintaining interest.

5. *Apply what you learn.* Think about it, write about it, talk about it to other persons, and fit it into every phase of your life that you can. Such application will make a subject real to you, it will give it a richness it could not otherwise attain, and it will make it vastly easier for you to grasp the significance of it and to remember it. Some students develop the bad habit of keeping each of their studies locked in separate little compartments of their minds. They open up the chemistry closet when it comes time to study chemistry, and when the time for this study has elapsed they carefully close it off from any other activity and do not allow any thought of it to encroach upon their other activities until class period or the next study period for chemistry arrives. Do not have any such sequestered cubicles in your mind. Let everything you learn have absolute freedom to wander anywhere in your thinking that it will, and you will be surprised to see how things which at first appeared abstract and useless will relate themselves to other things that you see and hear.

Follow these rules and you will discover that your college work points itself up in a surprising fashion. These are not merely hypothetical rules which are drawn from thin air. They were given to a number of students who were failing in their studies, and in almost every case where the student actually applied them he was enabled to make a remarkable improvement in his grades.

B

Make a program of activities. The five principles just discussed should become an intimate part of your life; they should become habitual attitudes which color your whole existence. While this is taking place you will need to work out specific programs of activity. Time spent in organizing your activities is time well spent.

Should you feel that you do not need to allot your time you can easily convince yourself that you do. Make up a detailed study of what you actually do by fifteen-minute periods. Do this for a week and then tabulate the results, and you will be astounded at how much time is spent in a sort of vacuum, time in which you have no fun, accomplish nothing, time in which you merely vegetate—that is, you have nothing more vital happen than does a potato.

Many students complain that they cannot get down to work. They are told that they must gain self-control and master themselves. They, therefore, go through a process of self-incrimination. They scold themselves, deny themselves pleasures, and virtually try to browbeat themselves into docile, submissive, hard-working students. The only outcome of such a procedure is the development of intense irritability, restlessness, discouragement, and eventually hatred of the whole educational procedure. They spend all their time "studying," so they say; whereas, if the truth were known, they spend all their time with books, but little of that in study. To sit with a book in front of you, your mind wandering everywhere under the sun, feverishly worrying why you cannot get the "stuff," is worse than useless.

The way some students study leads one to imagine what would happen if an industry were conducted in a similar fashion. Suppose a manager filled his factory with employees—good employees—but gave them no specific instructions. Instead he told them that it was up to them to work hard and to do their best and then success would be sure to crown their efforts. The result would be a tremendous waste of activity, with little or nothing accomplished. The manager in an industry avoids any such outcome by careful planning. It would pay each student to visit some manufacturing establishment and then make up his mind to plan his work so that things were turned out with the same efficient smoothness.

1. *Estimate time required to complete various assignments.* You cannot begin to make a schedule until you arrive at some sort of an estimate of how long will be required to complete the various assignments that you have been given. At first the estimates may be difficult to make and later events may show them to have been wrong. These difficulties can be corrected in later schedules and their existence simply argues for the necessity of making some sort of rational program of study.

2. *Determine the number of hours available for study.* This can be done by making a schedule for a week, assigning times for the necessary activities of life—that is, for sleeping, eating, playing, caring for clothing, and the like. If the hours available for study are fewer than the hours you estimate will be needed, some readjustment must be made. If you must shorten the time for preparation distribute the cuts throughout your whole course of study. Your job will be to see that each course gets a fair share of your time. Do not let your time distribution be determined by the greediness or the leniency of certain professors. Some few professors have the habit of giving students enough work to take their entire time. You go to college to study various courses of different fields, and

you should not let an over-ambitious professor interfere with balancing your program.

Another word of warning is essential. Some students tend to ignore recreation in making their schedule of activities. The only way they can get in any recreation is to steal it from the time assigned to some course. Allow plenty of time for wholesome recreation and fun, or you will find that your schedule will not function.

3. *Use short periods of study.* No absolute rule can be made here, but it is unwise to study any one subject for more than an hour consecutively. If you have three hours to study in a single stretch it would pay to take up three or more tasks in that time. If you have only two subjects to prepare in such a period alternate between them rather than complete one long assignment and then go to another long assignment. You will find such changes restful, and you will accomplish more with less effort. In addition, you will find that these changes will add to your ability to sustain your interest.

4. *Stick to your program.* A definite program will bring order out of chaos and make your study effective, just as planning will bring order into an assembly room in a factory.

A young man who had drifted throughout his academic year came to his senses about four weeks before the final examinations were scheduled to begin. He decided that he must get to work and set out to study. After a week he came to the personnel director of his university with a very elongated countenance and told him that he probably had better leave rather than wait until he failed in all his subjects. It did not look very hopeful, but the personnel officer went at the problem in the way we have suggested. He made a very definite program and marked out each hour which could be devoted to study up to the time of the last examination. He then decided how much of this total time could be devoted to each subject, allowing a greater proportion of time for those subjects which the student found hardest. He assigned times for the various subjects, changing from one to another as we suggested in number three. Furthermore, he allotted the time for each subject to specific parts of that subject. For example, he found that six hundred pages should be covered for one course and that he could only take fifteen hours to do this. This meant that he must cover forty pages in each hour. He distributed this reading throughout the three weeks. Granted he might not be able to study the forty pages thoroughly in an hour, he knew he could take no more time for that particular portion and so he set out to get all he could from the forty pages between, let us say, eight and nine on a specified day. The whole schedule was arranged in this fashion, with allowance for sufficient sleep and some recreation. As a result the boy passed all his examinations.

When you see a man floundering around in the water, splashing and struggling in a violent fashion, you can be sure that he does not know much about swimming or that something is wrong. He does not learn to swim by increasing his energy, by saying to himself, "I must swim," and telling himself to use more effort. He would do well to get to dry land in some fashion, and have some one explain to him—or figure out himself—just what he should do and how he should do it; then perhaps he can make some progress. If a man slashes at a golf ball with great zeal, cutting up the turf with some blows and fanning the air with others, he, too, could make more headway by cooling off and planning his activities.

The same principles apply in studying. Studying is merely a complex form of learning and it needs to be planned. As a high school student you had much of your studying planned for you, while in college you must plan for yourself. When you have to drive yourself you know you need to stop and organize. Fretting and most of the worry that comes to the student has its inception in this one thing—a failure to plan a definite program of study.

How to read efficiently. Most of your studying is done with books, that is, it is a form of reading. If you have trained yourself to read efficiently your work will go much more smoothly than if you have not trained yourself in this respect. Even if you think you are an efficient reader you probably have room for improvement. The following principles should be of assistance to any student whether he is a good reader or a poor one.

1. *Adapt your method of reading to the material to be studied.* Have you ever read a page of printed matter and then suddenly awakened to the fact that you had not the faintest notion of what you had read? Have you ever listened to a speaker drone on and on while your mind was a thousand miles away? Are not the two very similar? If you have listened to a man speak to you but have not comprehended his meaning you cannot be said to have heard his message. If you read a page and have no notion of the message of the writer you may have gone through the motions of reading but you have lost the primary purpose of the whole process. Every writer attempts to produce some effect upon you. The first function of the reader is to ascertain what effect the writer is trying to create.

Books of philosophy, history, fiction, poetry, science, biography, humor, folklore, romance, travel, and political intrigue all require a different reading attitude and a different manner of reading. If the author is trying to convince you of the truth of certain propositions try to follow the trend of his reasoning. If he is trying to give you the interrelation of certain historical events try to gain his historical perspective. Get in the mood for each type of material, if you would get the meaning of what you read.

2. *Learn the language of each author.* You will soon discover that subjects require a different terminology, some so widely different from that to which you have been accustomed that you may almost think you are reading a foreign language. To become accustomed to the vocabulary of each new subject is not so difficult as it may seem, providing you follow one very simple principle. Do not let a single word or phrase get by you without understanding its meaning. Arm yourself with a good dictionary and use it. The author may use a vocabulary which is new to you, but you will discover that the number of new terms is not as great as it seems to you at first. Master each new word as you come to it and then as it is used in different contexts its meaning will become enriched.

An extreme instance of this situation arose when a student enrolled in a course in systematic theology without adequate preparation. He encountered almost at once such terms as ontological, cosmological, teleological, inductive, deductive, and the like. He spent an hour attempting to grasp the meaning of the first page of a textbook of over six hundred pages. To make matters worse he sat through his first recitation period listening to the instructor and the other students bandying around these terms whose meaning was so hazy to him. He felt that some evil spirit must have transported him to some foreign country, and that he was in a class dealing with oriental magic. By a continued use of the dictionary and a valiant attempt to get accurate meanings for all the new terms, in a surprisingly short time he found himself quite at home in the use of the new dialect.

3. *Get a preliminary bird's eye view before you read for detail.* Many textbooks are outlined topically, and the topics are indicated by display type. It would be well to go over this display material in order to get a notion of what the reading is to be about, and to relate it to what you have already learned. Some books have no such helps, and you can get little more accurate notion than that given by a chapter heading. With such books it might be well to skim the assignment, reading only a sentence or two from each paragraph before giving it a thorough reading. A little time spent in this preliminary orientation will be found to be very profitable and actually to save time later. Remember, the purpose is to get the meaning and not just to say you have read the assignment. Use the preliminary orientation to help you get the full meaning of what you read.

4. *Be sure to understand the main point of each section.* A fine practice is to restate the main point *in your own words.* A good many students make it a practice to underscore the main sentence in each paragraph. In books where there is no display type to make the significant points stand out this may be a good practice. However, it is very likely to lead to slovenly thinking. You may think you have grasped a point when you can point to the sentence which states it, but you have not fully grasped it until you can restate it in your own words. You may object that you cannot state it as well as the author has done. Probably you cannot, but the object

at this point is not to strive for a better way of saying it but to say it in a way which makes it a part of you. Every truth can be stated in different ways and if you can think of no other way than that given by the author you have not done enough thinking on that point.

5. *Weigh the evidence upon which the author bases his points.* Does he merely make an assertion, expecting you to accept the statement on his authority? Does he quote other authorities and expect you to accept the weight of their testimony? Does he marshal facts to substantiate his point? If so, does he also cite contradictory facts? Does he get you into a mood where you want to believe what he says or does his presentation antagonize you? Do you feel receptive or antagonistic because of his presentation or because of a bias already formed? Does he use analogies and illustrations to make his points clear? If so, do you clearly recognize that such devices have value in making a subject clear and vivid but do not argue for the truth of a proposition? Keep these and similar questions in the background of your mind while you read, and you will soon find that your reading takes on richness as you grasp the signficance of the various rhetorical devices of your author.

A simple instance will illustrate the results of a failure to weigh the evidence. A student will often remember an illustration which has been used but forget entirely the truth the illustration was designed to make clear. He does not even know why the writer told the story which he did.

6. *Outline as you read.* Unless the author has already done it for you, make a logical, topical outline of what you read. This, of course, does not apply when you read poetry, fiction, mystery stories, and the like. Usually, however, if you are assigned such reading there is a pur-

pose in the assignment and you can make notes on items which fit in with the purpose for the reading.

Learn to read rapidly. The primary aim in reading should be to read efficiently by means of the methods just outlined. Granting that it is more important to be sure to get the real purpose of the author than it is to cover a great amount of territory, it is still valuable to be able to read rapidly. As a matter of fact, slowness in reading is too often merely evidence that the reader is not interested, is not gaining the meaning of the writer, nor fitting into the mood of the material he is reading. Increase in speed can be effected without assuming that all material should be read with equal rapidity.

1. *Do not articulate as you read.* Grasp the meaning of phrases without articulating the words either aloud or subvocally. If you move your lips as you read silently, or if you can detect movements of your larynx, you are an inefficient reader. Reading should not be rapid speaking, it should be an entirely different process. Children to-day are being taught to read by the "flash-card" method; that is, they are permitted to see a whole phrase and give the answer to it without pronouncing it at all. This should be carried through to most of our reading. If you have not trained yourself to "see" the meaning of phrases without "saying" them, it is time you began practicing.

2. *Make fewer and fewer stops per line of print.* In reading, the eye does not move smoothly and evenly along a line of print, but moves by jumps. During the movement nothing is seen. It is only during the pauses in movement that the reader may see any of the printed matter. A poor reader makes a great number of stops, the distances between stops is uneven, and he may even retrace his movements. The good reader, by learning to

grasp a longer phrase with one glance can make fewer stops per line. The aim of training should at first be to make as few stops as possible per line, and when this is accomplished the speed of comprehension at each stop may be improved. Obviously if one reads by slowly enunciating each syllable his eyes will make a great number of stops per line.

The ordinary rate of speaking is about 160 words per minute. If you do not exceed this speed in reading it is probable that you are merely talking to yourself as you read. The average reading speed of an educated adult who uses the silent reading method is about 250 words of the ordinary magazine article per minute.

3. *Keep a chart of your reading speed.* Practice silent reading continually, but each week make a test of your speed and keep a graphic record of your performance. You will be surprised at the amount of improvement you make and will be encouraged to continue practice.

The curve can be made as follows. Use ordinary coordinate paper. Let the height of each record represent the number of words per minute. Let regular intervals along the base line of the paper represent weekly periods. For each weekly period you will then record the average number of words you can read per minute. It would be well to make the test on several pages of material for a special book of ordinary difficulty which is set aside for this purpose alone. If you keep your time for reading several pages it is a simple matter to divide the number of words by the time required and obtain the rate per minute. Don't give up your practice until your curve shows signs of flattening out, thus showing you have reached an approximate limit. This flattening should not be much short of 250 words per minute.

The time taken to improve your reading will be time well spent and you will reap the reward of your efforts many times over before you finish your college course.

Memorizing efficiently. Do not identify memory with rote memory or mechanical memory. Comparatively few things must be learned in a mechanical fashion with no reference to the meanings involved. On the other hand, there is never an experience which does not leave its imprint upon us and, in a broad sense, that imprint is a type of memory trace. We will remember whether we attempt to do so or not. All we mean by efficient memorizing is guiding our mental processes so that we will remember the valuable things instead of letting the whole process be dominated by chance. The student who browses through his books, saunters to his classes, and lounges through his lectures will remember something; he may even once in a while be impressed by something that will be useful in writing an examination. He develops a sort of "approximate" memory. Called upon to state what nine times nine is, he is likely to reply that it is eighty or thereabouts; or he might happen to guess that it is eighty-one. Do not let your memory play you such tricks. Be boss of your memory, and do not let it boss you.

1. *Decide which method of memorizing suits your immediate purpose.* The methods of memorizing may be divided into four different types: immediate memory, rote or mechanical, logical, and associative memory. Each is valuable and has its place; but it is a mistake to use one type where another would be more appropriate. Let us get acquainted with each type.

a. Immediate memory. There are many times when you need to remember something for a minute or two and then to forget it. You look up a telephone number long enough to get the connection, but it would be a nuisance to have the number bobbing up the rest of the day. You remember what your bill came to long enough to pay it, but after you are sure you have the correct change its exact amount is of minor concern. Efficient use of your memory involves the ability to forget items readily as soon as they are no longer of any value to you.

b. Mechanical or rote memory. Mechanical memory is the name given to memorizing by sheer repetition. It is used when something needs to be remembered which is totally new, and which has no logical relationship to anything else you already know. It should be used only as a last resort. Unfortunately, this type of memorizing is too often used, and with some individuals it is the only memorizing process that they recognize. Consequently, when you hear a person disparaging memorizing, it is quite likely that it is this type to which he is referring. It has its value, but it should not occupy a dominant place in the memorizing of the college student. If there is no other way to learn a thing than by rote memory, set about it and learn it that way.

c. Logical memory. Probably the best way to memorize is to hunt for logical relationships between the different items involved. Each item then becomes a part of a unified whole and remembering it is relatively easy. The difference between mechanical memory and logical memory may be illustrated in memorizing a theorem in geometry. Should one use mechanical memory he would see no logical relationship between the different steps but would learn the sequence by sheer repetition. The whole thing would have no more meaning to him when he was through than would the sequence of nonsense syllables: duj—pim—sig—bex—bap. Study the logical relationships and the whole theorem becomes a functional unit, each step leads naturally into the next one and the memorizing is relatively easy.

A logical relationship, once discovered, is as valuable as hundreds of repetitions on a purely mechanical basis. The student who takes the time and devotes his energies toward discovering the logical processes will save time in the end, and will find his memorizing easy. Furthermore, things learned by logical memory are much more likely to have lasting value than are things learned by rote. Use rote memory when you have to, but be sure you cannot use logical memory before you revert to the mechanical method.

d. Associative memory. When any sort of relationship exists between the different items to be memorized we have associative memory. The relationship may be a logical one or it may be illogical, it may be an inherent part of the items or it may be highly artificial. Where any relationship exists it is much easier to memorize than when there is none. Consequently, it pays to hunt for some connecting link and even to create one should none exist. If the items sound alike, if they look alike, if they taste alike, if they are spelled similarly these similarities tie them together. Similarly, if they have contrasting characteristics it may help.

Classifying, building outlines, organizing items according to time or place, rhythm or rhyme, all these are devices to give relationship to items which might, otherwise, be totally unrelated and thus hard to memorize. The conclusion is, if you cannot find a logical tie to bind together the materials you must memorize, find some sort of connection, even an artificial one, and tie them together in this manner.

2. *Recite to yourself.* After going over the material to be memorized a few times attempt to recite. This will be much more effective than blind repetition. In reciting you will discover the weak spots, the places where the parts do not seem to hang together. Give these spots special consideration and hunt for associations to tie them up.

Taking examinations. "I know my lessons. I am sure that I understand the course; but when I come into the examination room I go to pieces, lose my head, forget what I do know and make a miserable showing. Why cannot I do myself justice in an examination?"

This is a common complaint of students. Sometimes, of course, it is the plaint of a student who knows nothing, who did not study, and who thinks he can thus play upon the sympathies of his teachers. Often, however, the complaint is real, and demonstrates ignorance of a few important principles.

1. *Get acquainted with examinations.* Your fear of examinations may be due to the fact that you are not intimately familiar with them. An examination is no guessing contest. The instructor is not trying to outwit you—he is trying to find out what you know. We have already suggested, as a means of efficient study, that you make up questions on each lesson, lay them aside, and then try to answer them at a later date. If you do this you will find the number of questions that can be asked is rather limited. You will get accustomed to the examination itself and will lose your fear of it.

Furthermore, if you observe closely you will discover that there are different ways of asking examination questions. Experiment with these different forms so that you are familiar with all of them. If, in any examination, you get a totally new form of question, note that form carefully and include it in the form of questions you use in making your own examinations. You simply cannot long be afraid of anything with which you are well acquainted. See if you cannot make up better examinations than your instructor and you will have no reason to fear his. You may or may not succeed in beating him, but you will have lost your fear of examinations in the attempt.

2. *Be absorbed with answering the questions instead of being absorbed with yourself.* Your fear may be merely a form of self-consciousness. You may come in to the examination asking yourself: "I wonder whether I will know the answers? I wonder if I shall pass? Will I get fussed again?" So long as you think such things you cannot refrain from being self-conscious, and this is a form of fear of a very exasperating sort. The only solution is to be more concerned with the examination than you are with yourself. The result will be that you will overcome the fear and will do better in the examination.

These two rules are simple but wonderfully effective if you will but persist until you are able to apply them.

Being your own boss. A good executive must accomplish three things: 1. He must determine clearly what it is he wishes to achieve. 2. He must devise specific procedures which will bring about his desired ends. 3. Finally, he must enlist the help of his subordinates in the execution of his plans.

The third of these is by far the most important. It does little good to know what one wants, or even to know just what steps need to be taken to get what one wants, if one is unable to enlist the help of those whose efforts are essential if these wants are to be fulfilled. This ability to get along with people, to coöperate with them and to gain their coöperation will be the subject of our next chapter; but the extension of executive ability to include others is not usually successful until we have learned the lesson of handling ourselves.

Suppose, as a student in college, you have fulfilled the first two steps of an executive with reference to your work. You have decided what you want, you have outlined a program of work, know some of the rules for getting the work done efficiently. Now, how are you going to get yourself to do it? You will find a number of impulses which run counter to the smooth fulfillment of the program you outline. They will pull you into all sorts of outside activities; movies, dances, "bull-sessions," and even just loafing, and cleaning your room, rather than the work you have planned and know you should be doing.

Here you have the beginnings of disharmony within yourself. You may win from the start or you may lose. Suppose you permit these irrelevant things to interfere with your program, and you find yourself getting swamped with so much work that as the school year advances you become emotionally upset about it all. Then you are very likely to revert to some of the defense mechanisms we have described. You may develop an inferiority feeling and think you are incapable of doing school work. You may blame it on the "system" or on the interference of your friends. You may pretend you are not well and develop a case of hysteria. You may philosophize about the futility of education and point to men who have succeeded without the benefits of college training. In short, you do everything except admit the real reason, which is your failure as an executive in controlling the forces within you.

The first impulse of a person who has it impressed upon him that he is a poor executive is to prove to himself that he is "boss." Being "boss" implies gaining obedience, to most of such persons, and so they set out to secure it. We are all familiar with the person who is given, for the first time, a little authority. In order to convince himself and others that he is really in a position of authority he outdoes himself in demanding subservience. He lords it over his subordinates in a senseless fashion and is very apt to arouse resentment, unless the prestige of his position is great enough to permit an actual revolt. Such a diminutive executive does not get things accomplished, he actually loses sight of achievement as an objective, and becomes blinded by the question of how implicitly he is obeyed.

The person who sets out to master himself in order to prove to himself that he is "boss" of himself is making just as big a mistake as the tiny executive who lords it over his workers. He makes himself do undesirable tasks as a form of self-discipline. He discovers what he would like to do and then does the opposite in order to show himself that he will not humor himself. Revolt, discord, and a waste of energy inevitably result from such a useless conflict. The good executive does not have an organization in which each person is doing as he pleases, pulling in opposite directions; nor does he have an organization in which everyone does his bidding but does it unwillingly with an eye open for a possible opportunity for revolt. He has an organization in which all subordinate individuals are doing what he wants them to do, but they are doing it willingly and view his will merely as a reflection of their own.

If you gain this inner harmony will it not often hap-

pen that you are forced to do many things you do not
want to do? Certainly, but you do unpleasant things
because they are essential if you are to reach the objectives you have set for yourself. This is vastly different
from doing things merely because they are unpleasant,
and in order to discipline yourself. The true executive
asks whether a task is necessary or unnecessary. If necessary it must be done whether pleasant or unpleasant.
The individual who is master of himself does the same
thing. Unpleasantness does not deter him from a necessary task. He keeps the objective before him and soon
the task which seemed unpleasant takes on interest and
even pleasure because it is getting him toward some desirable objective.

QUESTIONS

1. How does dependence upon others limit one's outlook?
2. What makes it hard to overcome the desire to remain dependent?
3. How is college particularly valuable in this connection?
4. What methods could you use to discover the purpose of a course?
5. Why is teaching better than reciting as a motivation for study?
6. What is the value of preparing examination questions?
7. Show how questioning develops interest.
8. The most important rule for effective study is: "Apply what you learn." Why?
9. What is meant by compartmentalized learning?
10. How can you test the need for organizing a time schedule?
11. Explain why "self-control" is little more than organization.
12. What is the first step necessary for making a schedule?
13. What two things may threaten the balance in your program?
14. How can short periods of study be scheduled efficiently?
15. Explain why organization is much more valuable than the determination to be industrious.
16. State in your own words the essential purpose of reading.

17. How does the accomplishment of this purpose vary with different kinds of reading material?

18. What do we mean by "learning the language of each author"?

19. Explain the value of preliminary orientation before reading for detail.

20. What is the value of translating what you have read into your own words?

21. Why should you evaluate critically what you read?

22. What is the value of a topical outline?

23. What is the usual significance of slow reading?

24. Distinguish between speaking and reading.

25. What mistaken method of reading results from failure to make this distinction?

26. How does the eye move in reading?

27. What bearing has this on improvement in reading speed?

28. What is the average rate of speaking? Of reading?

29. Describe how to make a chart to register your improvement in reading speed.

30. How does one develop slovenly memory habits?

31. Name the four types of memory.

32. Why is good memorizing not dependent upon never forgetting?

33. When should immediate memory be used?

34. Where should rote memory not be used?

35. Why is logical memory the best for long time retention?

36. How does logical memory reduce the required number of repetitions?

37. Name some kinds of associative memory.

38. Show how recitation is a form of "applying what you learn."

39. What method can be used to eliminate fear of examinations?

40. How get over self-consciousness in examinations?

41. Compare the task of a student with that of an executive in an industrial organization.

42. Show why both should place the major emphasis upon accomplishments and not on "control."

CHAPTER XIII

GETTING ALONG WITH PEOPLE

"Why is it I am losing all my good clients and why is it that a young, inexperienced upstart is getting them all?" asked a dentist who had been in the profession for ten years. He went on to say that he knew that he was a better dentist than this young man. This junior dentist was just out of college and had made some very serious blunders with patients; but somehow he laughed off his mistakes and the patients put up with him and soon forgot them. The complainant was probably right in his judgment of the relative inefficiency of his younger and more successful rival. When he first became conscious of the trend which was depleting his clientele he tried the harder to do good work, depending on the theory that excellence in the end would overcome all obstacles and that his customers would inevitably come back to him. After two years of this he admitted that something must be wrong, for they were going in greater numbers rather than returning. They were leaving an expert and experienced dentist in order to have their work done by a relatively inefficient and inexpert one.

More irritating still was the flippant attitude which this young rival took toward his patients. He would joke with them, and keep up a continual chatter about trivial subjects, such as baseball, prize fights, motor races, and the like, while he was doing his work. One needed to put his whole mind upon his work, so we were told by the failing dentist, or he could not do his best.

385

The thing which is probably obvious to the reader by this time was not apparent to this man at all. It is the fact that people liked the young man, but did not like him. When asked about this he replied with a show of irritation that he did not know, that he had never thought of that, and he could not see that it had anything to do with his problem anyway. People went to a dentist, according to him, to have their teeth repaired, and would go where they got the best work, and not to a man merely because they liked him. When asked where he learned that theory he became still more irritated, and said any one would know that. He had been taught in medical school to explain to the patient exactly what he was doing and why. Make them see what should be done and then give them assurance that it was being done in a perfect manner, and they could not help being pleased with the work.

Was he right? The fact that he was losing his clients was evidence that his theory was wrong, or that he did not know how to apply it. He thought it was the latter. He was later convinced it was the former. No matter what line of work you are in you must win the favor and coöperation of other people or your success is limited. If you want an employee and know two applicants of equal ability, you will select the one you like. If you wish to buy an article and may get the identical article from two places, you will patronize the man you like. If you know two equally efficient physicians, you are likely to take your ills to the one you like better. Of course you would not favor one with no ability merely because he has a pleasing personality; but, other things being equal, you do not hunt for people of surly dispositions to hire or to patronize, merely because they are efficient.

In short, success in any line of endeavor depends in large part upon your ability to get along with other people.

Why should people like you? You want people to like you but have you ever stopped to ask yourself why anyone should like you? Have you ever stopped to figure out why you like the persons you do? Usually we like certain persons and dislike others, know that certain people like us and that others do not, and let it go at that. Such ignorant acceptance of things as they are leaves us powerless to change affairs if they are not satisfactory. We must know the why of social relationships if we are to add to the circle of our friends. We told our dentist friend that he needed to make friends of his clients; but after he admitted this need, he was ignorant as to how to proceed.

Do people like us because of our good qualities? The dentist thought that people should like him because he was a good dentist. We are inclined to think that people should like us because we are comely, virtuous, intelligent, wealthy, successful, or efficient. Do they? Most of us have a wrong notion of the true state of affairs because of the way in which we were treated by our mothers and fathers. They made us feel that they loved us because we were good, because we got our lessons, because we were industrious, honest, and the like. Why did our goodness make our mothers like us? Because their job was to teach us to be good and we gave them a feeling of success when we were good. Did our goodness win for us the affection of our naughty brothers and sisters? Not much. They more likely hated us for gaining more approval than they themselves received. Our teachers like us when we do good work in school and appear to be intelligent. It makes them feel that they are successful

in their profession of teaching. But if we are too successful as students we are likely to incur the enmity of our
fellow students.

What can we do about this complex situation? Hold
up our heads? Be more virtuous and more studious and
ignore the jealousy and dislike of our comrades? Shall
we hunt for people like our mothers and teachers who
are appreciative, and cultivate their friendship, ignoring
those who are on about our level and who might become
jealous of us? You can see numbers of persons about
you who are proceeding on this basis and are limiting
their social horizon because of the short-sightedness of
such a policy.

Our mothers and fathers do not love us, and our brothers and sisters hate us because we are good. Our teachers
do not love us, and our classmates hate us because we
are studious. It is not the quality in us that counts, but
the emotion that trait or quality arouses in others. Our
goodness makes our parents love us because it makes
them feel happy; it makes our brothers and sisters hate
us because it makes them feel inferior. Our industry in
our studies makes our teachers feel happy and therefore
they like us; it makes our fellow students unhappy and
they dislike us. If we would make friends we must be
concerned with the effect we produce in others more
than we are concerned with developing any specific
traits in ourselves. We may argue that others should
develop an appreciation for the good things in life—we
being the good things—and that if they are deficient in
such appreciation we do not care for their friendship;
but candor will force us to admit that this is a weak excuse for failure in a very important aspect of life.

We are now in a position to answer our question:

Why do people like us? They like us when we do the things that make them feel happier, nobler, more efficient, or more intelligent. They dislike us when we make them feel unhappy, ignoble, inefficient, or unintelligent.

This principle underlies all we shall say concerning getting along with people. It may take different forms and be easy or difficult to apply in different cases; but the more you study social life the more clearly will you discover how essential this principle is for a complete understanding of social relationships.

How can you make people like you? People will like you when you do the things which will make them feel nobler and happier. How can this be accomplished?

1. *Learn to like other persons.* The dentist with whom we introduced this chapter admitted that he did not like people. He liked to fill cavities, and it seemed to be an unfortunate thing that cavities in teeth had to be in the mouths of persons. If he could have taken the jaws of his patients off into his laboratory he would have been happy. This was really the root of his difficulty. It might be possible to tell the reader a number of ways to make people respond favorably, but they would all be hollow unless they were backed by a genuine regard for the other persons. It is almost impossible to hide a dislike successfully over a long period of time. Even a child or a dog can tell when a person dislikes him, no matter how he tries to cover his feelings to please the mother of the child or the owner of the dog. You must have a genuine regard for other persons before you can expect them to like you.

2. *Try to understand the other person.* Study the people with whom you associate by listening to what they have to say, by noticing the things they do. Get acquainted with their hobbies, their interests, their hopes, their

fears, their loves, and their aversions. This knowledge will
have a twofold effect. In the first place, it will make you
like them more. It is a proved fact that the more we know
of people the more we like them even if they are very
peculiar in their personal characteristics. As you know
more about people you will find them fascinating. In the
second place, your more intimate knowledge of other
people will reflect itself in greater consideration for their
wishes and they will be pleased with your changed behavior.

A word of warning should be sounded here. Do not
gain information about other persons so that you may be
able to demonstrate your adroitness in learning about
them. Such boasting cannot be anything but irritating.
Your study should never take the form of prying into
what is none of your concern, nor should it lead to taking
advantage of the other person. Should you use your
information in these ways you will inevitably drive
people from you instead of drawing them closer to you.
You can make a person hate you by getting too much of
his confidence. He becomes afraid of you, and hates you
for taking advantage of a moment of weakness when he
was in a confidential mood.

3. *Do not treat people alike.* All people are different
and must be treated differently if you would get along
with them successfully. The person who makes such a
generalization as "all men love flattery" and then proceeds to flatter them in similar fashion will not get very
far. Suppose the generalization has some truth in it.
Each man may like to be flattered but he likes his flattery
served up to him in a particular form, and unless you
know just what that form is you had better refrain from
a bungling attempt at a compliment whose purpose will
be obvious to him.

To be able quickly to understand a person well enough to treat him differently and at the same time refrain from unwelcome intimacies is an art which will bring you hosts of friends. The emphasis should not be upon the personal treatment of the other person but in discerning his points of difference from other people. Everyone is familiar with the obnoxious back-slapper who mauls every stranger he meets in his bungling attempt to be cordial.

Barriers to social success. All the hindrances which block the path of the one who desires to make friends may be summed up in one general category—egocentricity or self-centeredness. The key to social success is the ability to become so interested in other people that you forget yourself. When you are so engrossed in yourself, in how you are impressing them, how you are winning their esteem, or any other personal problem, you cannot hope to make them feel comfortable and happy. In some cases egocentricity is quite apparent, in other cases it is subtly disguised. The results are the same in either case. Hence, it may be profitable to study the different forms that egocentricity may take.

1. *Plain selfishness.* Some persons want to make friends simply to exploit them. Only those persons who can be of advantage are cultivated. Such motivated exploitation is easily detected and individuals who use it are held in derision by anyone who observes them. The derogatory names which have been invented for such persons is evidence enough of our detestation of them: boot-lickers, earwigs, apple-polishers, clawbacks, flunkeys.

2. *Self-respect.* No one can make too apparent his good opinion of himself and hope thereby to attract friends. It is all right for an army officer to swagger or for a drum major to strut because it is a duty of these

officers to strut and swagger. Let them carry such behavior over to their personal lives and their friends will
drop away from them. We expect persons to feel proud of
themselves when they achieve some success; but we expect
them to keep their good opinions of themselves a private
matter. Even when we congratulate them upon their
good points we do not expect them to agree too heartily.
Your mother may tolerate bragging but do not expect
others to be so generous. You will never make friends
by parading your good qualities.

3. *Self-consciousness.* Self-consciousness simulates extreme modesty but it is anything but that. Instead of
being sensitive to the other person, the self-conscious
person is thinking of himself so intently that he makes
everyone around him uncomfortable. He makes blunders
of speech and of movement, he knocks over crockery,
spills his soup, trembles and blushes, all in a seemingly
strenuous effort to be agreeable and to cater to the other
person; but he is totally unaware of the other person
except as a witness to his behavior. When he gets over
the notion that he is so important that all eyes are centered
on him he will recover from his self-consciousness.

When you wear a new hat in public and are very self-
conscious about it, does it actually mean that people are
noticing your new hat and that their glances are what
produce your feelings of discomfort? No. If you will
observe fairly you will notice that few people know
whether you have a hat or not, much less that it is a new
or different one. They are concerned with themselves and
not with you. It is merely your conceit which makes you
think they see your hat.

4. *Emotional depression.* The person who pities himself is manifesting a selfishness which makes it hard for

him to make friends. If you tell people your troubles and then permit them to help you, they may get enough satisfaction from their generosity to make them like you; but very often depressed persons do not want help and will permit no one to do anything for them. They wish to appear as great sufferers—they parade their misfortunes and resent it when some kind-hearted soul attempts to alleviate their pain. The selfishness of the depressed person is just as real as that of the one who admits his greatness, but it is so cleverly disguised that he is seldom accused of selfishness. He is cordially disliked none the less.

5. *Domination.* Domination in open form is recognizable by anyone, but it is often disguised so as to appear as a form of service. When you hear a person complaining about the ingratitude of those for whom he has done a favor you can be sure that the service was not an unselfish one. The unselfish giver is not concerned with gratitude. If a person does us a favor we enjoy showing our gratitude until we know that he expects our thanks, and then we resent giving it because this expectation reveals to us the selfish motive behind his generosity. To enslave a person by means of benefactions is one of the meanest forms of slavery. It certainly wins us no permanent friends.

Egocentricity in any form is the greatest barrier to social harmony. If knowledge of the other person is used to further our own interest, whether we disguise our purpose or not, the results can be nothing but disappointing. Social immaturity is synonymous with selfishness; while social maturity is measured by the degree to which one is able to keep himself and his own personal interests in the background. You must get to the point where you desire to make friends because you like people, and not because they can be of service to you. Your objective is not to gain your own happiness directly, but to make the other person happy. When you reach this stage you will find that you are happier as a result, but you do not gain it by directly exploiting anyone else to get what you think you want.

How to use knowledge of other persons. We shall now consider various ways of applying the general principle of social control which we have already enunciated—namely, that you gain friends when you make the other person feel nobler, happier, more intelligent, or more efficient—but the reader must bear in mind that the happiness of the other person must receive prime consideration if these applications are to be effective. If they are applied as so many devices to gain selfish ends this motive will vitiate their effectiveness.

1. *Let the other person feel superior to you.* It took a long time for a young man who held a minor executive position to learn to let his boss have the credit for the bright ideas that grew out of their conferences. Until he did so he and the boss were at enmity. When he learned this lesson, his superior became very fond of him. It came about in this fashion.

When first placed in the position of authority he assumed, as many young men erroneously assume, that his prestige depended upon his ability to develop and "put over" with Mr. A——, the president of the organization, a stream of brilliant ideas. His job, he thought, was to convince Mr. A—— that he was capable. When he discovered that the president was not very cordial to his suggestions he determined that he must convince him that his schemes had merit. This lead to the collection of arguments and evidence that he was right, but the more he fought for his ideas the greater became Mr. A——'s opposition. He discovered also that some of the ideas were later used, but never as the result of his suggestions.

Here was a situation that he could not understand. He was employed to develop original ideas, and when he did he found his efforts blocked. He sought advice as to means for inducing his boss to appreciate him.

It may be seen that his attitude toward the whole situation and the direction of his endeavors were diametrically opposed to the fundamental principle of social adjustment which we have been explaining. Mr. A—— had decided that the ideas of this man were not so good. He wanted to make Mr. A—— eat his words, he wanted to convince him that he was able to produce good ideas. Had he succeeded it would have been humiliating to Mr. A——, but that is exactly what the man wanted.

He was urged to consider the feelings of Mr. A——. After all, the head of the organization should be the one to originate the excellent plans. He was told to give nothing more than suggestions, to give the president credit for all the good ideas, and that when he helped in organizing some new plan the president should be made to feel that he was the prime mover. His job should be to make Mr. A—— feel important, and not to convince him that he had a genius working for him.

When he mastered his pride and did this the whole situation was changed; Mr. A—— warmed up to him, there was no fighting between them but a harmonious attempt to improve the entire organization.

2. *Learn to receive favors.* Most of us have the impulse to bestow gifts upon those we like. The impulse is, no

doubt, a generous one and our object is to make the recipient happier. Under certain circumstances this may be the result; if the gift is not too large, if there are no real or implied obligations connected with the gift, and if it can be interpreted as no more than an indicator of the sincere regard of the donor, it will doubtless make the recipient happy. If this is the effect it is an excellent means of furthering a friendship.

Too often, on the other hand, gifts are not mere tokens of affection. The donor expects some consideration in return for his gift, and its acceptance places the recipient under obligations to him. Giving gifts in this fashion becomes nothing but an adaptation of the "unordered merchandise racket."

Too often we give gifts in order to make ourselves feel noble because of our generosity rather than with the purpose of making the recipient feel happier. When a parent reminds his child of the sacrifices he has made in his behalf, telling the child that he owes him something in return, the child has a right to be resentful. When he knows that the parent made the sacrifices with no expectation of a return he is naturally impelled to love his parent because of the love which such sacrifice implies. Love cannot be bought by forcing gifts on another, and each of us resents any attempt to gain our affection by such means.

On the other hand, you may win friends by learning to receive graciously any favors they care to grant to you. "Anyone can bestow a favor, but it takes a gentleman to receive a gift graciously."

No better illustration of this principle can be given than the one told by Benjamin Franklin in his autobiography. Having discovered that a man of considerable influence disliked him Franklin was very much disturbed, and cast about for some means of winning his friendship. How he did so he tells himself:

"I therefore did not like the opposition of this new member who was a gentleman of fortune and education with talents that were likely to give him great influence in the House which, indeed, afterward happened. I did not, however, aim at gaining his favor by paying any servile respect to him but, after some time, took this other method. Having heard that he had in his library a certain very scarce and curious book, I wrote a note to him, expressing my desire of perusing that book and requesting that he would do me the favor of lending it to me for a few days. He sent it immediately and I returned it in about a week with another note expressing strongly my sense of the favor. When next we met in the House, he spoke to me (which he had never done before) and with great civility; and he ever afterward manifested a readiness to serve me on all occasions, so that we became great friends and our friendship continued to his death." [1]

There are several reasons why this strategy on the part of Franklin made his enemy feel of greater importance. It flattered him to know that Franklin was interested enough in him to know that he loved rare books.   It pleased him to know that he possessed a book that Franklin desired, but could not obtain.   It placed him in a superior position to have Franklin ask a favor of him.   It made him feel generous to do a favor to one whom he opposed. He did not reason this out consciously, of course, but he could not help feeling somewhat more cordial to a man who had made him feel superior in so many ways.

[1] Franklin, Benjamin, *Autobiography*, Houghton Mifflin, 1886, pp. 126–127.

3. *Learn to listen to others.* How do your friends feel after a conversation with you? Is your conversation a means of demonstrating to them your superior wisdom, so that as they look back upon it they feel humiliated? Correspondence courses advertise that they can train you so effectively that you can lead a conversation in any gathering; should anyone else start to talk on any subject you can join immediately and demonstrate that you know more than he does, and thus win social esteem. Try such a method and your reward will be merely to increase your reputation as a snob. Instead, let your conversations arouse such emotions in your friends that they will desire to renew the opportunity of talking with you.

Remember, a conversation means talking with a person and not to one. There is such a thing as professional entertainment, but it is not conversation. A person may enjoy your entertainment but not regard you as his friend. If you want friends, learn to talk with them instead of entertaining them with your words of wisdom.

A man in the manufacturing business had occasion to make a call upon a professor of astronomy. The next day he made the remark that he was agreeably surprised by the cordiality that his host had demonstrated, that they had enjoyed a very pleasant conversation. Since the professor knew nothing about manufacturing and the manufacturer knew nothing about astronomy this seemed very unusual. Investigation showed that the professor, after a few awkward preliminaries, had opened the way for the manufacturer to describe the procedures used in his factory, and had then listened very attentively to what he had to say. Not being accustomed to such an appreciative audience, the manufacturer warmed up to his subject and gave the professor a very interesting hour.

There is nothing more flattering than attentive interest in what the other person says to you. If you want his good-will, listen to him. But let your listening be sincere, for there is no greater discourtesy that you can give to another than to give evidence that you are trying your best to attend to what he has to say but find it impossible to be interested.

4. *Show an interest in others.* Becoming interested in those with whom you are associating is an excellent cure for self-consciousness, as the following illustration will show:

A girl who for years had been very well poised, who had conducted herself with ease in a great variety of social situations, complained that when she was in the company of a particular man she was very self-conscious. She complained that her thoughts fled, her speech was tremulous and disjointed, and that she made a very awkward demonstration, to state it mildly. A little questioning showed that this situation did not result from any particular behavior on the part of the man. She confessed that he was the first man that she had particularly cared for, and that she had been very desirous of making a good impression. She concluded her story: "I think it is so strange that I can be poised, can converse easily, and make a good impression on those about whom I care little; but when I get with a person I would like to impress I make such a fool of myself."

Is it so strange? When she was with people for whom she cared little, as she expressed it, she was not concerned with the impression she was making on them, but was interested in them. When she went with this one man she thought only of one thing: "How am I impressing him?" This was a form of thinking about herself.

When she was told this she said: "All right. I'll admit that my self-consciousness is a way of thinking about myself; but how can I keep from thinking about myself?"

You cannot refrain from thinking about yourself by saying, "I won't think about myself. I won't think about myself." That is merely another way of continuing to think about yourself. Get something more interesting than yourself to think about. "If you admire this man as much as you say you do," she was told, "he should be a more interesting subject of thought than you are. Think about him. Whenever you find yourself getting self-conscious, make yourself think about his interests, his work, his manner of doing things, and the like."

This girl reported in a short time that she had solved her trouble in this manner. At first it was not so easy, but soon she learned to turn her attention from herself to him, and as soon as she did her poise returned. In addition, it had another result. The young man appreciated her interest in him, blossomed out under it, and they became fast friends.

5. *Indirect praise.* Most of us like to receive praise, but we hate to admit it too frankly. Consequently, when people are too obvious in their attempts to flatter us it is likely to produce a little irritation or resentment. Of course, if appreciation is so spontaneous that our admirers cannot contain themselves we do not consider such expression an affront. It is only where the purpose behind the applause is obviously to win our esteem that we dislike it. It is too much as though our flatterers said: "This fellow does not amount to much and I do not like him; but he is a conceited prig, and if I tell him he is good he will fall for it."

Praise, to be effective, must be genuine, and it is better if it is given indirectly. This does not imply in the least that we should withhold praise. If you must make an error in either direction it is better to be too generous with praise than too niggardly with it. To be sure, some persons are spoiled by too much praise, but this usually happens when the praise given to them has not been genuine.

As an illustration of the attitude which some persons take toward praise we can cite the case of a little boy who, at first glance, needed anything but praise. He was very arrogant in his behavior, did poor work in school but enjoyed bragging about what he could do, and delighted in disparaging the conduct and work of others. We discovered that all these performances were tricks on his part to cover up an underlying hunger for appreciation. His mother, father, and older sister were all extremely critical of him. When this situation was analyzed his mother was asked to praise him so as to increase his self-confidence. If he were praised by others he would have less need to brag about himself. She listened attentively to the analysis, agreed that he probably did need praise, and then added: "But he does nothing to merit any praise."

This statement was merely evidence that she had placed standards for the boy which were too high, and then proceeded to criticise him for not measuring up to them. Is it any wonder the boy became discouraged, and had to brag about his own good qualities? Perhaps you may think the other person is not as good as you in some trait; but that does not mean he does not deserve credit. He may have had greater handicaps than you. Do not be too stingy in your genuine appreciation of the accomplishments of others if you would get along with them.

Perhaps the best way to praise a person is to manifest appreciation without saying much about it directly. A good way, also, is to praise people behind their backs.

An executive broke up a great deal of disharmony in his organization by this method of indirect praise. He discovered the enmity which existed between various employees and determined to break it down. When he discovered that A and B were at swords' points he would, in a conference with A about other matters, induce him to make some complimentary remark about B. Then, in conference with B, he would repeat the flattering remark A had made about him. He would, likewise, get B to make a favorable comment about A, and then repeat this remark to A at some later time. In short, by keeping to himself all the mean things the men said about each other and passing on the good things they said, he created a situation of harmony. When A heard that B had complimented him he could not help feeling a little less enmity for him; and when B heard the nice things A had said, he warmed up likewise. Besides, they thought more of the executive.

Some persons hope to gain favor by peddling all the mean things they hear. They come to you and tell you that X made a disparaging remark about you. They hope by such whispers to gain your favor. Usually they do not. It is poor procedure to peddle scandal if you wish to make friends.

6. *Make it easy for people to say "yes" to you.* Before you can gain any real coöperation from another person you must make him *want to* coöperate. His estimation of himself must increase at the prospect of being of assistance to you and, after he has helped you, he must have a better estimate of himself than he would if

he had refused to coöperate. If you are in an extremely superior position, recognizedly head and shoulders above most other persons, it may be such an honor to help you that all you find it necessary to do is to give others the opportunity to help you in anything you plan to do. Few of us are in such exalted positions, however, so that we cannot have people to flock to our banners and do our bidding. We must pave the way to make them want to help us.

One great obstacle to the obtaining of coöperation is the fact that we take delight in the homage of other persons. We try to obtain their help so as to increase our own prestige, our own feeling of superiority. Nothing will arouse the ire of those who might be willing to help us so much as giving them the impression that we feel nobler because of their servitude.

Then, after we have aroused their resistance, we give them arguments or reasons why they should do our bidding. These arguments usually have no real validity but are trumped up to support our authority. If our position is strongly enough entrenched we may be enabled to enforce our desires by such means, but we can be sure, when we have secured obedience or submission, that it is unwilling and will continue only as long as we have the backing to enforce it. It is because so few of us know how to gain willing coöperation that we must have executive offices which carry with them enough prestige to enforce our will upon others. We cannot do it alone, so fall back upon rank and position to help us out. The true leader of men needs neither rank nor position to gain and keep the good-will and to secure the help of his fellows.

If we start our program for obtaining help by antagonizing the person we are approaching, about the only thing he can do and "keep his face" is to continue to refuse. Dress up your request so that it will fit in with what he already wants to do and you need worry no more about how to make him change front.

As an illustration of the point we have in mind, suppose a mother desires to get her boy, who is playing with his electric train, to go to the store on an errand for her. Suppose she begins thus: "Johnny, will you please leave your train for a little while and go to the store for me?" The chances are that he will not want to go, but he may overcome his antagonism if he is on particularly good terms with her. She is taking a chance of opposition, however. The more peremptory she is in her demands the more likely she is to be met by opposition. Should he refuse she has the task of trying to change his viewpoint.

How could you make him want to leave his train? In the first place you should not call to his attention what he is sacrificing in obeying you. Why say anything about leaving his train? Stop and figure out something he wants to do very badly. Perhaps he has been saving his money to buy materials to make an aëroplane. If so, why not say: "Johnny, do you want to earn a nickel?" Now, there is only one answer to that. He does. He may not fancy the method you propose but he can say nothing but "yes" to your question. You have him coming your way. Follow it with: "Come here and I'll tell you how you can do it." The prospect of earning the money is enough, quite probably, to take him away from his train with no mention of his train or what he is giving up.

Such procedures take a little thought, especially in the more complex situations in life, but it takes a little thought to enable us to accomplish the things that are worth while. Isn't it important enough that we gain the coöperation of others to give it some thought?

To put this problem in other words, you need to be conscious not so much of what you want done as of what the other person likes to do, and make sure that when a thing is proposed to him it fits closely into this desire of his. Modify your own desires as much as you like but do not do violence to his if you would gain his hearty coöperation. The problem is not—How can I make him do my bidding? It is—How can I present my plans so that he will want to do as I desire?

Social conduct is largely emotional. Usually we feel called upon to explain rationally why we like one person and dislike another, why we criticise the behavior of one person and applaud that of another, but these explanations seldom reach the real reason for our social prejudices. Most of our social prejudices are irrational and go back to early experiences which we have had.

In our early childhood there were certain persons who were good to us and whom we learned to like. There were others of whom we were afraid or whom we disliked. We developed attitudes of love or hate toward these persons and, at the same time, we extended these emotions toward a great number of characteristics connected with them—the tone of voice, mannerisms, dress, features, moral attitudes, and the great host of characteristics which comprise the personality. These incidental and sometimes trivial characteristics often were given values which they did not deserve in and of themselves, merely because they were connected with personalities we learned to know.

For example, suppose the woman who was kindest to us and did the most for us happened to have long, black hair. Long, black hair became at first a part of mother.

We need not be told to connect such hair with mother; but our experience makes the connection without any effort on our part. Now, if we meet a strange woman with hair which is like that of our mother, we tend to have the same attitude toward her that we had toward our mother. We tend to trust and love her—this new woman—just as we did our mother. If she is vicious in her attitude toward us, we lay ourselves open to unscrupulous exploitation by our faith in her.

The reverse situation may lead to opposite results. Suppose some person who injured us in our youth, whom we learned to hate and fear, has a particular formation of teeth—suppose, for illustration, that the upper teeth protrude. Unconsciously, we tend to identify everybody who has protruding teeth with this person and cordially fear and hate him. We may thus lose a potential friend because of original hostility based on a cue which we learned to adopt when we were infants, but which has no meaning as far as understanding people is concerned.

Strong positive and negative prejudices of this sort do great harm in social adjustments. Those who possess them attempt to account for them in various ways, but usually they give them some supernatural significance and imagine that they are endowed with some mysterious gift which enables them, at sight, to understand human nature. This is a most dangerous supposition. None of us have any power which will enable us to size up a person correctly on the basis of his appearance alone. The only way we can understand people is by observation of what they do and say, and this observation should be extended over a period of time.

In other words, if we are to succeed in our adjustment to other persons we must control these hasty emotional reactions toward them because they are irrational prejudices carried over from youthful experiences with totally different persons who have slight or marked resemblance to them. Instead of responding to our own emotions we should observe the emotional behavior of the other person toward us. We can observe by little emotional expressions which he makes whether he likes us or hates us, whether he trusts or distrusts us, whether he admires or despises us, whether he would like to help us or harm us. These expressions which he gives, probably without being aware that he is telling us how he feels, will enable us to do the thing which will promote the favorable attitudes and dispel the unfavorable ones.

In short, social understanding is dependent upon controlling our own emotional reactions and studying the significance of the emotional expressions of the other person.

Normal social adjustments. Our ability to control our own emotional expressions in the presence of other persons and our skill in applying the rules of social adjustment which we have been studying depends primarily upon the attitudes we have developed toward others. These attitudes, whether they are beneficial or harmful, are habits which we have learned by our contact with people and our accumulated experiences with them. If we understand the significance of these attitudes, which are harmful and which are beneficial, and know the type of experience which leads to their development, we should be able to organize our living so as to make the most wholesome social adjustment.

1. *Can you trust people?* There are all degrees of difference in trustfulness among people, from those who are suspicious of everybody to those who will place implicit trust in total strangers. Which is most dangerous, to be

too suspicious or too trustful? We have an answer to this question if we study the presence of these two attitudes in those who have become mentally unbalanced. Suspiciousness is a dominant characteristic of one group of mentally abnormal persons, those that are called paranoid. These persons are likely to have delusions of persecution; they explain their failure by detailing the mischief which other people have perpetrated upon them. If it had not been for the malicious influence of others, so they argue, they would be normal. These people are very hard to treat because they have escaped responsibility by placing the blame on other persons. We can answer one side of our question by saying that the tendency to be suspicious of other persons is an extremely dangerous tendency, and great care should be taken to prevent the development of a chronic attitude of suspicion.

What happens if we trust people too implicitly? About the worst a person who is extremely trustful can do is to make himself ridiculous or annoying. Trustfulness is not a dominant attitude of any of the groups of persons that must be committed to institutions for mental disorders. You do not become insane because you have trusted people too much. If you must be either too trustful or too suspicious, it will pay to be too trustful. Of course, it is better to be neither. The solution is to learn to understand people and to learn something of each one before you take either attitude toward him. Your trust should not be based on how you feel toward others but on evidence which you obtain by intelligent contact with each individual.

2. *Do you prefer companionship or solitude?* Here again we find all degrees from one extreme to the other. There are those who go to such an extreme of withdrawal

from others that they retreat to solitary parts of the earth; or, if they are forced to be surrounded by people, withdraw into themselves and ignore those around them. Extreme withdrawal from people is a prominent characteristic of a very serious mental disease known as hebephrenic schizophrenia. This disease is just as vicious as the name sounds. The reader should not infer from this that, if he tends to enjoy his own company more than the company of others, that he has this disease or even a tendency toward it. All that is implied is that it is well to avoid an attitude which is such a prominent characteristic of those who are so afflicted.

A normal person must adjust his social life to the circumstances he happens to be in. A college student, for example, might have very social tendencies and enjoy being with others. Some college work demands quiet and solitude and such a person must forego what he would most desire in order to accomplish the essential purpose of college life. On the other hand, a student who shuns companionship is very prone to take his lessons as an excuse for refraining from all social contacts. Hating to be with people, he stays away from them by preference and uses the press of college work as an excuse.

Here again, balance is obtained not by particular reference to one's own habits—his tendency to be sociable or to isolate himself—but by a sympathetic understanding of other persons. Each person should be so sensitive to others that he learns how to enjoy himself with some individuals and understands why it is he does not crave the companionship of others. Balance does not imply lack of discrimination, nor should excessive discrimination be used as a cloak to cover excessive self-centeredness which prevents adjustment to others.

3. *Can you coöperate with others?* Coöperation depends upon an understanding of yourself as well as of
other people. If you do not understand yourself you will
have all sorts of attitudes which make adjustment to
others in a common enterprise very difficult. On the other
hand, even though you understand yourself, you cannot
adjust to others unless you understand something of their
personalities. It takes two or more for coöperation, just
as it takes two or more to have a fight. Consequently,
when difficulty arises it will pay neither to fall into the
habit of always blaming the friction on the peculiar
traits in the other person, nor of always blaming yourself.

If, however, you cannot get along with anybody, it
would pay to look for the trouble in yourself. If the other
fellow demonstrates that he cannot get along with anybody, do not feel too much chagrin if you find him difficult.

We have pointed out that egocentricity is the primary
cause for failure in social coöperation. As we become less
self-centered we naturally find it easier to coöperate.

Most of us can get along if the other fellow comes halfway, and most of us should not be expected to do more
than that; but, in this connection, there is an ideal of
social adjustment which it is probably worth attempting to
attain, and that is, the ability to get along with despicable
creatures.

There is a man of marked ability who now occupies a
position of executive responsibility, but who has had
difficulty of one sort or another with every person with
whom he has come into contact. For years it has been the
custom of those who have had dealings with this man to
get together and have a "gab-fest" and pour out their
ill-feelings toward him. They all agree that he has ability,
but that is the only favorable characteristic they will

grant to him. They all justify their inability to get along with him on his mean traits and perhaps they are right, but their complete self-justification is spoiled by the fact that he has succeeded in his line of work and, in addition, there is one man who has kept in his good graces.

For the first few years of this young man's success with the "old reprobate" the disgruntled ones ridiculed the methods they assumed he must be using. They thought he must be resorting to trickery, that he must be "licking the old man's boots" and the like. Now, after the passage of many years, they admit that this young man has done nothing of the sort. He has simply been clever enough to understand the difficult old gentleman.

The work done in psychopathic hospitals has demonstrated that it is possible to get along with persons who are extremely ill in their mental lives by the simple process of attempting to understand them, so why cannot the same principle be applied in everyday life? It can if one but makes the attempt.

We can escape from a social difficulty by blaming the trouble on the personality of the one with whom we have the difference, but it is much more of a challenge to use the difficulty as an incentive to study the other person with more zeal and intelligence.

Summary. Some of the principles involved in getting along with people may be summarized as follows:

1. People respond favorably to us when we do things to make them feel nobler, to make them feel more efficient, to make them feel more intelligent, or to make them happier.

2. You can arouse these feelings in people by studying them, learning what they desire, their attitudes, and their little personal habits. Knowing these you can act in such a way as to leave them better pleased with themselves.

3. Do not make the mistake of trying to impress people with your good characteristics if you would make lasting friends. Do not put yourself on a pedestal, for people will not look up to you very long. It will hurt their necks and they will want to knock you off your high perch. "The higher you soar the smaller you look to those whom you left behind."

4. Learn to be sensitive to other people's feelings rather than to expect them to be sensitive to yours. Know when you please them and when you irritate them, even though they may try to be civil to you and to hide their feelings when you are thoughtless.

5. Try to overcome your own egocentricity, for it is the greatest barrier to social harmony.

6. Let all your attempts to get along with people be based on a genuine love for them. It is folly to attempt to master some social tricks to gain the friendship of people for whom you do not have a genuine regard. Eventually they will sense the true feelings you have for them.

QUESTIONS

1. List a number of positions in life where it is very essential for one to have an attractive personality.

2. List any positions which are in no way influenced by the personality of the individual occupying them.

3. How important would you consider the ability to get along with people?

4. Where do we get the belief that people should like us because of our good qualities?

5. What is likely to be the effect upon other persons when we "show off"?

6. How can it come about that being "good" makes our parents love us at the same time that it makes others dislike us?

7. Why do people like us?

8. How can you make people like you?

9. Why is it important to like other persons before you can expect them to like you?

10. In what two ways may understanding affect your personal relationships?

11. What warning needs to be recognized in carrying out our attempt to understand other persons?

12. What is the significance of individual differences in gaining the good-will of people?

13. What importance would you ascribe to egocentricity as a barrier to social success?

14. What is the general attitude toward persons who are undisguisedly egocentric?

15. Explain how self-respect may be a disguised form of egocentricity.

16. What is the general cause for self-consciousness?

17. What is the best method for overcoming self-consciousness?

18. How can emotional depression be used to disguise selfishness?

19. What may be a selfish motive behind giving favors?

20. State what is meant by social maturity.

21. State six methods of applying the knowledge of others to gain their good-will.

22. What general attitude should underlie the application of these methods?

23. What is the greatest barrier to permitting the other person to feel superior to you?

24. How are gifts often misused by the giver?

25. What ill-effects may gifts have upon the recipient?

26. How may the proper acceptance of a gift win the friendship of the giver?

27. Explain the importance of learning to listen to others.

28. How can self-consciousness block social adjustments?

29. Can you think of methods of giving praise indirectly other than the one cited in the text?

30. Why is it that those who peddle gossip seldom form many lasting friendships?

31. What is meant by getting a "yes-response"?

32. Think of various situations where you might gain the coöperation of stubborn individuals in a positive manner.

33. Describe how childhood emotional prejudices account for later social reactions.

34. What is necessary in connection with our own emotional behavior if we would gain friends?

35. What is it necessary for us to do in connection with the emotional behavior of our friends if we would gain their friendship?

36. Describe the danger of being too suspicious of others.

37. Explain why it is less dangerous to be too trustful than it is to be too suspicious.

38. Explain why sociability is more wholesome than solitude.

39. Upon what does coöperation depend?

40. Summarize the principles involved in getting along with people.

CHAPTER XIV

SELF–CONFIDENCE

"Yes, I think I can drive a car. You have taught me how to start the motor, how to manipulate the gears, how to reverse, and how to steer. I can drive around here but I will never be able to drive down Michigan Avenue in Chicago."

So spoke a débutante after the automobile salesman had informed her that she was capable of driving her shining new car. Is there really such a difference between driving on the side streets of Lake Forest and through the traffic on Michigan Avenue?

"All you need to do," the salesman replied, "is to practice what I have taught you until your movements are automatic, until the car becomes a part of you. When you have learned to handle your car you can devote your attention to the other drivers around you, and when you can do that you can consider yourself an expert."

That this girl learned her lesson is demonstrated by an episode which happened two years later. A traffic cop, after chasing her down Michigan Avenue, made her pull up along the curb and yelled at her:

"Hey, Miss! Where is the fire?"

"In your eyes, you great big handsome man!" she beamed.

Do you think she had learned her way about? What had become of her panicky fear of driving in traffic? She had taken the salesman's advice and had learned self-

415

confidence by practicing, under easy driving conditions, the simple principles of driving and had discovered that driving in traffic was simply a different application of the same principles.

Learning your way in life. The same rule applies when it comes to making your way in life. The principles we have been teaching may sound so simple that you do not see their significance. They are easily applied in your home or in college but, some pessimist may have told you, when you get into the hard, cold world things will be different.

They will not be different in kind, merely in quantity and complexity. The principles will be the same in the most complicated phases of life. To be sure, if the débutante had started through the thick of traffic before she knew how to handle her car she would have encountered difficulties. That is precisely the reason why you should learn the principles of mental health when you are young, and in a situation of less confusion and stress. It is easy to apply the principles now, they are very simple. Do not, however, make the mistake of isolating yourself and thinking practice is unnecessary, hoping for some mysterious guiding hand to take you through the stresses of life when they do come. Take every chance you can get to adjust to the simple situations in the very best possible manner and the cruel world will have no threat for you—it will be but a delightful challenge.

Why are people afraid of insanity? In spite of what we have said many people are afraid of mental diseases. They have been told wild stories, usually by persons who know not what they are saying, until they have come to look upon insanity as a sort of ghost which may come upon them at any time out of the unknown. This fear makes them refrain from facing life, from practicing living, and thus they do not develop the stamina which can only come through experience, and which they need to meet life as an adult human being should.

The girl in our illustration got over her fear of traffic by getting out and driving, not by sitting in her home wondering about the terrible traffic jams on Michigan Avenue. The insane hospital offers no threat to one who has learned to live. As we have said before, ignorance is the father of fear, and it is the ignorance of life that breeds the fear of insanity.

The lessons for living which we have presented were learned by studying the mistakes of those whose mental balance has been undermined. We have told you how to profit by their mistakes. If scientists discover that an infectious disease is spread by contaminated milk and teach the health authorities how to keep the milk pure, we can all profit by this knowledge. Now that we know the cause of the disease and that we are protected from contamination we should no longer have any fear. Any vestige of fear that might remain could only be a fear of negligence on the part of the health officers and not a fear of the disease itself nor of milk. The fear, through knowledge, is directed toward the proper place.

Various causes of mental disease. All the various kinds of mental disease that are known today may be classified into twelve groups. It is not important for you to know these groups but it may serve to allay any lurking fear you may have if we list them and indicate the general factors which tend to cause each type.

It is quite possible that one reason that mental diseases appear so fearsome to the layman is because they are designated by tremendous names of unknown meaning.

These words sound revolting merely because we do not know what they mean. Therefore, we shall give a common sense synonym or equivalent for each group, placing the technical name in parenthesis.

1. *Feeblemindedness* (Hypophrenosis). Feeblemindedness may be present at birth from unknown reasons, among which may be: hereditary factors, glandular disturbances of parents, pre-natal malnutrition, birth injuries, or some disease of the mother during gestation. It may be caused by degenerative diseases of the brain, some types of poisoning, gross injury to the nervous substance, or some diseases of childhood. In short, feeblemindedness is a general term given to any individual who has a marked intellectual deficiency, no matter what factors may have contributed to that deficiency.

Feeblemindedness should be no cause for worry to the ordinary individual. There are great individual differences in intellectual ability even in normal persons, and the job of each person is to make the most of what he has and not to torment himself wondering just how much he has or how he came to have it. Make the most of what you have and do not hide behind an excuse that you should have had more, nor get bombastic because you think you have too much.

2. *Brain diseases* (Infectious psychoses). There are some micro-organisms which may invade the nerve substance and cause injuries which affect the mental life of the one infected. The prevention of these diseases is a medical problem and should not cause any more worry to the average person than the fear of any infectious disease. General physical hygiene, with enough medical supervision to detect any possible infection, is the solution of mental disorders of this group.

3. *Brain injuries* (Traumatic psychoses). Injuries which result from falls, bruises, gunshot wounds, and the like may have their effect on the mental life of the individual. These involve no mystery.

4. *Old age deterioration* (Senile psychoses). As we age our brain begins to function less and less effectively. This is inevitable, and about all any man can do about it is to live as wholesomely as he can, so that old age will not come prematurely, and make the best of it when his intellectual powers do begin to wane. There is no more occasion to worry about the ageing of the brain than about the ageing of any other part of the body.

5. *Bodily malformations* (Somatopsychoses). In this group are placed various kinds of bodily disturbances. Probably the commonest are those caused by maldevelopment of some of the ductless glands. These conditions usually show themselves by gross bodily changes and have little personal concern for the ordinary man.

6. *Poisons* (Toxic psychoses). Various poisons may injure brain tissue. Some of these are secreted within the body and may be secondary results of some infectious disease. Others, such as lead, alcohol, morphine, and cocaine, are taken into the body from without. The means of prevention of mental disturbances from such sources is obvious.

7. *Epilepsy* (Epileptopsychoses). Not all epilepsy is accompanied by brain disorders, but some types are. There is much to be learned about epilepsy, and as we learn more about it our fears on this score will diminish. There is a general feeling that much may be done for this disorder by means of proper nutrition.

Note: It can be seen that all of the above seven groups depend upon some physical condition or disease, that prevention is a problem of physical hygiene, and that treatment is synonymous with treatment of the physical condition which underlies the mental disease. None of them will sneak up on you like a thief in the night any more than any other disease will. The best prophylaxis against these is rational care of the body.

The next five groups comprise those individuals who have become pathological due to the exaggeration of one or more of the conditions we have been discussing in this text. As far as is known their condition does not depend upon any physical disease or any injury to the nervous system. It is caused by unfortunate ways of meeting life which have become an habitual part of the individuals through repetition, and the exclusion of the more desirable means of responding that we have tried to stress throughout the text.

8. *Shattered personalities* (Schizophrenia or dementia præcox). These are the persons who refuse to face reality, who build up false ways of reacting to situations which confront them, or who refuse to respond at all and live in a world of their own. They begin by setting up false values in life and then determining to maintain the fiction that things are as they have designed them, ignoring anything which does not fit in with their little plan. There are different types, depending upon the method they adopt to evade real life. Some merely become indifferent drifters; the "happy hooligans" and "ne'er-do-wells." Others regress and live in the past. Others blame their failures on other persons. Still others react to a part of life and ignore the rest, becoming warped and twisted personalities.

One need have no fear of this disease if he forms the habit of meeting the varied situations of life as they arise.

It is to enable the student to avoid this type of disorder that we have urged objective behavior.

9. *Emotional extremists* (Cyclothymoses or manic-depressive). In this group are placed those persons who have built up an extreme habit of going to emotional excesses. Instead of meeting the factors in life which produce emotional tensions in the way we have suggested in the chapter on Emotional Maturity, they feed upon their emotions and let the external situation continue to incite them. Meeting the objective situation directly is the only valid way of making an emotional adjustment. Instead, they will go from the extreme of wild excitement to that of deep depression; building up their emotional life rather than building up a way of meeting life's difficulties.

This type does not lead to as serious a condition as the shattering type which results from evasion (the schizophrenics), and one need have no fear of it if he learns to meet objectively the situations in life which cause emotions.

10. *Intellectual extremists* (Paranoia). These persons evade the issues of life by building up defenses which appear reasonable but which are rationalizations. They are dominated by "wishful thinking" and tend to develop delusions. When things go wrong they build up a system of persecutory delusions which appear so valid that the outsider is inclined to believe them.

The way to avoid this tendency is to learn the habit of facing life instead of hiding behind the excuse that the other person is always to blame.

11. *Evaders* (Psychoneurotics). These persons escape difficulties by devices which deceive both themselves and other persons. In most cases the trickery is not

conscious but is adopted because they are not heroic
enough to face life as it is. There are four types:

a. Those with fears and compulsions (Psychasthenia).
These are victims of abnormal fears (phobias) and uncontrollable tendencies (compulsions) to do inane and
absurd acts.

b. Those with chronic fatigue (Neurasthenia). These
get out of meeting life by making the excuse that they
are tired. They fill sanitaria and are on the lookout
continually for rest cures of one sort or another.

c. Disease hunters (Hysteria). These escape mental
conflicts by developing symptoms of specific diseases
and by the other devices which we have already described in detail.

d. Worriers (Anxiety neuroses). These distract themselves and others from the real conflict by calling attention to numerous trivialities which form the basis of
their worries.

The evaders seldom become abnormal enough to be
committed to a hospital for the insane. Their personalities are not likely to become shattered in the sense that
those persons in group eight are shattered, but their
evasions are not wholesome and should be supplanted
by more desirable types of adjustment.

12. *Queer personalities* (Psychopathic personalities).
In this group are placed mild cases who are too queer to
be called normal, who usually have intelligence enough
to know what should be done but too little consideration
for others to do the sensible thing. If they run athwart
the law they may become criminals.

Importance of facing reality. An examination of this
classification of mental disorders will indicate to the
reader the reason for the stress we have given to the ne-

cessity of facing reality. After excluding those groups which are due to actual diseased conditions—that is, groups 1 to 7, inclusive—the remainder are due to failure to face life as it is. The classification is based largely on the type of subterfuge which the patient uses and, while some methods are more harmful than others, normality comes when the problems of life are faced squarely and frankly.

Life is a game. When we are born we are entered in that game and there is only one thing for us to do—play the game. Those who get functional mental disorders, groups 8 to 12, inclusive—are simply persons who refuse to play it or who refuse to play according to the rules.

If a person will not play according to the rules it is not his fault, of course. It is because some one has induced him to do differently. Some one has taught him to attempt to stay out, to evade playing, to cheat, to sneak in dirty little foul plays, or to play as though no one else were in the game. If you have come to the age of a college student and have been taught any such tricks, it is up to you to change your attitude, to unlearn such devices, and to face life squarely from this point on.

How personality growth is accomplished. The kind of person we are at the present moment is the result of the manner in which we have met the varying experiences of life in the past and the type of person we shall be in the future will depend upon how we meet them from this point. As an infant each individual is very much undeveloped but has the possibility of great expansion provided he takes advantage of the opportunities offered him.

To make graphic the different forms that personality development may take, let us try to imagine the growing self, or ego, as expanding in space. In the accompanying diagram, the small sphere in the center represents the ego of the little child. Let us imagine him as a perfect

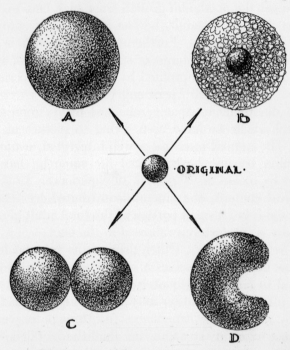

DIFFERENCES IN PERSONALITY DEVELOPMENT

Schematic diagram to illustrate how the infantile personality (Original) may grow into a well-unified individual (A); into a shattered personality (B) where the infantile personality remains almost intact, with all later additions adhering to this infantile segment but with no organic relationship; into a dual personality (C); and into a distorted personality (D).

sphere, every point on the surface of which is sensitive to his environment.

1. *The well-integrated person.* Let us further imagine that every contact with the environment leads to development and that such development may be symbol-

ized by an enlargement of the ego at that point. If he has a great number of experiences, if they are equally distributed on all surfaces of the sphere, and if he responds so as to get the maximum growth from each one, we can imagine that, as an adult, he has grown to the proportions of the sphere A. Furthermore, the growth is not only to be reckoned in terms of size but in terms of symmetry as well. He has profited by all types of experience and is a "well-rounded" personality.

Such development (that symbolized by A) represents the ideal which we have been trying to picture in this book. The normal man has a well-integrated, a unified personality because he has faced life squarely, has developed by means of every type of experience. In terms of cubical content, the amount contributed by the infantile ego is but a small portion of the total adult person. The baby is completely swallowed in the man.

2. *The dwarfed ego.* Other persons, as infants, learn to throw around themselves a wall of separation so that they fail to respond adequately to contact with the outside world. This isolation may be begun through fear, through unfortunate experiences, or through perverted teachings which make them feel that the world is vile; but whatever its source the individual strives to maintain his infantile personality in its original state.

Even after such a person reaches physiological maturity his adult ego is no larger than his infantile one. The only change is that the shell around this tiny sphere has become harder and more impervious to stimulation from without. He has not met life but has kept himself separated from it. Experiences beckon for admission but are denied entrance; so they attach themselves to the outside shell like so many barnacles on the hull of an

old ship. These extraneous elements may grow to such
an extent that, on the outside, the individual may appear
to be about as large as a well-integrated individual. Examination of the internal structure will show the original
tiny infantile ego unchanged, with the rest of the sphere
composed of unintegrated foreign substance—merely
so many parasites hanging on to the outside. This type
of person is represented by B in our diagram. Group 8
of our classification of abnormal types most nearly fits
this kind of personality.

3. *Dual personality.* Other individuals begin, very
early in their lives, to classify experiences into distinct
classes; usually as good or bad. They determine to react
openly and whole-heartedly to the good experiences and
to refrain from responding to the bad. In order to make
such a judgment there is some response necessary, so
that the individual gets somewhat acquainted with so-
called bad things, but soon discards them from the realm
of conscious behavior. In response to the good experiences
his personality grows much as the normal person grows
and we have represented in A. If the bad experiences
constitute but a minor part of the total they will adhere
to the side-wall of the main personality as a sort of wart.
If, however, he classifies many such items in the undesirable group and attempts to push them all out with equal
vigor the "wart" may grow to such proportions that it
is about as large as the main personality. Such a situation, illustrated in C, gives the background for the dual
personality.

In such a personality the two systems cannot act in
unison. Either the part considered normal has control of
all conscious behavior or the person may shift to the ostra-
cized portion and act as though he were a different per-

sonality. Sometimes there is a minor shift from one to the other and then we can discern inconsistencies in conduct.

4. *The distorted personality.* Finally, instead of growing into a well-rounded and balanced personality, it is possible for a person to grow into all sorts of distorted forms. As an illustration of how a warped individual may be initiated let us suppose that the tiny infantile ego (represented by the center sphere) has an unpleasant experience. It might be a terrible fright, some unkind act on the part of mother or friend, or the like. As a result a portion of the ego develops scar tissue which does not function as the rest does, and is irresponsive to experiences of the nature which caused the injury. The ego cannot develop in this direction and remains forever dwarfed. Such a possible instance is pictured in D. One part of the childhood ego did not grow and, consequently, a deep indentation is found in the adult personality. Seen from one side such an individual may appear to be well integrated and thoroughly normal. It is only when we get a view which discloses the side which has been injured that we see the distortion. It can also be understood that the types and degrees of distortion can vary tremendously.

Can a person help himself? The four trends of development which we have described represent extremes which probably never occur in actuality. What we find in any individual is a trend in one of these four directions or a combination of two or more.

The type of personality we now possess is the result of thousands of experiences, but that does not mean it will remain the same in the future. Each of us is destined to have thousands of other experiences, and it is with these that we should concern ourselves. How can we make the future yield the best results?

The first essential is to get clearly in mind just what we want the future to accomplish for us. To know this we should exercise the greatest frankness in discerning what sort of person we are. If you have profited by the teachings of this book you should now be able to state whether you are primarily the type of person represented by A, B, C, or D in our diagram. But do not stop at this point. Determine to make yourself as much like A as you possibly can.

If you are a type B, afraid of every phase of life, attempting to keep your infantile ego in its original form, you will need to make a heroic struggle to break down the wall which separates you from life. You may not be able to do this in a brief space of time, but if you see clearly what your objective is, you can achieve it in time. The type B requires the greatest change of front because the very nature of the previous reactions has tended to make such a person afraid of life and he must gradually overcome such fear.

The C type should be able to make an adjustment by fitting together and comparing the two opposed types of attitude and behavior which he fosters. The result will be a sort of compromise between the two extremes and the effect on his personality will be to weld the two spheres together into a united and symmetrical one.

The D type should search for the particular phase of his personality which is distorted, and then build it up by experiences which negate the deteriorating work of the earlier ones. Friends are valuable in discovering twists in our organization and, if we will but encourage them a little, will be willing to show us wherein we are warped.

Why be afraid of life? Having organized your life in such a rational fashion, what is there to fear? You are no more afraid of life than an experienced driver is of handling his car. Meeting the various phases of life is merely a part of your everyday program. If you ever had any leanings toward abnormality of any sort it is because you were too afraid to meet life at some point (or at all points) and devised some evasive method to escape it. When you learn to adjust to that phase of life, it ceases to be a problem and the fear vanishes.

Being a unified personality you will, nevertheless, meet new problems every day of your life, but they will come as challenges, not as threats, because meeting life in the past has given you confidence that you can meet it in the future. Perhaps some unusual event will get you down for a while, but it cannot keep you down. Past opposition has made you as resilient as a rubber ball, and you naturally bounce back on your feet ready for the fight.

Your greatest opposition will come from people. Social adjustments are by far the hardest to accomplish, but you will get more and more experience with people, and each successful encounter will add to your social poise. You will find the fear of people vanishing as you come to know them better, and as they come to like you because of your understanding of them.

Finally, mental soundness is not static. Life is ever changing and new adjustments must always be made. You must steer through a great number of seething forces, but your course will be smooth because you are one of the forces and the whole system is unified. You are not a monkey-wrench in the wheels of progress, you are one of the cogs. You have achieved mental soundness when you are willing to be a part of life.

QUESTIONS

1. How does the application of a principle to a simple situation enable one to solve complex problems?

2. Give two reasons why people are afraid of insanity.

3. How can one overcome his fear of insanity?

4. Into how many groups may all sorts of mental disorder be classified?

5. Why should not the college student live in any fear of feeblemindedness?

6. Explain how brain diseases constitute a problem in medicine and not education.

7. The first seven groups of mental disorders are called organic as distinguished from the latter ones which are called functional. Explain this difference.

8. Explain what is meant by a shattered personality.

9. How can one eliminate the fear of becoming a shattered personality?

10. How can one prevent himself from becoming an emotional extremist?

11. Distinguish between intellectual proficiency and intellectual extremism.

12. Why is not "wishful thinking" facing reality?

13. Distinguish the four types of "evaders."

14. Groups 8 to 12 are arranged from the most dangerous to the mildest. Show how this arrangement fits in with the degree of adjustment to reality.

15. The first seven groups fall into one general class. How would you state a simple principle of hygiene to avoid these?

16. State the simple principle of hygiene which will safeguard an individual from falling into any one of groups 8 to 12.

17. State in your own words why the problem of mental health is a problem of adjustment to the outside world.

18. State why it is not a problem of internal adjustment without relation to the external world.

19. State in your own words what is meant by a unified, integrated, or well-rounded personality.

20. Can you think of certain aspects of the training of children that would foster the dwarfed ego?

21. If you know an individual with a dwarfed ego, outline some specific kinds of situation which might tend to break down his "wall of separation."

22. What other kinds of distinction, besides good and bad, might tend to give rise to a dual personality?

23. Can you cite some warping influences with which the ordinary person has to cope?

24. To what extent can a person choose his own environment?

25. Upon what basis should he make such a choice?

26. It has been contended that the basis of fear is ignorance. Is there any phase of mental adjustment and mental health which continues to frighten you? If so, outline a program for learning more of that phase.

27. If social environment is the most important influence in the development of stability or instability, what effect do you suppose you exert on the adjustments of those around you?

28. State in your own words how your attitudes toward life have changed since beginning this course.

REFERENCES FOR FURTHER READING

Bagby, English, *The Psychology of Personality*, Henry Holt.

Beers, Clifford, *A Mind That Found Itself*, Doubleday, Doran.

Blanchard, Phyllis, *The Adolescent Girl*, Moffat Yard.

Charters, Jessie A., *The College Student Thinking It Through*, Abingdon Press.

Dearborn, G. V. N., *How to Learn Easily*, Little, Brown.

Dewey, John, *How We Think*, D. C. Heath.

————, *Human Nature and Conduct*, Henry Holt.

Elkind, Henry, editor (symposium), *The Healthy Mind*, Greenberg.

Fishbein, Morris, and White, Wm. A., *et al.*, *Why Men Fail*, Century.

Fryer, Douglas, *Vocational Self-Guidance*, Lippincott.

Green, George H., *Psychanalysis in the Classroom*, G. P. Putnam's Sons.

Groves, E. R., *Personality and Social Adjustment*, Longmans Green.

————, and Blanchard, Phyllis, *Introduction to Mental Hygiene*, Henry Holt.

Hart, Bernard, *The Psychology of Insanity*, Cambridge Univ. Press.

Healy, William, *Mental Conflicts and Misconduct*, Little, Brown.

Hollingworth, Leta, *Psychology of the Adolescent*, Appleton.

Kornhauser, Arthur W., *How to Study*, Univ. of Chicago Press.

Marston, W. M., *Defense Mechanisms*, Ency. Brit. (14th ed.).

Menninger, Karl A., *The Human Mind*, Crofts.

Morgan, John J. B., *The Psychology of Abnormal People*, Longmans Green.

————, *The Psychology of the Unadjusted School Child*, Macmillan.

Overstreet, H. A., *About Ourselves*, Norton.

Richmond, Winifred, *The Adolescent Girl*, Macmillan.

Russell, B. A. W., *The Conquest of Happiness*, Horace Liveright.

Tracy, Frederick, *The Psychology of Adolescence*, Macmillan.

Vaughan, Wayland F., *The Lure of Superiority*, Henry Holt.

Webb, E. T., and Morgan, John J. B., *Making the Most of Your Life*, Long and Smith.

———, *Strategy in Handling People*, Doubleday, Doran.

White, William A., *Principles of Mental Hygiene*, Macmillan.

Williams, E. H., and Hoag, E. B., *Our Fear Complexes*, Bobbs-Merrill.

INDEX

Absences, description of, 124–125.
Achievement: sense of, 115; substitutes for, 117–120.
Activity, as a foe of emotional depressions, 351–352.
Altruism: as a goal, 198; development of, 188–190.
Ambition: as a stimulus, 101–103; contrasted with daydreaming, 115–117; making effective, 113–115.
Analogies, misuse of, 221–222.
Applause, desire for, 151.
Application, aid in study, 365.
Attitudes: as indicators of mental health, 10; causing crime, 310–326; changing of, 44–46; clues to disguises of, 58–60; development of, 42–44; distortion of, 55–57; diversity of, 47–48, 51; essentially habits, 44, 47; evaluation of, 48–56; persistence in, 50–51; questioning, 210–211; racial differences in, 51; source of, 49–50; unconscious, 56–58.

Beliefs: criticism of, 206–207; independent of truth, 203–204; willingness to change, 207.
Believe, wish to, 207–209.
Bias, effect on reasoning, 217–219.
Blame, shifting to others, 228–229.
Blood pressure, increased with fear, 86.
Blushing, caused by fear, 88–89.
Burnham, William H., 242.

Case to illustrate: ambition, importance of, 99–101; crime as a defense mechanism, 317–318; crime caused by deprivation, 310–311;

crime caused by fear, 309–310; crime caused by repression, 315–316; crime, compulsive, 313–314; compensation by contrast, 249; compensation by substitution, 251; compensation, direct, 244; deafness, functional, 288–289; delusion of disease, 231–232; delusion of persecution, 223–226; depression to gain love, 354–355; double personality, 285, 286; emotional bias, 235; emotional depression, 349–351; epilepsy, feigned, 282; fainting spells, 283; fear, cause for, 63; grief, exaggerated, 330; hate, development of, 261–262; hate, disguised, 321–322; how to receive favors, 397; illness, exaggerated, 268–269, 273–274, 275; imaginings, excessive, 122–123; interest in others, 399–400; making other person feel superior, 394–395; nausea, functional, 293–294; needless break, 1–2; obsession, 126–127; overcoming handicaps, 239, 257–258; paralysis, functional, 292; perspective to fight, 349–351; praise, effect of, 401–402; psychopathic personality, 299–301; reasoning, perverted, 215–216; reforming others, 252–254; regression, 171, 197; self-confidence, 415–416; selfishness, parental, 189; self-punishment, 356–358; sleep walking, 279–280; social adjustment, poor, 385–386; stealing, egocentric, 325–326; wish to believe, 219–220; zeal, excessive, 342–343.
Change, certainty of, 10, 139–141.